Software Abstractions: Logic, Language, and Analysis

Software Abstractions

Logic, Language, and Analysis

Daniel Jackson

The MIT Press
Cambridge, Massachusetts
London, England

MIT Press books may be purchased at special quantity discounts for business or sales promotion use. For information, please email *special_sales@ mitpress.mit.edu* or write to Special Sales Department, The MIT Press, 55 Hayward Street, Cambridge, MA 02142.

This book was set in Adobe Warnock and ITC Officina Sans, by the author, using Adobe Indesign and his own software, on Apple computers. Diagrams were drawn with OmniGraffle Pro. Printed and bound in the United States of America.

Library of Congress Cataloguing-in-Publication Data
Jackson, Daniel.
Software abstractions : logic, language, and analysis / Daniel Jackson.
   p. cm.
Includes bibliographical references and index.
ISBN 0-262-10114-9 (alk. paper)
1. Computer software—Development. I. Title.
QA76.76.D47J29 2006 005.1—dc22 2005056155

10 9 8 7 6 5 4 3 2 1

to Claudia

Contents

5: Analysis   139

6: Examples   169

Appendix A: Exercises   229

Appendix B: Alloy Language Reference   253

Appendix C: Kernel Semantics   291

Appendix D: Diagrammatic Notation   295

Preface

As a programmer working for Logica UK in London in the mid-1980's, I became a passionate advocate of formal methods. Extrapolating from small successes with VDM and JSP, I was sure that widespread use of formal methods would bring an end to the software crisis.

One approach especially intrigued me. John Guttag and Jim Horning had developed a language, called Larch, which was amenable to a mechanical analysis. In a paper they'd written a few years earlier [21], and which is still not as widely known as it deserves to be, they showed how questions about a design might be answered automatically. In other words, we would have real software "blueprints"—a way to analyze the essence of the design before committing to code. I went to pursue my PhD with John at MIT, and have been a researcher ever since.

As a researcher though, I soon discovered that formal methods were not the silver bullet I'd hoped they would be. Formal models were hard to construct, and specifying every detail of a system was too hard. Theorem proving, the kind of analysis that Larch relied on, could not be fully automated. Even now, after 20 more years of research, it still requires the careful guidance of a mathematical guru. In my doctoral work, therefore, I took a more conservative route, and worked on automatic detection of bugs in code. But I kept an interest in the more ambitious world of formal methods and design analysis, and hoped one day to return to it.

In 1992, I visited Carnegie Mellon University. By then, I'd become enamored, like many in the formal methods community, with the Z language. The inventors of Z had dispensed with many of the complexities of earlier languages, and based their language on the simplest notions of set theory. And yet Z was even less analyzable than Larch; the only tool in widespread use was a pretty printer and type checker.

On that visit, Ken McMillan showed me his SMV model checker: a tool that could check a state machine of a billion states in seconds, without any aid from the user whatsoever. I was awestruck.

With the invention of model checking, the reputation of formal methods changed almost overnight. The word "verification" became fashionable again, and the adoption of model-checking tools by chip manufacturers showed that engineers really could write formal models, and, if the benefit was great enough, would do it of their own accord.

But the languages of model checkers were not suitable for software. They were designed for handling the complexity that arises when a collection of simple state machines interacts concurrently. In software design, complexity arises even in a single machine, from the complex structure of its state. Model checkers can't handle this structure—not even the indirection that is the essence of all software design.

So I began to wonder: could the power of model checking be brought to a language like Z? Here were two cultures, an ocean apart: the gritty automation of SMV, reflecting the steel mills and smokestacks of Pittsburgh, the town of its invention, and the elegance and simplicity of Z, reflecting the beautiful quads of Oxford.

This book is the result of a 10-year effort to bridge this gap, to develop a language that captures the essence of software abstractions simply and succinctly, with an analysis that is fully automatic, and can expose the subtlest of flaws.

The language, Alloy, is deeply rooted in Z. Like Z, it describes all structures (in space and time) with a minimal toolkit of mathematical notions, but its toolkit is even smaller and simpler than Z's. Alloy was also strongly influenced by object modeling notations (such as those of OMT and Syntropy). Like them, it makes it easy to classify objects, and associate properties with objects according to the classification. Alloy supports "navigation expressions," which are now a mainstay of object modeling, with a syntax that is particularly simple and uniform.

The analysis, embodied in the Alloy Analyzer, actually bears little resemblance to model checking, its original inspiration. Instead, it relies on recent advances in SAT (boolean satisfiability) technology. The Alloy Analyzer translates constraints to be solved from Alloy into boolean constraints, which are fed to an off-the-shelf SAT solver. As solvers get faster, so Alloy's analysis gets faster and scales to larger problems. Using the best solvers of today, the analyzer can examine spaces that are several hundred bits wide (that is, of 10^{60} cases or more). Hardware advances must also get some of the credit. Even had this technology been available 10 years ago, an analysis that takes only seconds on today's machines would have taken an hour back then. (Incidentally, Alloy was by no means the first application of SAT to this kind of problem. SAT had been used for analyzing railway control systems [66], for checking hardware [67], and for planning [43, 15]. Since its adoption in Alloy [31], it has been incorporated into model checkers too [5].)

The experience of exploring a software model with an automatic analyzer is at once thrilling and humiliating. Most modelers have had the benefit of review by colleagues; it's a sure way to find flaws and catch omissions. Few modelers, however, have had the experience of subjecting their models to continual, automatic review. Building a model incrementally with an analyzer, simulating and checking as you go along, is a very different experience from using pencil and paper alone. The first reaction tends to be amazement: modeling is much more fun when you get instant, visual feedback. When you simulate a partial model, you see examples immediately that suggest new constraints to be added.

Then the sense of humiliation sets in, as you discover that there's almost nothing you can do right. What you write down doesn't mean exactly what you think it means. And when it does, it doesn't have the consequences you expected. Automatic analysis tools are far more ruthless than human reviewers. I now cringe at the thought of all the models I wrote (and even published) that were never analyzed, as I know how error-ridden they must be. Slowly but surely the tool teaches you to make fewer and fewer errors. Your sense of confidence in your modeling ability (and in your models!) grows.

You can use analysis to make models not only more correct but also more succinct and more elegant. When you want to rework a constraint in the model, you can ask the analyzer to check that the new and old constraint have the same meaning. This is like using unit tests to check refactoring in code, except that the analyzer typically checks billions of cases, and there are no test suites to write.

I sometimes call my approach "lightweight formal methods" [37], because it tries to obtain the benefits of traditional formal methods at lower cost, and without requiring a big initial investment. Models are developed incrementally, driven by the modeler's perception of which aspects of the software matter most, and of where the greatest risks lie, and automated tools are exploited to find flaws as early as possible.

But at the same time as I have argued against some of the assumptions of traditional formal methods, my experience in the last decade—teaching software engineering to students at Carnegie Mellon and MIT, building tools with students, and consulting on industrial developments—has convinced me of the validity of their central premise. As Tony Hoare famously put it in his Turing Award lecture [29]:

> *There are two ways of constructing a software design: One way is to make it so simple there are obviously no deficiencies and*

the other way is to make it so complicated that there are no obvious deficiencies.

A commitment to simplicity of design means addressing the essence of design—the abstractions on which software is built—explicitly and up front. Abstractions are articulated, explained, reviewed and examined deeply, in isolation from the details of the implementation. This doesn't imply a waterfall process, in which all design and specification precedes all coding. But developers who have experienced the benefits of this separation of concerns are reluctant to rush to code, because they know that an hour spent on designing abstractions can save days of refactoring.

In this respect, the Alloy language and its analysis are a Trojan horse: an attempt to capture the attention of software developers, who are mired in the tar pit of implementation technologies, and to bring them back to thinking deeply about underlying concepts.

That is why I have chosen the title *Software Abstractions* for this book. The lure of coding, and pressure to deliver elaborate features on short schedules, often draw programmers away from designing abstractions to coping with the intricacies of transient technologies, and to inventing clever tricks to overcome their limitations. If we focused instead on the underlying concepts, and struggled not for small performance gains or ever more complex features, but for simplicity and clarity, our software would be more powerful, more dependable, and more enjoyable to use. Like the best artifacts of civil and mechanical engineering, the best software systems would be a marriage of utility and beauty. And as software designers, we'd have more fun: we'd spend less time working around basic structural flaws in our software, and our ideas would have more lasting impact.

Acknowledgments

I am deeply grateful to the many friends and colleagues who have helped in the writing of this book:

To Ilya Shlyakhter, who invented the modeling idiom that expresses dynamics by adding a column of state atoms to each relation (leading to the design of the signature construct, and making possible Alloy's precarious balance of expressiveness and tractability), and who designed and built the key algorithms of the Alloy Analyzer.

To Manu Sridharan, who contributed extensively to the language, designed and implemented large parts of the analyzer, was an enthusiast for Alloy before we had credible examples, and has continued to help out despite having left MIT long ago.

To the many undergraduate and masters students who contributed to the tool implementation: Arturo Arizpe, Emily Chang, Joseph Cohen, Sam Daitch, Greg Dennis, David Kelman, Daniel Kokotov, Edmond Lau, Likuo Lin, Jesse Pavel, Uriel Schafer, Ian Schechter, Ning Song, Emina Torlak, Vincent Yeung, and Andrew Yip; and to those who were guinea pigs in evaluating Alloy in early case studies: Ryan Jazayeri, Sarfraz Khurshid, Edmond Lau, Robert Lee, SeungYong Albert Lee, Kartik Mani, Tina Nolte, Suresh Toby Segaran, Tucker Sylvestro, Mana Taghdiri, Allison Waingold, Hoe Teck Wee, and Jon Whitney; and to MIT's UROP office for coordinating the undergraduate research program.

To the current members of my research group—Felix Chang, Greg Dennis, Jonathan Edwards, Lucy Mendel, Derek Rayside, Robert Seater, Mana Taghdiri, Emina Torlak, and Vincent Yeung—not only for their intellectual company, but for their many contributions to the Alloy project big and small; especially to Derek who, on his own initiative, took on the task of resolving release problems and platform dependences; to Emina, now Alloy's lead developer, and Vincent, for their continuing work on the Alloy Analyzer; to Jonathan, who led the design of Alloy's new type system; to Robert, for his help teaching Alloy; and to Greg, for his work on the Alloy library modules and for answering queries from users. To Viktor Kuncak, for developing the theory behind the "unbounded universal quantifier" problem.

To my colleagues who have taught Alloy in their courses, especially Matt Dwyer, John Hatcliff, Cesare Tinelli, and Michael Huth, who developed extensive material when Alloy was much rougher than it is today.

To the readers who gave me comments and suggestions on drafts of the book: Paul Attie, Daniel Le Berre, Paulo Borba, Jin Song Dong, Rohit Gheyi, Tony Hoare, Michael Lutz, Tiago Massoni, Walden Mathews, Joe Moore, Sanjai Narain, David Naumann, Norman Ramsey, Mark Saaltink, Martyn Thomas, and Mandana Vaziri; and especially to Michael Jackson, Jeremy Jacob, Viktor Kuncak, Butler Lampson, Chris Wallace, David Wilczynski, and Pamela Zave, who read the book in its entirety and together found something to fix on almost every page. They have saved me from many embarrassments and the reader from countless frustrations and confusions.

To the National Science Foundation, NASA, IBM, Microsoft, and Doug and Pat Ross, for their support of my research.

To Rod Brooks, Eric Grimson, John Guttag, Rafael Reif, and Victor Zue, for their role in creating the wonderful research and teaching environment that nurtured this work.

To Michael Butler, John Fitzgerald, Martin Gogolla, Peter Gorm Larsen, and Jim Woodcock for contributing solutions in their own languages to the hotel locking problem for appendix E.

To Bob Prior at MIT Press, for his confidence in this book, and his sage advice; to Katherine Almeida, its editor; and to Yasuyo Iguchi, design manager, for her advice on typography.

To my father, Michael Jackson, for his endless encouragement; for the inspiration he has been for me since I joined the family business; and for his tolerance of so many papers, and now a book, where rigor in logic often seems to take precedence over rigor in method. To my mother, Judy Jackson, the most prolific author in the family, whose uplifting emails continued to come even when replies became short and infrequent. To my brother, Adam Jackson, who insisted that my text be optically aligned (and showed me how to do it).

And finally, to my wife Claudia, to whom I dedicate this book, who has taught me so much, especially that analysis isn't everything (and that the New Yorker is much more fun than the Economist). And to my children Rachel, Rebecca and Akiva, who will grow up, I hope, in a world of better and simpler software than we have today.

1: Introduction

Software is built on abstractions. Pick the right ones, and programming will flow naturally from design; modules will have small and simple interfaces; and new functionality will more likely fit in without extensive reorganization. Pick the wrong ones, and programming will be a series of nasty surprises: interfaces will become baroque and clumsy as they are forced to accommodate unanticipated interactions, and even the simplest of changes will be hard to make. No amount of refactoring, bar starting again from scratch, can rescue a system built on flawed concepts.

Abstractions matter to users too. Novice users want programs whose abstractions are simple and easy to understand; experts want abstractions that are robust and general enough to be combined in new ways. When good abstractions are missing from the design, or erode as the system evolves, the resulting program grows barnacles of complexity. The user is then forced to master a mass of spurious details, to develop workarounds, and to accept frequent, inexplicable failures.

The core of software development, therefore, is the design of abstractions. An abstraction is not a module, or an interface, class, or method; it is a structure, pure and simple—an idea reduced to its essential form. Since the same idea can be reduced to different forms, abstractions are always, in a sense, inventions, even if the ideas they reduce existed before in the world outside the software. The best abstractions, however, capture their underlying ideas so naturally and convincingly that they seem more like discoveries.

The process of software development should be straightforward. First, you design the abstractions, from a careful consideration of the problem to be solved and its likely future variants. Then you develop its embodiments in code: the interfaces and modules, data structures and algorithms (or in object-oriented parlance, the class hierarchy, datatype representations, and methods).

Unfortunately, this approach rarely works. The problem, as Bertrand Meyer once called it, is *wishful thinking*. You come up with a collection of abstractions that seem to be simple and robust. But when you implement them, they turn out to be incoherent and perhaps even inconsistent, and they crumble in complexity as you attempt to adapt them as the code grows.

Why are the flaws that escaped you at design time so blindingly obvious (and painful) at coding time? It is surely not because the abstractions you chose were perfect in every respect except for their realizability in code. Rather, it was because the environment of programming is so much more exacting than the environment of sketching design abstractions. The compiler admits no vagueness whatsoever, and gross errors are instantly revealed by executing a few tests.

Recognizing the advantage of early application of tools, and the risk of wishful thinking, the approach known as "extreme programming" [4] eliminates design as a separate phase altogether. The design of the software evolves with the code, kept in check by the rigors of type checking and unit tests.

But code is a poor medium for exploring abstractions. The demands of executability add a web of complexity, so that even a simple abstraction becomes mired in a bog of irrelevant details. As a notation for expressing abstractions, code is clumsy and verbose. To explore a simple global change, the designer may need to make extensive edits, often across several files. And pity the reviewer who has to critique design abstractions by poring over a code listing.

An alternative approach is to attack the design of abstractions head-on, with a notation chosen for ease of expression and exploration. By making the notation precise and unambiguous, the risk of wishful thinking is reduced. This approach, known as *formal specification*, has had a number of major successes. Praxis, a British company that develops critical systems using a combination of formal specification and static analysis, offers a warranty on its products, boasts a defect rate an order of magnitude lower than the industry average, and achieves this level of quality at a comparable cost.

Why isn't formal specification used more widely then? I believe that two obstacles have limited its appeal. The notations have had a mathematical syntax that makes them intimidating to software designers, even though, at heart, they are simpler than most programming languages. A second and more fundamental obstacle is a lack of tool support beyond type checking and pretty printing. Theorem provers have advanced dramatically in the last 20 years, but still demand more investment of effort than is feasible for most software projects, and force an attention to mathematical details that don't reflect fundamental properties of the abstractions being explored.

This book presents a new approach. It takes from formal specification the idea of a precise and expressive notation based on a tiny core of simple and robust concepts, but it replaces conventional analysis based on theorem proving with a fully automatic analysis that gives immediate feedback. Unlike theorem proving, this analysis is not "complete": it examines only a finite space of cases. But because of recent advances in constraint-solving technology, the space of cases examined is usually huge—billions of cases or more—and it therefore offers a degree of coverage unattainable in testing.

Moreover, unlike testing, this analysis requires no test cases. The user instead provides a property to be checked, which can usually be expressed as succinctly as a single test case. A kind of exploration therefore becomes possible that combines the incrementality and immediacy of extreme programming with the depth and clarity of formal specification.

This volume introduces the key elements of the approach: a logic, a language, and an analysis:

- The *logic* provides the building blocks of the language. All structures are represented as relations, and structural properties are expressed with a few simple but powerful operators. States and executions are both described using *constraints* ("formulas" to the logician, and "boolean expressions" to the programmer), allowing an incremental approach in which behavior can be refined by adding new constraints.

- The *language* adds a small amount of syntax to the logic for structuring descriptions. To support classification, and incremental refinement, it has a flexible type system that has subtypes and unions, but requires no downcasts. A simple module system allows generic declarations and constraints to be reused in different contexts.

- The *analysis* is a form of constraint solving. *Simulation* involves finding instances of states or executions that satisfy a given property. *Checking* involves finding a counterexample—an instance that violates a given property. The search for instances is conducted in a space whose dimensions are specified by the user in a "scope," which assigns a bound to the number of objects of each type. Even a small scope defines a huge space, and thus often suffices to find subtle bugs.

This book is aimed at software designers, whether they call themselves requirements analysts, specifiers, designers, architects, or programmers. It should be suitable for advanced undergraduates, and for graduate students in professional and research masters programs. No prior knowledge of specification or modeling is assumed beyond a high-school–level familiarity with the basic notions of set theory. Nevertheless, it is likely to appeal more to readers with some experience in software development, and some background in modeling.

Throughout the book, I use the term "model" for a description of a software abstraction. It's not ideal, because a software abstraction need not be a "model" of anything. But it's shorter than "description," and has come to have a well established (and vague!) usage.

To keep the text short and to the point, I've relegated discussions of trickier points and asides to question-and-answer sections that are interspersed throughout the text. For the benefit of researchers, I've used these sections also to explain some of the rationale behind the Alloy language and modeling approach.

In the book's appendices you'll find a series of exercises designed to help develop modeling and analysis skills; a reference manual for the Alloy language; a summary of the semantics of the logic; and a comparison of Alloy to some well-known alternatives.

There's no better way to learn modeling than to do it. As you read the book, I recommend that you try out the examples for yourself, and experiment to see the effects of changes.

The Alloy Analyzer is freely available at *http://alloy.mit.edu* for a variety of platforms. It can display its results in textual and graphical form, and includes a visualization facility that lets you customize the graphical output for the model at hand.

All the examples in the book are available for download at the book's website, *http://softwareabstractions.org*, along with other supplementary material.

2: A Whirlwind Tour

This chapter describes the incremental construction and analysis of a small model. My intent is to explain just enough to impart the flavor of the approach, so don't expect to follow all the details.

I've chosen an example that should be familiar to most readers: the design of an address book for an email client. Although I've kept the model small to simplify the presentation, this example isn't atypical in the amount of effort involved. A ten-line program can't do very much, and has almost nothing in common with a thousand-line program. But a ten-line model can be very useful, and doesn't differ that much from a hundred-line model, which is often all that's needed to explore a difficult design issue.

By developing the example in a series of small additions and modifications, I've attempted to convey the lightweight and incremental spirit of the approach. The immediacy of the feedback that the tool provides is much harder to get across; to experience this, you'll need to try the example yourself, running analyses and seeing how they react to your own modifications.

An email client's address book is a little database that associates email addresses with shorter names that are more convenient to use. The user can create an *alias* for a correspondent—a nickname that can be used in place of that person's address, and which need not change when the address itself changes. A *group* is like an alias but is associated with an entire set of correspondents—the members of a family, for instance. When defining a group, a user will often insert aliases rather than actual email addresses, so that a change in a person's email address can be corrected in just one place, even if it appears implicitly in many groups.

The tour starts with a simple address book with aliases and no groups. It shows how to declare the structure of the state of a system, and how to generate sample instances of the state (section 2.1). Then it adds dynamic behavior, and shows how to model an operation with constraints, how to simulate it, and how to check properties of operations (section 2.2).

The tour then takes a turn into more sophisticated territory. The state of the address book is elaborated to allow names (that is, groups and aliases) to refer to other names, forming naming chains of any length (section 2.3). The model uses an idiom that design pattern afficionados call *Composite*. The analyses of the simple address book are reapplied, and now turn up some potential problems.

Finally, the model is extended with traces, so that now analyses and simulations show entire executions involving a series of operations, rather than single operation steps (section 2.4). I included this section to show the flexibility of the approach, especially for readers familiar with model checking, although in practice it's often fine just to analyze operations one at a time.

2.1   Statics: Exploring States

We're going to explore a simple address book for an email client that maintains a mapping from names to addresses. Here's our first model:

```
module tour/addressBook1

sig Name, Addr {}
sig Book {
    addr: Name -> lone Addr
    }
```

That's a complete Alloy model. It introduces three *signatures—Name*, *Addr*, and *Book*—each representing a set of objects. The *Book* signature has a field *addr* that maps names to addresses. In fact, *addr* is a three-way mapping associating books, names, and addresses, containing the tuple *b -> n -> a* when, in book *b*, name *n* is mapped to address *a*. The expression *b.addr* denotes the mapping from names to addresses for book *b*.

The keyword *lone* in the declaration indicates *multiplicity*—in this case that each name is mapped to at most one address. For now, we're just modeling simple aliases; later we'll consider groups.

This model contains no commands, so there's no analysis that can be done (beyond simple static semantic and type checks). Our first analysis will be to get some samples of the possible states. To do this, we add a *predicate*, and a *command* to find an instance of the predicate:

```
pred show () {}
run show for 3 but 1 Book
```

The predicate has an empty body; later we'll add some constraints. The command specifies a *scope* that bounds the search for instances: in this case, to at most three objects in each signature, except for *Book*, which

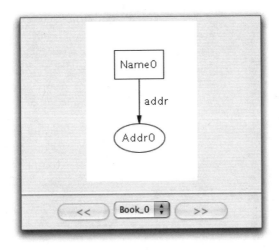

FIG. 2.1 Simulating the address book: a first instance.

is limited to one object, since, for now, we're only interested in seeing a single address book. The scope is for the purpose of analysis alone; the model doesn't limit the size or number of address books.

Running the command produces the *instance* of fig. 2.1. Outputs can be shown in a variety of forms, textual and graphical. Here, I've chosen to have the output displayed as a graph, and I've instructed the analyzer to "project" the instance on *Book*, which means that it shows a separate graph for each book object.

You may wonder why this particular instance was chosen. In fact, the tool's selection of instances is arbitrary, and depending on the preferences you've set, may even change from run to run. In practice, though, the first instance generated does tend to be a small one. This is useful, because the small instances are often pathological, and thus more likely to expose subtle problems. You can ask the tool to produce a series of instances without repeats, but in our tour, we'll always make do with the first one.

This instance shows a single link from a name to an address. To see an instance with more than one link, we can add a constraint to the predicate:

```
pred show (b: Book) {
    #b.addr > 1
    }
```

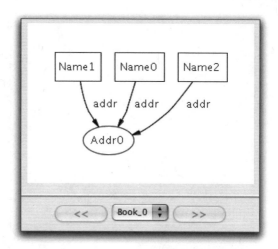

FIG. 2.2 A second address book instance.

So that we can talk about a particular book, I've added an argument *b* of type *Book* to the predicate. The expression *b.addr* is the mapping from names to addresses for this book, and *#b.addr* is the number of associations in this mapping. So the constraint asks for an instance in which the book *b* has more than one name/address association.

Running the command again now gives the instance of fig. 2.2. We see that our model allows two names (three in this case!) to map to one address. Does our model allow one name to map to two addresses? If we add a constraint asking for such a name

```
pred show (b: Book) {
  #b.addr > 1
  some n: Name | #n.(b.addr) > 1
  }
```

the analyzer tells us that the predicate *show* is now inconsistent—at least in this scope—and has no instances. This is not surprising, since the constraint we added contradicts the multiplicity in the declaration of *addr*.

Even if we can't have one name map to two addresses, we would like to make sure that it's possible to have more than one address in the address book. So we replace the inconsistent constraint by a weaker one:

```
pred show (b: Book) {
  #b.addr > 1
  #Name.(b.addr) > 1
  }
```

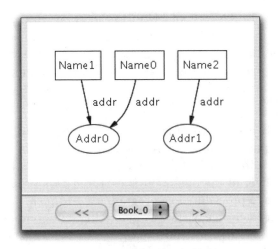

FIG. 2.3 A third address book instance.

Whereas the bad constraint used the expression *n.(b.addr)* for looking up a single name *n* in address book *b*, this constraint uses *Name.(b.addr)* for looking up the entire set of names. This expression therefore denotes the set of all addresses that may result from lookups. One of the nice features of Alloy is that the operators are defined very generally, and any operator that can be applied to a scalar can also be applied to a set.

Running the command gives the instance of fig. 2.3. These little simulations are useful because, with minimal effort on the user's part, they confirm that the model doesn't inadvertently rule out obvious cases, and they present other cases that might not have been considered at all.

So far, we've defined a state space and generated some sample states. It's time to look at some behaviors.

2.2 Dynamics: Adding Operations

Let's add to the model a description of what happens when an entry is added to an address book:

```
pred add (b, b': Book, n: Name, a: Addr) {
    b'.addr = b.addr + n -> a
}
```

The predicate *add*, like the predicate *show*, is just a constraint. In this case, though, it represents an *operation*, and describes dynamic behavior. Its arguments are an address book before the addition (*b*), an address book after (*b'*), a name (*n*), and an address (*a*) the name is to be mapped to. The constraint says that the address mapping in the new book is equal to the address mapping in the old book, with the addition of a link from the name to the address.

The way this operation is described will probably strike you as odd if you're used to imperative programming languages and haven't seen modeling languages before. There's no explicit mutation here; instead, the before and after states of the book are given different names (*b* and *b'*), and the effect of the operation is captured by a property relating them. Whereas a procedure in a program is *operational*, and describes how to *produce* a change of state by modifying state components, Alloy is *declarative*, and describes how to *check* whether a change of state is valid, by comparing the before and after values.

Even though Alloy is declarative, it can still be executed much like an operational language. To execute the operation, we run a command such as

> **run** add **for** 3 **but** 2 Book

This time we've limited the scope to just 2 books (for the before and after values). The result, in fig. 2.4, shows the prestate (the state of the book before the operation) above, and the poststate (the state after) below. In the prestate, the book is empty; in the poststate, there is a new link from *Name0* to *Addr0*.

Note how the name node is marked with the label *add_n* and the address node with *add_a* to show which objects are bound to the arguments *n* and *a* of the *add* operation. These labels will become more important later when they show witnesses to the violation of an assertion.

Following the same strategy we used for states, we can explore more interesting transitions by adding constraints. We could elaborate the predicate *add* itself, but it's better to create a new predicate, making a clear distinction between the operation itself and constraints written for the purpose of exploration:

```
pred showAdd  (b, b': Book, n: Name, a: Addr) {
  add (b, b', n, a)
  #Name.(b'.addr) > 1
  }
```

> **run** showAdd **for** 3 **but** 2 Book

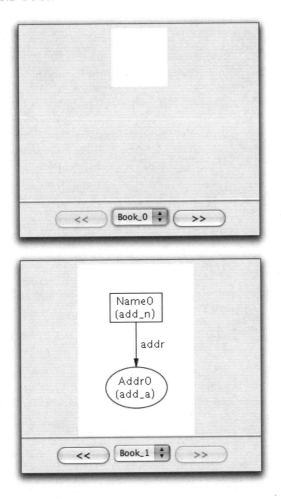

FIG. 2.4 A generated transition for *add*.

The new predicate *showAdd* "invokes" the existing predicate *add*. The effect is no different from including the constraints of *add* directly (but it's more modular to do it this way). We've added a constraint that asks for a transition in which the address book after has more than one address mapped to (using the same constraint we used when simulating states). The result is shown in fig. 2.5. Note that it's just as easy to constrain the state *after* as constraining the state *before*: the analyzer is "executing" this operation backward.

Let's move on, and write some more operations, for deleting entries, and for lookup:

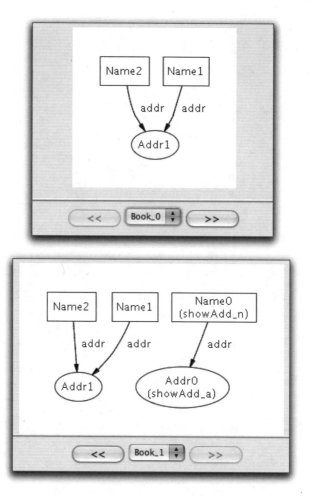

FIG. 2.5 A generated transition for *showAdd*.

pred del (b, b': Book, n: Name) {
  b'.addr = b.addr - n -> Addr
  }

fun lookup (b: Book, n: Name): **set** Addr {
  n.(b.addr)
  }

The deletion operation says that the after-book is the before-book with all links from the name *n* to any address removed. The lookup operation is written as a *function* rather than a predicate: its body is an expression rather than a constraint, and says that the result of a lookup is whatever set of addresses the name *n* maps to under the *addr* mapping of *b*.

We could simulate these operations too, but let's do something different, and write some assertions about how combinations of operations in sequence behave. Our first assertion says that deletion is an undo operation for addition:

```
assert delUndoesAdd {
    all b,b',b": Book, n: Name, a: Addr |
        add (b,b',n,a) and del (b',b",n) implies b.addr = b".addr
}
```

An *assertion* is a constraint that is intended to be valid—that is, true for all possible cases. This one says that an addition from book *b* resulting in book *b'*, followed by a deletion using the same name *n*, results in a book *b"* whose address mapping is the same as that of the original book *b*.

To check the assertion, we issue the following command to the analyzer:

```
check delUndoesAdd for 3
```

This instructs the analyzer to search not for an example, but for a *counterexample*—a scenario in which the assertion is violated. And indeed, it finds one, as shown in fig. 2.6. Strangely, there are only two distinct states in this scenario. As the diagram at the bottom shows (produced by the visualizer with different settings), *b* and *b'*, the values of the book in the first and second states, are both *Book0*, shown above on the left. The reason is that the name/address link to be added is already present, so the execution of *add* has no effect. The execution of *del*, on the other hand, removes the link, resulting in the empty book, shown on the right.

Sometimes the failure of an assertion will point to a flaw in the model proper. In this case, however, the model seems reasonable, and given our decision to allow additions for existing entries, it's not surprising that deletion doesn't act as an undo. (At least, it's not surprising in retrospect. Many of the issues raised by analysis are like bugs in code—perfectly obvious once you've already seen them.) To check that our hypothesis is right, we can modify the assertion, restricting the claim to cases in which no entry already exists for the name *n*:

```
assert delUndoesAdd {
    all b,b',b": Book, n: Name, a: Addr |
        no n.(b.addr) and add (b,b',n,a) and del (b',b",n)
            implies b.addr = b".addr
}
```

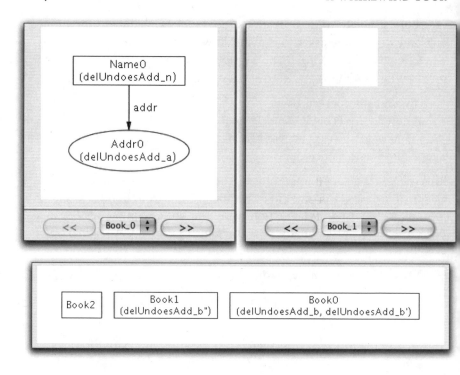

FIG. 2.6 A counterexample to *delUndoesAdd*.

Executing the check now finds no counterexample. The assertion may still be invalid, though. Since the analyzer only considered cases involving three books, three names, and three addresses, it's possible that there is a counterexample involving more.

So we crank up the scope. There's no point considering more than three books, but we allow 10 names and 10 addresses:

> **check** delUndoesAdd **for** 10 **but** 3 Book

Executing this takes longer than the previous analyses (about 3 seconds on a 2GHz Macintosh G5). As you increase the scope, the space of cases to consider grows dramatically. With 10 names and addresses, there are 11 possibilities for each name, so the starting state alone has 11^{10} possible values. And because the operations don't have to be written in an executable style, the tool has to search over the possible values of all three books, so there are over 10^{30} cases to consider.

Now you can see why this kind of analysis is more effective than testing. Of course, the analyzer doesn't construct and check each case individually; even if it used only one processor cycle per case, 10^{30} cases would still take longer than the age of the universe. By pruning the tree of possibilities, it can rule out large subspaces without examining them fully.

We still haven't *proved* the assertion is valid. But, intuitively, it seems very unlikely that, if there is a problem, it can't be shown in a counterexample with 10 names and addresses. How far to go is a pragmatic judgment you have to make as a modeler. Eventually, as you increase the scope, the analysis becomes intractable.

The tradeoff is no different in principle from the one you face when deciding whether you've tested a program enough. In practice, though, exhausting a scope of 10 gives more coverage of a model than handwritten test cases ever could. Most flaws in models can be illustrated by small instances, since they arise from some shape being handled incorrectly, and whether the shape belongs to a large or small instance makes no difference. So if the analysis considers all small instances, most flaws will be revealed. This observation, which I call the *small scope hypothesis*, is the fundamental premise that underlies Alloy's analysis.

There are many other examples of assertions in this "algebraic" style. Here are two. The first checks that *add* is idempotent—that repeating an addition has no effect:

```
assert addIdempotent {
    all b,b',b": Book, n: Name, a: Addr |
        add (b,b',n,a) and add (b',b",n,a) implies b'.addr = b".addr
}
```

The second checks that *add* is local; that adding an entry for a name *n* doesn't affect the result of a lookup for a different name *n'*:

```
assert addLocal {
    all b,b': Book, n,n': Name, a: Addr |
        add (b,b',n,a) and n != n' implies lookup (b,n') = lookup (b',n')
}
```

Checking these assertions gives no counterexamples.

The final version of the model discussed in this section is shown in fig. 2.7. Note that it includes the simulation predicates and assertions and their associated commands. These play the same role that test drivers and stubs play for code; they are an integral part of the development. When you make a change to a model, you can recheck the assertions and rerun the simulations just as you would run regression tests after modifying code.

module tour/addressBook1

sig Name, Addr {}
sig Book {addr: Name -> **lone** Addr}

pred show (b: Book) {
  #b.addr > 1
  #Name.(b.addr) > 1
  }
run show **for** 3 **but** 1 Book

pred add (b, b': Book, n: Name, a: Addr) {b'.addr = b.addr + n -> a}
pred del (b, b': Book, n: Name) {b'.addr = b.addr - n -> Addr}
fun lookup (b: Book, n: Name): **set** Addr {n.(b.addr)}

pred showAdd (b, b': Book, n: Name, a: Addr) {
  add (b, b', n, a)
  #Name.(b'.addr) > 1
  }
run showAdd **for** 3 **but** 2 Book

assert delUndoesAdd {
  all b,b',b": Book, n: Name, a: Addr |
    no n.(b.addr) **and**
    add (b,b',n,a) **and** del (b',b",n) **implies** b.addr = b".addr
  }

assert addIdempotent {
  all b,b',b": Book, n: Name, a: Addr |
    add (b,b',n,a) **and** add (b',b",n,a) **implies** b'.addr = b".addr
  }

assert addLocal {
  all b,b': Book, n,n': Name, a: Addr |
    add (b,b',n,a) **and** n != n'
      implies lookup (b,n') = lookup (b',n')
  }

check delUndoesAdd **for** 10 **but** 3 Book
check addIdempotent **for** 3
check addLocal **for** 3 **but** 2 Book

FIG. 2.7 Final version of model for simple address book.

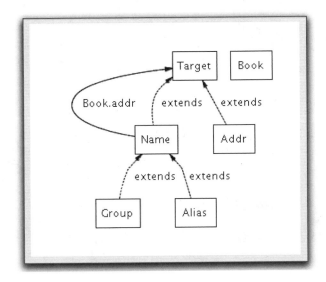

FIG. 2.8 Model diagram for hierarchical address book.

2.3 Classification Hierarchy

In a realistic address book application, you can create an alias for an address, and then use that alias as the target for another alias. And an alias can name multiple targets, so that a group of addresses can be referred to with a single name.

Rather than elaborating our existing model, we'll just start afresh and reuse fragments of the old model as needed. We start with a classification hierarchy showing the various sets of objects and their relationship to one another:

module tour/addressBook2

abstract sig Target {}
sig Addr **extends** Target {}
abstract sig Name **extends** Target {}

sig Alias, Group **extends** Name {}
sig Book {addr: Name -> Target}

Fig. 2.8 shows a *model diagram*, a graphical representation of the model's declarations, generated automatically by the analyzer from the text above. Note that the *addr* field of *Book* now maps names to targets. A

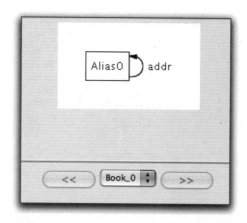

FIG. 2.9 First instance for hierarchical address book.

target is either just an address, as before, or a name itself; names are either groups or aliases.

Just as we did for the simple address book, we can explore the state space with simulation predicates. For example, if ask to see a nonempty book

pred show (b: Book) {**some** b.addr}
run show **for** 3 **but** 1 Book

the analyzer responds with the instance of fig. 2.9, in which an alias is mapped to itself. This is the first simulation we've done that clearly reveals a flaw to be remedied. We add a *fact*—a constraint that's assumed always to hold—stating that, for any book, there is no name that belongs to the set of targets reachable from the name itself:

fact {
all b: Book | **no** n: Name | n **in** n.^(b.addr)
}

The expression *n.^(b.addr)* denotes the targets reachable from *n*, using the transitive closure *^(b.addr)* of the address book mapping of *b*. You can think of *x.r* as a navigation from object *x* through one application of relation *r*, and *x.^r* as a navigation from object *x* through one or more applications of *r*.

Facts like this, that apply to every member of a signature, are better written as *signature facts*, in which the quantification, and the reference to the particular member, are implicit:

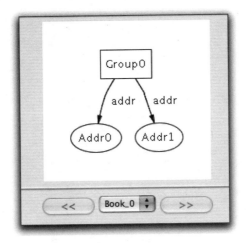

FIG. 2.10 Second instance for hierarchical address book.

sig Book {addr: Name -> Target}
{**no** n: Name | n **in** n.^addr}

Note that, like a reference to a field of a receiver in an object-oriented program, *addr* now implicitly refers to *this.addr*, the address book mapping of an archetypal book, and the *all* quantifier has gone.

Running the command again, we now get a situation, shown in fig. 2.10, in which a group contains two addresses. We'd like to see an alias mapped, so we change the predicate's constraint to say that there should be some targets resulting from mapping all aliases:

pred show (b: Book) {**some** Alias.(b.addr)}

Now, in fig. 2.11, we have an alias mapped to two addresses. This is undesirable; a name mapped to more than one target should be a group, not an alias. So we add another fact:

sig Book {addr: Name -> Target}
{
no n: Name | n **in** n.^(addr)
all a: Alias | **lone** a.addr
}

Executing the command again, we see a new problem, shown in fig. 2.12: an alias maps to an empty group. This means that if you look up a name, you might get no addresses back at all, even though the name is in the

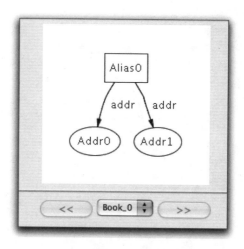

FIG. 2.11 Third instance for hierarchical address book.

address book! In fact, many address book applications allow this, and then (unhelpfully) report a failure only later when the message is sent.

Let's make this issue explicit in our model. First, we elaborate the *Book* signature to make explicit the set of names that are in the book, by adding a field (*names*) to represent this set, and by changing the declaration of the address mapping (*addr*) to say that it maps only names in this set, and maps each to at least one target:

```
sig Book {
    names: set Name,
    addr: names -> some Target }
    {
    no n: Name | n in n.^(addr)
    all a: Alias | lone a.addr
    }
```

Then we add an assertion claiming that every lookup of a name in the book yields some results:

```
assert lookupYields {
    all b: Book, n: b.names | some lookup (b,n)
    }
```

(We'll define *lookup* shortly.) Checking this assertion will give a counterexample just like fig. 2.12. The problem isn't so easy to fix. We could simply add a fact stating, for example, that groups can't be empty. But

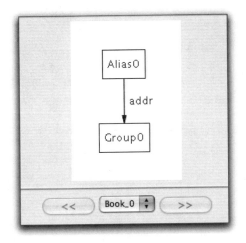

FIG. 2.12 Fourth instance for hierarchical address book.

it's not obvious how to maintain such a property, so we'll put it off for now and return to it later.

Let's update the operations to match the new, more elaborate address book:

> **pred** add (b, b': Book, n: Name, t: Target) {b'.addr = b.addr + n -> t}
> **pred** del (b, b': Book, n: Name, t: Target) {b'.addr = b.addr - n -> t}
> **fun** lookup (b: Book, n: Name): **set** Addr {n.^(b.addr) & Addr}

The differences are minor. The *add* operation now takes a target rather than an address, and *del* now also takes a target in addition to a name. At first I didn't see the need for the second argument of *del*, but while exploring the model with the analyzer, I realized that without it you wouldn't be able to remove just one target from a group. The *lookup* operation is more interesting now, being generalized to arbitrary depth: it follows the address mapping any number of times, rather than just once, obtaining a set of targets, which it then intersects with the set of addresses, thus returning all addresses reachable from the name.

We can now check the old assertions. The assertion *delUndoesAdd* (with the extra condition that the name added is not already mapped) still passes, as does *addIdempotent*. But *addLocal* now fails, as shown in fig. 2.13. Note the labels indicating which objects act as witnesses to the violation: *n'* is *Group1*, whose associated addresses are changed by an *add* applied to *n*, which is *Group0*. Now that we have indirection, changing

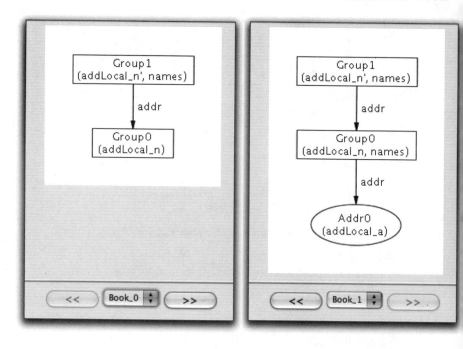

FIG. 2.13 Counterexample to *addLocal* for hierarchical address book.

the binding of one alias or group can affect another. This seems reasonable, and we decide that the model doesn't need to be fixed.

The final version of the model discussed in this section is shown in fig. 2.14.

2.4 Execution Traces

Let's return to the problem of empty lookups—cases in which a name that is in the address book corresponds to no addresses. This time, we'll examine not only the bad situations but also how they might arise. Rather than considering the effect of individual steps, we consider entire traces, consisting of multiple steps from an initial state.

The body of the model remains unchanged. All we need to do is add an ordering on address books, constrained so that the first book satisfies some initial conditions, and any adjacent books in the ordering are related by an operation.

```
module tour/addressBook2

abstract sig Target {}
sig Addr extends Target {}
abstract sig Name extends Target {}

sig Alias, Group extends Name {}
sig Book {
  names: set Name,
  addr: names -> some Target }
  {
  no n: Name | n in n.^(addr)
  all a: Alias | lone a.addr
  }

pred add (b, b': Book, n: Name, t: Target) {b'.addr = b.addr + n->t}
pred del (b, b': Book, n: Name, t: Target) {b'.addr = b.addr - n->t}
fun lookup (b: Book, n: Name): set Addr {n.^(b.addr) & Addr}

assert delUndoesAdd {
  all b,b',b": Book, n: Name, t: Target |
    no n.(b.addr) and
      add (b,b',n,t) and del (b',b",n, t) implies b.addr = b".addr
  }
check delUndoesAdd for 3

assert addIdempotent {
  all b,b',b": Book, n: Name, t: Target |
    add (b,b',n,t) and add (b',b",n,t) implies b'.addr = b".addr
  }
check addIdempotent for 3

assert addLocal {
  all b,b': Book, n,n': Name, t: Target |
    add (b,b',n,t) and n != n'
      implies lookup (b,n') = lookup (b',n')
  }
check addLocal for 3 but 2 Book

assert lookupYields {
  all b: Book, n: b.names | some lookup(b,n)
  }
check lookupYields for 4 but 1 Book
```

FIG. 2.14 Final version of model for hierarchical address book.

Here's what the new model looks like (with ellipses for the old declarations and operations):

```
module tour/addressBook3
open util/ordering [Book]
...
pred init (b: Book) {no b.addr}

fact traces {
    init (first ())
    all b: Book - last () | let b' = next (b) |
        some n: Name, t: Target | add (b, b', n, t) or del (b, b', n, t)
    }
```

The ordering on books is provided by the library module *util/ordering*. This module is generic—that is, it can order a set of any type—so when opened it must be instantiated with a type (in this case, *Book*). The module has its own signatures and fields, but is accessed through the functions *first*, *next* and *last*, giving the first element in the order, the element following a given element, and the last.

The predicate *init* gives the initial condition—that the address book is empty. The fact *traces* specifies the constraints that make the ordering a trace: that the initial condition holds for the first book in the trace, and that any book *b* (except the last) and its successor *b'* are related by the constraints of the *add* or *del* operation.

To see a sample trace, we ask for an instance satisfying an empty predicate:

```
pred show () {}
run show for 4
```

The analyzer generates the trace, shown in fig. 2.15, with three additions in a row. The last one (making *Group0* a member of *Group1*) is interesting: it creates two routes to the same address. Again, we see how simulation generates cases that are thought-provoking, even when they don't expose obvious flaws.

To investigate the empty lookup problem, we can check the same assertion as before:

```
assert lookupYields {all b: Book, n: b.names | some lookup(b,n)}
check lookupYields for 3 but 4 Book
```

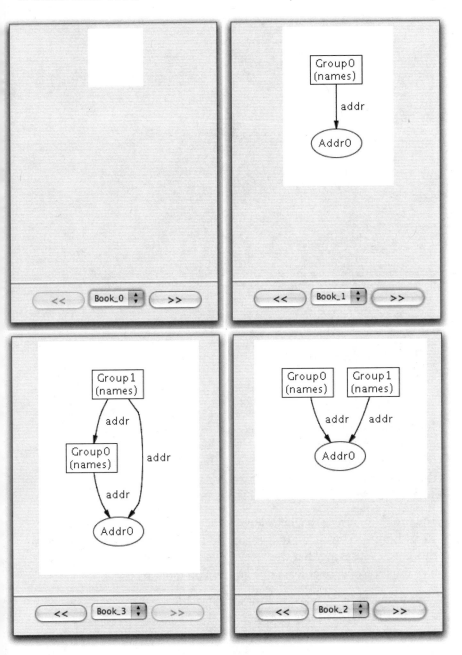

FIG. 2.15 Sample trace for hierarchical address book: each panel represents a state, starting with the initial state in the top left, and moving clockwise around.

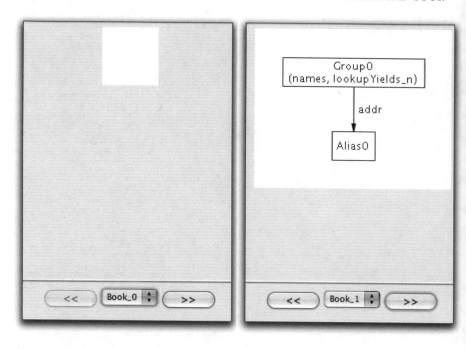

FIG. 2.16 Counterexample trace violating *lookupYields* with one step of *add*.

This time, however, the set of books is constrained to form a trace, so the counterexample, shown in fig. 2.16, shows how a sequence of operations can result in a bad state. Note the label *lookupYields_n* indicating the witness to the violation—*Group0*. The violation actually occurs after the very first step, in state *Book1*, so I've omitted the other two states. A smaller scope would have sufficed.

The problem here is that *add* allows a meaningless alias—one that refers to nothing—to be added to a group. To fix this, we might add a precondition to *add*, saying that the target given must either be an address, or else must resolve to at least one address on lookup:

```
pred add (b, b': Book, n: Name, t: Target) {
    t in Addr or some lookup (b,t)
    b'.addr = b.addr + n -> t
    }
```

Checking the assertion again, we get the counterexample of fig. 2.17. This time the problem is with deletion: we've deleted the last member of a group. We can fix this, albeit in a rather draconian manner, by forbidding such a deletion with a precondition:

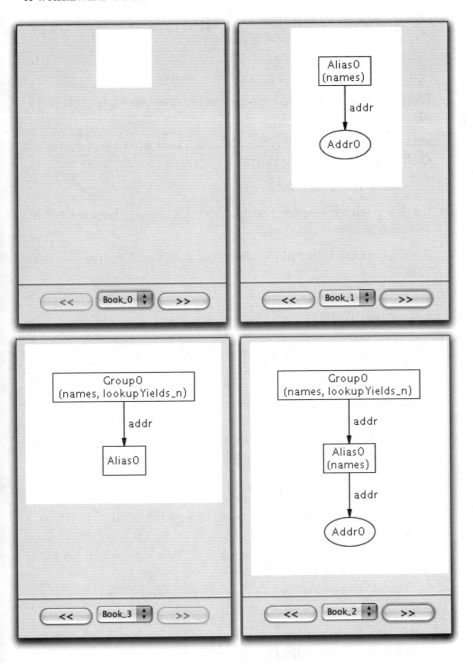

FIG. 2.17 Counterexample trace violating *lookupYields* with deletion of last member of a group; each panel represents a state, starting with the initial state in the top left, and moving clockwise around.

```
pred del (b, b': Book, n: Name, t: Target) {
  no b.addr.n or some n.(b.addr) - t
  b'.addr = b.addr - n -> t
  }
```

The precondition says that *n* isn't itself mapped to, or it's mapped to some target besides *t*.

Now, no counterexample is found. So we crank up the scope to 6, and analyze for all scenarios involving 6 targets and 6 address books:

```
check lookupYields for 6
```

This is a much larger space, and analysis takes almost 2 minutes, but still no counterexample is found.

The final version of the model discussed in this section is shown in fig. 2.18.

2.5   Summary

The purpose of this short tour wasn't to demonstrate how much can be accomplished with this style of modeling. Indeed, when you've read this book and have had some practice, you'll be able to write more sophisticated models of more interesting things. Its purpose was instead to show how little you actually need to do to get some insight into a software design problem. Our most complex model was only a page long, but that was sufficient to explore some issues that arise in a real system.

It's easy to dismiss the kinds of issue we looked at as trivial and obvious. They often are—in retrospect, at least. Indeed, the hardest, and most rewarding, challenge in software design is reducing a mass of complicated, incongruous details to a few simple generalities. Simplicity is the key to good software design.

Looking back at this modeling exercise, it's instructive to recall not so much what we did, but what we didn't do:

- We didn't write an elaborate model, and only then analyze it. Our first analysis was applied to a model less than ten lines long. We developed the model incrementally, as we explored it with the analyzer.

- We didn't use any complicated mathematics or unfamiliar symbols. The Alloy language is based on simple notions of basic logic, and a

```
module tour/addressBook3
open util/ordering [Book]

abstract sig Target {}
sig Addr extends Target {}
abstract sig Name extends Target {}
sig Alias, Group extends Name {}

sig Book {
  names: set Name,
  addr: names -> some Target }
  {
  no n: Name | n in n.^(addr)
  all a: Alias | lone a.addr
  }
pred add (b, b': Book, n: Name, t: Target) {
  t in Addr or some lookup(b,t)
  b'.addr = b.addr + n -> t
  }

pred del (b, b': Book, n: Name, t: Target) {
  no b.addr.n or some n.(b.addr) - t
  b'.addr = b.addr - n -> t
  }

fun lookup (b: Book, n: Name): set Addr {
  n.^(b.addr) & Addr
  }

pred init (b: Book) {no b.addr}
fact traces {
  init (first ())
  all b: Book - last () | let b' = next (b) |
    some n: Name, t: Target | add (b, b', n, t) or del (b, b', n, t)
  }

pred show () {}
run show for 4

assert lookupYields {
  all b: Book, n: b.names | some lookup (b,n)
  }
check lookupYields for 3 but 4 Book
check lookupYields for 6
```

FIG. 2.18 Final version of model for traces over hierarchical address book.

special dot operator for navigating along relations, similar to (but more flexible than) the dereferencing dot of Java.

· We didn't need to write any executable code to get sample states, nor even to get sample traces. A major advantage of this, which we didn't exploit in this tour, is that you can write a very partial description of an operation that allows many different behaviors.

· We didn't write any test cases. The assertions that we wrote are like test oracles that check the result of a test. An assertion is rarely more trouble to write than a single test case, but has the coverage of an unimaginably huge test suite.

· We didn't guide the analyzer in any way, beyond giving a scope to bound the analysis. No proof steps, no lemmas, no heuristics to suggest.

· We didn't have to worry about false alarms. Although the analysis of an assertion might not find a counterexample—because one only exists in a larger scope—it will never report a spurious one. (Of course, it may still be irrelevant because the assertion wasn't what we intended, or the model didn't express the behavior we had in mind.)

It's also instructive to consider how this experience would have been different if it had been conducted entirely by pencil on paper. Without extraordinary discipline and perseverance, it's hard to motivate yourself to explore tricky issues, and even if we had done so, we probably would not have articulated them in a form that was precise enough to share with others (or for us to recall for ourselves later).

Alternatively, think about conducting this exercise in code, in a language such as Java. We would have needed at least five files (just to represent the classification hierarchy). The one-line *lookup* operation would require a loop or recursion, accessing a hashtable, and accumulating results in another data structure. The only analysis we could have performed would have been the execution of a few fixed test cases—no generation of arbitrary samples, no exhaustive checking within bounds, no visual display of results.

2.5.1 Questions

Is this style of modeling new?

Jim Horning and John Guttag described a very similar approach in a paper in 1980, in which a theorem prover was used to answer questions interactively about a candidate design [21]. That paper was a major source of inspiration for Alloy. The Z notation [65], developed at Oxford in the 1980's, was designed to encourage incremental specification, as illustrated by many published Z examples. Several tools—such as the USE tool for UML [71] and VDMTools [2]—animate specifications by executing operations and evaluating constraints from given initial states.

Aren't the problems you explored trivial?

With hindsight, most software design problems are trivial. But if you don't address them head-on, trivial issues have a nasty habit of becoming nontrivial. At the time of writing, most email clients I know of don't handle the issue of empty lookups very gracefully. The Apple mail client, for example, lets you create empty groups and aliases in the address book, but refuses (without an explanatory warning) to let you include them in a message header. If you create a group whose sole member is an empty alias, it allows you to include the group in a header, and passes an ill-formed message to the SMTP server, which is then bounced back.

How do you select the scope for an Alloy analysis?

Every command (to check an assertion or run a predicate) specifies a scope that puts a bound on the number of elements of each signature. There's a tradeoff: a small scope may miss an instance, but a large scope takes longer to analyze (and tends to produce larger, and less intelligible, instances). So a good way to work is to start with a small scope, and increase it if no instances are found. Often the scope on some signatures is clear. For example, only two books are needed to analyze transitions that involve a single state change from one value of an address book to another.

Why isn't a notion of execution built into Alloy?

Not hardwiring a particular notion of execution allows the notation to be used in many different idioms. In chapter 6, for example, two versions of a model of a scheme for hotel locking are developed. One uses the idiom of this chapter, in which the execution steps satisfy named operations, but the operation names themselves are not part of the execution; the other uses an idiom in which the execution is a sequence of concrete, named events.

Why don't you just use diagrams?

Diagrams are very useful representations, but they're limited in their expressiveness. I often use a diagram to sketch the structure of a model, and then transcribe it into Alloy text. Graphical input is not very convenient in practice: within a tool, it's usually less work to enter text than to draw a diagram, and it's easier to exchange models in textual form. Graphical output, on the other hand, is indispensable. The Alloy Analyzer can display instances in graphical form, or in textual form, or as an expanding tree. It can also generate model diagrams from model text.

When the analyzer displays an example of a transition as a pair of graphs, how do you know which is the prestate and which is the poststate?

The analyzer includes an editor for customizing visualizations. In the visualizations I've chosen, the binding of pre- and poststate variables b and b' to atoms, such as *Book0* and *Book1*, isn't shown. Typically, the atoms are bound in lexicographic order, so *Book0* will be assigned to b, and *Book1* to b', but this is easily confirmed by selecting a different visualization, or by examining the output in textual form.

In a trace, are the states always in the order their names suggest?

Yes, when states are ordered, as the books were in the last version of the model, the lexicographic order of the states will always match their order in the trace. Here, for example, *Book0* was the first state, *Book1* the second, and so on. This is because the tool uses a special symmetry-breaking optimization for the library module *util/ordering* that ensures that it always orders atoms in their lexicographic order. (See the discussion following subsection 5.2.1 for more explanation.)

3: Logic

At the core of every modeling language is a *logic* that provides the fundamental concepts. It must be small, simple, and expressive. A "working logic," designed for expressing abstractions, unlike a logic designed for theoretical investigations, cannot be completely minimal, but must be flexible enough to allow the same idea to be expressed in different ways.

This chapter introduces a *relational logic* that combines the quantifiers of first-order logic with the operators of the relational calculus. It's easy to learn—especially if you're familiar with basic set theory, or with relational query languages—and surprisingly powerful.

Although designed for software abstractions, the logic has been kept free of any notions that would tie it to a particular programming language or execution model. Its key characteristic, which distinguishes it from traditional logics, is a generalization of the notion of relational join. As in a relational database, a relation is a set of tuples. Sets are represented as relations with a single column, and scalars as singleton sets. Consequently, the same join operator can be applied to scalars, sets, and relations, and changing the "multiplicity" of a relation (that is, whether it maps an element to a scalar or a set) in its declaration does not require a change to the constraints in which it appears. Dispensing with the distinction between sets and scalars also makes constraints more uniform and easier to write, and eliminates the problem of partial function application, so there's no need for special "undefined" values. There are a few other novelties too, such as the ability to nest multiplicities in declarations.

3.1 Three Logics in One

Our logic supports three different styles, which can be mixed and varied at will. In the *predicate calculus* style, there are only two kinds of expression: relation names, which are used as predicates, and tuples formed from quantified variables.

In this style, the constraint that an address book, represented by a relation *address* from names to addresses, maps each name to at most one address might be written

> **all** n: Name, d, d': Address |
>   n -> d **in** address **and** n -> d' **in** address **implies** d = d'

In the *navigation expression* style, expressions denote sets, which are formed by "navigating" from quantified variables along relations. In this style, the same constraint becomes

> **all** n: Name | **lone** n.address

In the *relational calculus* style, expressions denote relations, and there are no quantifiers at all. Using operators we'll define shortly, the constraint can be written

> **no** ~address.address - **iden**

The predicate calculus style is usually too verbose, and the relational calculus is often too cryptic. The most common style is therefore the navigational one, with occasional uses of the other styles when appropriate.

Discussion

Which choice would you actually make for this constraint?

None of these. Multiplicity constraints of this kind are so common that our logic has some special syntax that allows the constraint to be included in a declaration. In this case, you'd write

> address: Name -> **lone** Address

Where is the predicate calculus style used?

A common use is in comprehension expressions, which allow you to construct a set or relation from a constraint. For example, if you have a relation r that relates three elements from sets A, B and C, and you want the columns instead in the order B, A, C, you can define a new relation by comprehension:

> r' = {b: B, a: A, c: C | a -> b -> c **in** r}

The predicate calculus style can also be appealing when writing a very subtle constraint, because it's so concrete and straightforward, and the quantifications often match a formulation of the constraint in natural language.

Where is the relational calculus style used?

Experienced modelers find it useful for some commonly recurring constraints that can be expressed more concisely this way, writing, for example, *no ^r & iden* to say that the relation *r* is acyclic. Also, you might write a constraint in the navigation style and notice that a quantified variable can be "cancelled out." For example, the constraint

> **all** p: Person | p.uncle = p.parent.brother

can be written more concisely as

> uncle = parent.brother

(so long as *uncle* and *parent* only map members of the set *Person*).

Do the styles have equivalent expressive power?

No. The navigational style is the most expressive. Predicate calculus lacks transitive closure, so reachability properties can't be expressed. The relational calculus has no quantifiers, and not all occurrences of the quantifiers of predicate calculus can be expressed purely relationally.

Does the style have an impact on the performance of the analysis?

Not in general. Basic modeling decisions about how many relations to use, and how many columns each relation has, have a far bigger impact.

3.2   Atoms and Relations

All structures in our models will be built from *atoms* and *relations*, corresponding to the basic entities and the relationships between them.

3.2.1 Atoms

An atom is a primitive entity that is

· *indivisible*: it can't be broken down into smaller parts;

· *immutable*: its properties don't change over time; and

· *uninterpreted*: it doesn't have any built-in properties, the way numbers do, for example.

Elementary particles aside, very few things in the real world are atomic; this is a modeling abstraction. So what do you do if you want to model

something that *is* divisible, or mutable, or interpreted? You just introduce relations to capture these properties as additional structure.

3.2.2 Relations

A relation is a structure that relates atoms. It consists of a set of tuples,
each tuple being a sequence of atoms. You can think of a relation as a
table, in which each entry is an atom. The order of the columns matters,
but not the order of the rows. Each row must have an entry in every
column.

A relation can have any number of rows, called its *size*. Any size is possible, including zero. The number of columns in a relation is called its
arity, and must be one or more. Relations with arity one, two, and three
are said to be *unary*, *binary*, and *ternary*. A relation with arity of three
or more is a *multirelation*.

A unary relation corresponds to a table with one column; it represents
a *set* of atoms. A unary relation with only one tuple, corresponding to a
table with a single entry, represents a *scalar* .

> *Example.* A set of names, a set of addresses, each of size 3, and a
> set of address books of size 2:
>
> Name = {(N0), (N1), (N2)}
> Addr = {(D0), (D1), (D2)}
> Book = {(B0), (B1)}

> *Example.* Some scalars:
>
> myName = {(N0)}
> yourName = {(N1)}
> myBook = {(B0)}

> *Example.* A binary relation from names to addresses, for modeling
> a world in which there is only one address book (and therefore no
> need to model address books explicitly), with size 2:
>
> address = {(N0, D0), (N1, D1)}

> *Example.* A ternary relation (as used in chapter 2) from books to
> names to addresses, for modeling a world in which there are mul-
> tiple address books, each with its own name to address mapping:
>
> addr = {(B0, N0, D0), (B0, N1, D1), (B1, N1, D2), (B1, N2, D2)}

Book   Name   Addr

Book	Name	Addr
B0	N0	D0
B0	N1	D1
B1	N1	D2
B1	N2	D2

size = 4

← *arity = 3* →

FIG. 3.1 A ternary relation viewed as a table.

Book *B0* maps name *N0* to address *D0*, and name *N1* to address *D1*; book *B1* maps name *N1* and name *N2* to address *D2*. Fig. 3.1 shows this relation as a table.

A relation with no tuples is *empty*. A unary relation with at most one tuple—that is, a relation that is either a scalar or empty—is called an *option*.

Example. An email application might store the user's email address, and, optionally, a distinct address used for the "reply-to" field of messages. The former might be modelled as a scalar *userAddress*, and the latter as an option *replyAddress*, which either contains an address or is empty.

In the Alloy logic, all values are relations, so a tuple will be represented by the relation containing it, in the same way that a scalar is represented by a singleton set. We'll therefore use the term *tuple* to describe a singleton relation—a relation containing exactly one tuple.

Example. Two scalars, and the tuple that associates them:

    myName = {(N0)}
    myAddress = {(A1)}
    myLink = {(N0, A1)}

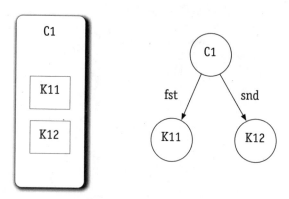

FIG. 3.2 A key card containing two keys (left)
represented with atoms and relations (right).

3.2.3 Expressing Structure with Relations

With relations, you can express structures in space and time, overcoming the apparent limitations of atoms as a modeling construct.

Although the only objects in the logic are indivisible atoms, you can model a composite object with atoms for the components and a relation to bind them together.

Example. To say that directories can contain files, you could introduce a relation *contents* that maps directories to the files they contain, which would include the tuples *(D0, F0)* and *(D0, F1)* when directory *D0* contains the files *F0* and *F1*.

Example. Hotel key cards, each holding two cryptographic keys, can be modeled as a set *Card* of cards, a set *Key* of keys, and two relations *fst* and *snd* from *Card* to *Key*. If a card *C1* has *K11* and *K12* as its first and second keys respectively, and a card *C2* has *K21* and *K22*, the relations would have these values:

fst = {(C1, K11), (C2, K21)}
snd = {(C1, K12), (C2, K22)}

This is illustrated, for card *C1*, in fig. 3.2.

When the content of an object is itself a relation, a multirelation is used to model containment.

Example. The relation *addr* mentioned in the previous section associates address books, names and addresses. Each address book can be viewed as containing a name/address table.

Although atoms are immutable, you can model mutation, in which the value of an object changes over time, by separating the identity of the object and its value into separate atoms, and relating identities, values and times.

Example. The history of values of some stocks might be represented by a relation *value* that includes the tuple *(S0, V0, T0)* if stock *S0* has value *V0* at time *T0*, and *(S0, V1, T1)* if it has value *V1* at time *T1*.

Example. An address book's changing contents could be modeled with a relation *addrT* on names, addresses and times, with a value such as

addrT = {(N0, D0, T0), (N1, D1, T0), (N2, D2, T1)}

if the book maps name *N0* to addresses *D0* and *D1* at time *T0*, and *N2* to *D2* at time *T1*.

When a model concerns only a single object and its changing value, a set of atoms can be used for that object to represent its value at different times.

Example. The *addr* relation of chapter 2 associated books, names and addresses. It could be used to model a static world in which there are several address books, each containing its own name/address table. In fact, however, it was used to represent the changing value of a single address book, with the book atoms playing the same role as the time atoms of *addrT*.

Finally, although atoms are uninterpreted, you can give them properties by introducing relations between them.

Example. The sequence numbers in a network protocol might be represented by atoms of a set *SeqNumber = {(N0), (N1), ...}*, and ordered by a relation *precedes*, which contains the tuple *(N0, N1)* when sequence number *N0* comes before sequence number *N1*.

Example. The book atoms in the model of section 2.4 were ordered *B0, B1, ...* with *B0* representing the value of the book initially, *B1* the value after one step, and so on. The ordering was imposed by importing a library module that includes a relation *next* mapping *B0* to *B1*, *B1* to *B2*, etc.

Example. Image-editing programs such as Adobe Photoshop allow you to apply color transformations to images. To explore the particular properties of one transformation, one would need a detailed model of colors and transformation functions. But to explore the abstractions underlying such a scheme, application of transformations to partial image selections, combining transformations with layers, undoing and redoing transformations, and so on, it may be sufficient to take a more abstract view, in which an image is just a mapping from pixel locations to RGB values, and a color transformation is a function from RGB values to RGB values. A relation

transform = {(RGB0, RGB1), (RGB1, RGB0)}

might model the transformation that exchanges the RGB values *RGB0* and *RGB1*.

Discussion

Are the names of the atoms significant?

No. Atom names never appear in models; they're only used to describe instances produced by simulation or checking. The Alloy Analyzer lets you assign your own names to the atoms of each set, but by default uses the full name of the set. So the atoms of *Book* will be *Book0, Book1*, and so on, rather than *B0, B1*, and so on.

What does an expression such as {(N0, D0), (N1, D1)} mean?

It's an expression in the language of traditional mathematics. In this case, it denotes the set consisting of two tuples, the first tuple having *N0* as its first element and *D0* as its second element, and the second tuple having *N1* as its first element and *D1* as its second element. The terms *N0, N1, D0*, and *D1* are names for atoms. None of this belongs to the logic itself; I'm using it just to explain the meaning of the fundamental notions. In Alloy, you can't refer to atoms explicitly at all. You could, however, declare scalar variables *N0, N1, D0*, and *D1*, and then, as we shall see, this relation could be denoted by the expression *N0->D0 + N1->D1*.

Why the extra parentheses in a set expression such as {(N0)}?

In Alloy, all structures are relations, and a set is simply a relation all of whose tuples contain only one element. The set *{N0}* would be modeled as this relation in Alloy; it cannot be represented directly. Because this kind of expression never appears in a model, the extra syntax of the parentheses is not inconvenient. In fact, on the contrary, the unification of sets and relations makes the syntax simpler, since there is no need to convert between sets and relations, or between scalars and sets.

Can relations contain relations?

No. Our relations are flat, or *first order*, meaning that entries are always atoms, and never themselves relations. Take the relation *addr*, from the example of section 3.2.2, which we used to model the idea that address books contain name/address mappings. In our flat representation, the relation's value was a ternary relation associating books, names and addresses:

addr = {(B0, N0, D0), (B0, N1, D1), (B1, N1, D2), (B1, N2, D2)}

More conventionally, this might be represented as a function from address books to a function from names to sets of addresses:

addrC =
{(B0, {(N0, {D0}), (N1, {D1, D2})}),
(B1, {(N1, {D2}), (N2, {D2})})}

The relation *addrC* is not directly representable in Alloy. We'll see later in this chapter (in subsection 3.4.3) that the name/address mapping for book *b*, which would conventionally be written *addrC(b)*, can be written *b.addr* in Alloy.

Why not admit higher-order relations?

The restriction to flat relations makes the logic more tractable for analysis. Flat relations, as the relational database community has discovered, are expressive enough for almost all applications, and their simplicity and uniformity is appealing. The lack of symmetry in *addrC* (above), for example, means that it cannot be accessed from the right as easily as from the left. The expression *addr.a* denotes the mapping from address books to the names they use for address *a*, and *addr.n.Addr* denotes the set of address books that have an entry for name *n*; for *addrC*, both would require a more complex construction.

Is there a loss of expressive power in the restriction to flat relations?

Yes, there is, but it can usually be worked around. Almost always, a situation that seems to call for a higher-order relation can be reformulated without one. Suppose we're modeling the prerequisite structure of a university course catalog, in which each course has a set of prerequisites, and, for admission to a course, a student is required to have taken all the courses in at least one of the course's prerequisites. In a higher-order setting, this structure could be represented as a relation from courses to sets of courses. For example, the relation

$$prereqC = \{(C3, \{(C0), (C1)\}), (C3, \{(C0), (C2)\})\}$$

would indicate that a student wanting to take course $C3$ must have taken either $C0$ and $C1$, or $C0$ and $C2$. Simply flattening this relation to

$$prereqBad = \{(C3, C0), (C3, C1), (C3, C2)\}$$

won't work, because it loses the grouping of the prerequisites. The solution is to introduce a new set of atoms to model prerequisites, along with a relation mapping prerequisites to their constituent courses:

$$prereq = \{(C3, P0), (C3, P1)\}$$
$$courses = \{(P0, C0), (P0, C1), (P1, C0), (P1, C2)\}$$

This retains the essential structure: course $C3$ now has two possible prerequisites, $P0$, consisting of course $C0$ and $C1$, and $P1$, consisting of course $C0$ and $C2$.

There is another respect, by the way, in which a higher-order relation is more expressive than a flat relation. A function that maps atoms drawn from a set A to sets of atoms drawn from a set B can include a mapping from an atom to the empty set, thus distinguishing an atom being mapped to nothing and an atom not being mapped at all. A binary relation from atoms in A to atoms in B cannot make such a distinction. Instead, you'd declare an additional set: the address books with empty mappings, for example, would belong to the set *Book* but would not be mapped by *addr*.

Why not include composite objects as a language construct?

Traditional specification languages such as VDM and Z allow you to model composite objects directly with composite mathematical objects. For example, an address book might be represented not as an atom, but as a relation from names to addresses. A relationship between an address book and another object would then be expressible only with a higher-order relation. The reasons for excluding composite objects in their own right are thus the reasons we've already given for preferring flat relations. Also, mathematical objects have no identity distinct from their value; if you want to talk about the values of different address books at different times, you need to introduce atoms representing the identities of the books anyway.

Can you really work without interpreted atoms such as the integers?

Yes, almost all the time. And it turns out that on most occasions that you might think you need integers, it's cleaner and more abstract to use atoms of an uninterpreted type with some relations to give whatever interpretation is needed. Alloy does actually support integers, albeit in a limited way. You can take the size of a relation, add, subtract, and compare integers (but not multiply or divide them). The treatment of integers is explained in sections 3.7 and 4.8.

Can relations have infinite size and arity?

Nothing in our logic precludes relations of infinite size, but for all the models we'll look at, it's sufficient to consider only finite instantiations. A relation must have a finite arity, though.

Are multirelations useful in practice?

Yes, because relations are flat rather than nested, arities greater than two are very common. To model execution traces of a system whose state involves relationships will require ternary relations: two columns for the relationship at a given time, and an additional column for the time. Relations of arity four are less common; as an example, the states of a network routing table might relate the host at which the table resides (1), a second host that is the desired destination of an incoming packet (2), the port to be used in forwarding the message (3), and the time at which this table entry is present (4). Arities of five or greater are rare.

Why don't the columns in a relation have names?

If you're more familiar with relational databases than relational logic, you may find it odd that the columns of a relation are identified by their position rather than by name. In modeling, relations tend to have much smaller arities than relations in a database; it's rare for a relation to have more than four columns. Moreover, in the constraints of a model, joins tend to be applied to a relation on particular columns, in a particular order. By arranging the columns carefully, almost all joins can be made to be on the first or last column of a relation. Consequently, treating columns positionally rather than by name is more convenient, and results in more succinct and natural expressions.

If the order of columns matters, how do you represent an unordered relationship?

An unordered relationship can be represented in different ways. The simplest way is to use a relation r (ordered, as always), and add a constraint $r = \sim r$ that makes it symmetric—the same forward and backward. For example, *spouse* = *~spouse* says that if you're my spouse, I'm your spouse. This trick may be philosophically dubious, but in practice it's fine, and much easier than introducing additional constructs.

Is the idea of treating scalars and sets as relations new?

No. It goes back to Tarski's foundational work on the relational calculus [70]. All of Tarski's relations were binary, however, so his encoding was a bit less natural: a set was a relation that mapped each atom in the set to every possible atom. Rick Hehner's "bunches" [27] have a similar flavor, but unify scalars and sets in a new kind of algebraic structure.

Isn't it confusing to treat scalars as sets?

On first encountering this idea, some people are disturbed. After all, isn't the distinction between a set and its elements the very foundation of set theory? In a first-order logic, however, in which sets of sets are never used, no confusion arises. And in practice, breaking down the distinction between sets and scalars brings a nice uniformity. When writing a navigation expression, you don't have to worry about whether an expression represents a set or a scalar. The grandfathers of person p, for example, can be written *p.parents.father*, in which the dot operator is applied to a scalar such as p in exactly the same way it is applied to a set such as *p.parents*.

Combined with the treatment of partiality, this allows us to write p's mother-in-law as *p.wife.mother + p.husband.mother* (or equivalently as *p.(wife + husband).mother*), without worrying that if p has no wife the expression *p.wife* may be undefined.

Which terms are Alloy specific, and which are standard in logic and set theory?

All the terms introduced so far are standard, with the exception of *multirelation* (for a relation with more than two columns) and *option* (for a set that is empty or singleton).

Is Alloy's option like the option of the ML programming language?

Rather than treating options as singleton or empty sets, most modeling and programming languages use a union type. ML's option is such a union: a tagged value that is either a scalar or some special null value. For modeling, this is less convenient, because the tagging wraps the value and changes its type. Consider, for example, a model of an email application with a scalar *userAddress* representing the user's address, and an option *replyAddress* representing a separate address to be used in the "reply-to" field of messages. In Alloy, these variables have the same type, and can be combined and compared with set operators;

>   userAddress = replyAddress

for example, is true if *replyAddress* is defined and equal to *userAddress*. In the traditional approach, the two variables have distinct types, and cannot be compared without projecting *replyAddress* first.

So there aren't really any scalars in Alloy?

Not in the standard sense. Whereas a conventional language would distinguish *a* (a scalar), *{a}* (a singleton set containing a scalar), *(a)* (a tuple), and *{(a)}* (a relation), Alloy treats them all as the same, and represents them as *{(a)}*.

Why is the term "option" useful? Isn't every option either a scalar or empty?

The term is used to describe a *variable* whose value is unknown, rather than a particular value, in the same way that you might refer to a "vehicle" without knowing whether it's a car or a truck. By definition, every scalar is also an option; both are sets; and every set is a relation. But, typically, you want to use the term that tells you most about a relation, so you don't call it a "relation" if you know it's a set, or a "set" if you know it's a scalar.

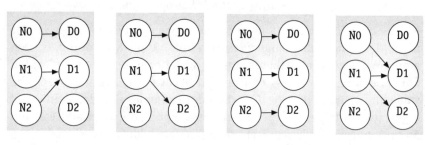

FIG. 3.3 Functional but not injective.

FIG. 3.4 Injective but not functional.

FIG. 3.5 Functional and injective.

FIG. 3.6 Neither functional nor injective.

3.2.4 Functional and Injective Relations

A binary relation that maps each atom to at most one other atom is said to be *functional*, and is called a *function*. A binary relation that maps at most one atom to each atom is *injective*.

Example. Here are four possible values of a relation mapping names to addresses, illustrated in figs. 3.3–3.6:

    address1 = {(N0, D0), (N1, D1), (N2, D1)}
    address2 = {(N0, D0), (N1, D1), (N1, D2)}
    address3 = {(N0, D0), (N1, D1), (N2, D2)}
    address4 = {(N0, D1), (N1, D1), (N1, D2)}

The first is functional but not injective; the second is injective but not functional; the third is both functional and injective; and the fourth is neither. An empty binary relation is functional and injective.

Discussion

Where does the idea of treating functions as relations come from?

The idea of treating functions as relations has been pioneered in modeling by the specification language Z [65]. Its use goes back at least to Zermelo and Fraenkel's set theory (hence the "Z" in Z). Alloy is actually more minimalist than Z. Although Z doesn't distinguish functions and relations, it does distinguish scalars, sets, and tuples from each other. In Alloy, everything's a relation.

Is it standard to treat functions as relations?

No. Most other modeling languages distinguish functions from other relations. In UML's constraint language OCL [53], for example, navigating through an association can either produce an empty set or an undefined value, depending on the multiplicity of the association.

Is an injective relation an injection?

The term "injection" is traditionally applied only to a relation that is both functional and injective, so I try to avoid using it. Unfortunately, there isn't a common name for an injective relation.

3.2.5 Domain and Range

The *domain* of a relation is the set of atoms in its first column; the *range* is the set in the last column.

> *Example.* A relation with its domain and range:
>
> address = {(N0, D0), (N1, D1), (N2, D1)}
> domain (address) = {(N0), (N1), (N2)}
> range (address) = {(D0), (D1)}

A relation of higher arity has a domain and range too.

> *Example.*
>
> addr = {(B0, N0, D0), (B0, N1, D1), (B1, N2, D2)}
> domain (addr) = {(B0), (B1)}
> range (addr) = {(D0), (D1), (D2)}

Discussion

Are domain and range special operators?

No, but they are predefined for binary relations as functions in the Alloy library. They're easily expressed with the other operators (introduced later): the domain and range of a binary relation *r* are *r.univ* and *univ.r* respectively.

Are the domain and range functions commonly used?

They are used less frequently than in languages such as Z, because of Alloy's rich language of declarations (see section 3.6), which encourages you to introduce sets that explicitly represent a relation's domain and range.

What about total and partial functions?

The term "domain" is often used to refer to the set of atoms that *might* be mapped by a relation or function. In that case, a total function is one that maps every member of its domain. This notion requires that a set be associated implicitly with a relation. (Alternatively, a total function relation might be one that maps every atom in the universe, but this is a very rare case.) Our logic is simpler than this: the relation is just its tuples, and the domain and range of the relation are determined by this set of tuples. I do occasionally use the terms "total" and "partial" informally, referring to whether a relation is total or partial over the set that appears in its declaration.

3.3   Snapshots

Particular values of sets and binary relations can be shown graphically in a *snapshot*. You create a node for each atom, and draw an arc for each tuple connecting the nodes corresponding to the first and second atoms in the tuple. To show several relations, you label each tuple arc with the relation it belongs to. Sets can be shown in two ways: either by an extra label in a node naming a set it belongs to, or by drawing a labelled contour around some nodes.

> *Example.* A multilevel address book modeled by a relation *address* mapping names to targets, where targets are names or addresses, and names are aliases or groups, might be represented textually by
>
> address = {(G0, A0), (G0, A1), (A0, D0), (A1, D1)}
> Target = {(G0), (A0), (A1), (D0), (D1), (D2)}
> Name = {(G0), (A0), (A1)}
> Alias = {(A0), (A1)}
> Group = {(G0)}
> Addr = {(D0), (D1), (D2)}
>
> or graphically by the snapshot of fig. 3.7.

Multirelations can be shown as graphs by *projecting* out one or more columns. Projection takes two steps. Suppose just one column is being projected out. In the first step, the column is moved to the front, so that it becomes the first column of the relation; each tuple is permuted accordingly. In the second step, the relation is split into an indexed collection of relations. For each atom that appears in the first column, we associate the relation consisting of all those tuples that begin with that

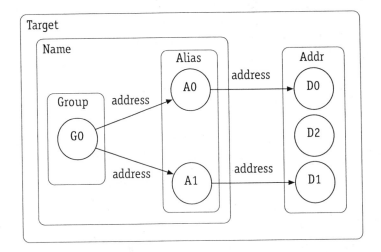

FIG. 3.7 A sample snapshot.

atom, but with the atom removed. For an atom *a* and relation *r*, this new relation is given by the expression *a.r* (using the join operator defined in subsection 3.4.3).

Example. A world of several multilevel address books modeled by the relation *addr* mapping books to names to targets, where targets are names or addresses, and names are aliases or groups, might be represented textually by

addr = {(B0, G0, A0), (B0, G0, A1), (B0, A0, D0), (B0, A1, D1),
    (B1, A0, D1)}
Book = {(B0), (B1)}

(and with appropriate assignments to the other sets as in the previous example.) Its projection onto the first column gives

B0.addr = {(G0, A0), (G0, A1), (A0, D0), (A1, D1)}
B1.addr = {(A0, D1)}

which could be shown visually as two graphs, the one for *B0* being that of fig. 3.7 (but with *addr* for *address*).

Examples. All of the diagrams generated by the Alloy Analyzer in chapter 2 are snapshots. The analyzer lets you customize how instances are displayed; you can select a set and project all relations in the instance onto the columns associated with that set. In this case, a projection using the set *Book* was chosen. Under projection, a binary relation becomes a set; this is why, for example, the relation *names* from books to the names they map appears as a label in fig. 2.13. The analyzer can show sets only by labeling nodes; it can't currently draw contours.

3.4 Operators

The language of arithmetic consists of constants (such as *0, 1, 2 ...*) and operators (such as +, -, ×). Likewise, the language of relations has its own constants and operators.

Operators fall into two categories. For the *set operators*, the tuple structure of a relation is irrelevant; the tuples might as well be regarded as atoms. For the *relational operators*, the tuple structure is essential: these are the operators that make relations powerful.

3.4.1 Constants

There are three constants:

none	empty set
univ	universal set
iden	identity

Note that *none* and *univ*, representing the set containing no atom and every atom respectively, are unary. To denote the empty binary relation, you write *none->none*, and for the universal relation that maps every atom to every atom, *univ->univ* (using the arrow operator defined in subsection 3.4.3). The identity relation is binary, and contains a tuple relating every atom to itself.

Example. For a model in which there are two sets

Name = {(N0), (N1), (N2)}
Addr = {(D0), (D1)}

the constants have the values

none = {}
univ = {(N0), (N1), (N2), (D0), (D1)}
iden = {(N0, N0), (N1, N1), (N2, N2), (D0, D0), (D1, D1)}

Note that *iden* relates all the atoms of the universe to themselves, not just the atoms of some subset.

Discussion

Are these constants implicitly parameterized by type?

No. In some modeling languages, these constants are actually indexed collections of constants, and the appropriate instance must be selected by some means, either implicit or explicit. In Z, for example, the identity relation takes an explicit type parameter, and the empty relation is polymorphic. In Alloy, these constants are just three simple constants, with the values of *iden* and *univ* determined by the values of all the declared sets. Consequently, it's rare to use *iden* and *univ* without qualification; you'll usually write *s <: iden*, for example, to give the identity relation on the set *s* (using the restriction operator defined in subsection 3.4.3.6). If you forget to do this, you may get some surprises. For example, *iden in r* not only says that the relation *r* is reflexive but also that it maps every atom in the universe, which is likely to be inconsistent with *r*'s declaration.

Are these constants useful?

The identity relation is essential to the relational calculus style. For example, the constraint *no ^r & iden* says that the relation *r* is acyclic. A common use for the empty relation is for instantiating predicates (see subsection 4.5.2) that take sets as arguments, as in the frame conditions of section 6.2.

Aside from these cases, the constants are rarely used. To say a relation is empty or non-empty, it's better to use the expression quantifiers (explained in subsection 3.5.2) than the constant *none*, writing *no r*, for example, rather than *r = none*. Universal relations are usually limited to particular sets, so instead, you'd write *Name->Addr*, for example, for the relation that maps all names to all addresses.

Do the constants add any expressive power?

A subtle point for those interested in language design issues. You might think that these constants could be omitted, and defined instead in a library module. The universal relation can't be defined in this way, since all quantifiers and comprehensions require explicit bounds. You could define the universal relation explicitly as the union of all the free set variables (the top-level signatures; see subsection 4.2.1), but then you'd have to change the definition whenever a new set is introduced.

The other two constants can in fact be defined. The identity relation, for example, can be expressed as the comprehension *{x, y: univ | x = y}*.

But they were included because it's more convenient to use constants than library functions, and because the analyzer can exploit their special properties more readily this way.

3.4.2 Set Operators

The set operators are

+   union
&   intersection
-     difference
in   subset
=   equality

and here is what they mean:

- a tuple is in $p + q$ when it is in p *or* in q (or both);
- a tuple is in p & q when it is in p *and* in q;
- a tuple is in $p - q$ when it is in p but *not* in q;
- p *in* q is true when every tuple of p is also a tuple of q;
- $p = q$ is true when p and q have the same tuples.

These operators can be applied to any pair of relations so long as they have the same arity. Because scalars are just singleton sets, the braces used to form sets from scalars in traditional mathematical notation aren't needed. For scalars a and b, for example, the expression $a + b$ denotes the set containing both a and b.

Examples. Given the following sets

```
Name = {(G0), (A0), (A1)}
Alias = {(A0), (A1)}
Group = {(G0)}
RecentlyUsed = {(G0), (A1)}
```

- Alias + Group = {(G0), (A0), (A1)}
  gives the set of atoms that are aliases or groups;

- Alias & RecentlyUsed = {(A1)}
  gives the set of atoms that are aliases and have been recently used;

- Name - RecentlyUsed = {(A0)}
  gives the set of atoms that are names but have not been recently used;

· RecentlyUsed **in** Alias
  says that every thing that has been recently used is an alias, and is
  false, because of the tuple *{(G0)}*, which is recently used but not
  an alias;

· RecentlyUsed **in** Name
  says that every thing that has been recently used is a name, and is
  true;

· Name = Group + Alias
  says that every name is a group or an alias, and is true.

Examples. Given the following relations, representing portions of
an address book cached in memory and stored on disk,

  cacheAddr = {(A0, D0), (A1, D1)}
  diskAddr = {(A0, D0), (A1, D2)}

· cacheAddr + diskAddr = {(A0, D0), (A1, D1), (A1, D2)}
  is the relation that maps a name to an address if it's mapped in
  the cache *or* on disk;

· cacheAddr & diskAddr = {(A0, D0)}
  is the relation that maps a name to an address if it's mapped in
  the cache *and* on disk;

· cacheAddr - diskAddr = {(A1, D1)}
  is the relation that maps a name to an address if it's mapped in
  cache but *not* on disk;

· **none in** diskAddr
  says that the empty relation is contained in the relation *diskAddr*,
  and is true, irrespective of the value of *diskAddr*;

· cacheAddr = diskAddr
  says that the mappings in the cache are the same as those on disk,
  and is false, because of the tuple *(A1, D1)* in *cacheAddr* and *(A1, D2)*
  in *diskAddr*.

Examples. Given the following scalars,

  myName = {(N0)}
  yourName = {(N1)}

· myName + yourName = {(N0), (N1)}
  is the set of atoms that are either my name or your name;

· myName = yourName
  says that my name is the same as your name, and is false;

· yourName **in none**

says that there is no name that is your name, and is false also.

Discussion

Is the set operator equals sign the one you used before?

No. Statements like *cacheAddr = {(A0, D0), (A1, D1)}* are used in this chapter alone to explain the meaning of the logic, and always have an Alloy expression on the left, and a description of a relation (in conventional mathematical notation) on the right. In this case, the equals sign is a special definitional symbol, and is not symmetric: it would make no sense to write *{(A0, D0), (A1, D1)} = cacheAddr*.

A statement like *Name = Group + Alias*, on the other hand, is a constraint in the Alloy logic, and the equals sign is the set operator defined in this section. This equality notion is symmetric, and the statement is equivalent to *Group + Alias = Name*. I could have used a different symbol for the definitional equals, but that seemed a bit pedantic.

Is equality structural equality or reference equality?

A relation has no identity distinct from its value, so this distinction, based on programming notions, doesn't make sense here. If two relations have the same set of tuples, they aren't two relations: they're just one and the same relation. An atom is nothing but its identity; two atoms are equal when they are the same atom. If you have a set of atoms that represent composite objects (using some relations to map the atoms to their contents), you can define any notion of structural equality you want explicitly, by introducing a new relation. (And for those C^{++} programmers out there: no, you can't redefine the equals symbol in Alloy.)

Aren't there type constraints on these operators?

Not the conventional ones. In some simply typed languages, such as Z, the two arguments to a set operator must have the same type. So an expression such as *Book + Addr*, representing the union of the set of address books and the set of addresses, would be illegal. In Alloy, such expressions are not in general illegal, and can be put to good use. In modeling the value of a Java variable v of type C, for example, you might introduce a singleton set *Null* containing the null reference, and then declare

v: C + Null

to say that *v* is either null or a reference in the set *C*. In type systems that don't allow unions of this form, it can be hard to express this constraint with a declaration, and it may be necessary to weaken it to allow a reference to any class, or to distinguish null values of different types.

Alloy does impose some constraints, though. The arities of the arguments must match, so an expression like *addr* + *Name* is illegal. And if it can be shown, from declarations of variables alone, that an expression can be replaced by an empty relation without affecting the value of the constraint in which it appears, that expression is deemed to be ill-formed, even though its meaning is clear. For example, both *Name & Book* and *Name & (Alias + Book)* would be ill-typed because the occurrences of *Book* in both (and also *Name* in the first) could be replaced by *none* without affecting their meaning.

Why the keyword in?

The keyword *in* was carefully chosen for its ambiguity. Because scalars are represented as singleton sets, *in* will sometimes denote *membership* (between a scalar and a set, or a tuple and a relation), conventionally written ∈, and sometimes *subset* (between two sets or two relations), conventionally written ⊆.

3.4.3 Relational Operators

The relational operators are

->	arrow (product)
.	dot (join)
[]	box (join)
~	transpose
^	transitive closure
*	reflexive-transitive closure
<:	domain restriction
:>	range restriction
++	override

3.4.3.1 Arrow Product

The *arrow product* (or just *product*) *p*->*q* of two relations *p* and *q* is the relation you get by taking every combination of a tuple from *p* and a tuple from *q* and concatenating them.

When *p* and *q* are sets, *p*->*q* is a binary relation. If one of *p* or *q* has arity of two or more, then *p*->*q* will be a multirelation.

When p and q are tuples, $p \rightarrow q$ will also be a tuple. In particular, when p and q are scalars, $p \rightarrow q$ is a pair.

Example. Given the following names, addresses, and address book mapping

> n = {(N0)}
> n' = {(N1)}
> d = {(D0)}
> d' = {(D1)}
> address = {(N0, D0), (N1, D1)}

we have

·   n -> d = {(N0, D0)}
    is the tuple mapping name n to address d;

·   address = n -> d + n' -> d'
    says that *address* maps n to d and n' to d' (and maps nothing else), and is true.

Example. Given the following sets of names, addresses, and address books

> Name = {(N0), (N1)}
> Addr = {(D0), (D1)}
> Book = {(B0)}

we have

·   Name -> Addr = {(N0, D0), (N0, D1), (N1, D0), (N1, D1)}
    is the relation mapping all names to all addresses;

·   Book -> Name -> Addr =
      {(B0, N0, D0), (B0, N0, D1), (B0, N1, D0), (B0, N1, D1)}
    is the relation associating books, names and addresses in all possible ways.

Example. Given the following address book mappings and address books

> address = {(N0, D0), (N1, D1)}
> address' = {(N2, D2)}
> b = {(B0)}
> b' = {(B1)}

$b \rightarrow address + b' \rightarrow address' = \{(B0, N0, D0), (B0, N1, D1), (B1, N2, D2)\}$
is the relation that associates book b with the name-address mapping *address*, and b' with *address'*.

3.4.3.2 Dot Join

The quintessential relational operator is *composition*, or *join*. Let's see how to combine tuples before we combine relations. To join two tuples

$$s_1 \to \dots \to s_m$$
$$t_1 \to \dots \to t_n$$

you first check whether the last atom of the first tuple (that is, s_m) matches the first atom of the second tuple (that is, t_1). If not, the result is empty—there is no join. If so, it's the tuple that starts with the atoms of the first tuple, and finishes with the atoms of the second, omitting just the matching atom:

$$s_1 \to \dots \to s_{m-1} \to t_2 \to \dots \to t_n$$

Examples. Here are some example of joins of tuples:

{(N0, A0)} . {(A0, D0)} = {(N0, D0)}
{(N0, D0)} . {(N0, D0)} = {}
{(N0, D0)} . {(D1)} = {}
{(N0)} . {(N0, D0)} = {(D0)}
{(N0, D0)} . {(D0)} = {(N0)}
{(B0)} . {(B0, N0, D0)} = {(N0, D0)}

The *dot join* (or just *join*) p.q of relations p and q is the relation you get by taking every combination of a tuple in p and a tuple in q, and including their join, if it exists. The relations p and q may have any arity, so long as they aren't both unary (since that would result in a relation with zero arity).

When p and q are binary relations, p.q is their standard relational composition.

Example. Given a relation *to* that maps a message to the names it's intended to be sent to, and a relation *address* that maps names to addresses

to = {(M0, N0), (M0, N2), (M1, N2), (M2, N3)}
address = {(N0, D0), (N0, D1), (N1, D1), (N1, D2), (N2, D3), (N4, D3)}

the relation *to.address* maps a message to the addresses it should be sent to:

to.address = {(M0, D0), (M0, D1), (M0, D3), (M1, D3)}

and is illustrated in fig. 3.8 overleaf.

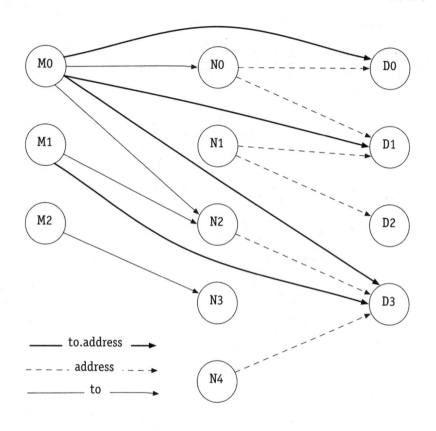

FIG. 3.8 A snapshot illustrating a dot join of two relations: feint arcs for the relation *to*; dashed arcs for *address*; and solid arcs for their join *to.address*.

If p and q are functions, $p.q$ will be a function too, and in this case dot is equivalent to functional composition.

Examples. Given a function *address* mapping names to addresses, a function *user* mapping an address to its username portion, and a function *host* mapping an address to its hostname portion

address = {(N0, D0), (N1, D0), (N2, D2)}
user = {(D0, U0), (D1, U1), (D2, U2)}
host = {(D0, H0), (D1, H1), (D2, H2)}

the expressions *address.user* and *address.host* are the functions that map a name to the corresponding user and host respectively:

address.user = {(N0, U0), (N1, U0), (N2, U2)}
address.host = {(N0, H0), (N1, H0), (N2, H2)}

When *s* is a set, and *r* is a binary relation, *s.r* is the image of the set *s* under the relation *r*; this image is the set you get if you follow the relation *r* for each member of *s*, and collect together in a single set all the sets that result. This is perhaps the most common use of dot, and is called *navigation* in object modeling parlance.

When *x* is a scalar, and *r* is a binary relation, *x.r* is the set of atoms that *x* maps to. For a function *f* and a scalar *x* in its domain, *x.f* is the scalar that *f* maps *x* to. So in this case, join is like function application, but note that *x.f* will be the empty set when *x* is not in the domain of *f*. Traditionally, a function applied outside its domain gives no result at all, and an expression involving such an application may therefore be undefined. In our logic, there are no undefined expressions.

You can navigate in both directions; *s.r* is the image of the set *s* going forward through *r*, and *r.s* is the image going backward.

Example. Given a multilevel address book represented by a relation *addr*, and sets of aliases, groups, and addresses

address = {(G0, A0), (G0, A1), (A0, D0), (A1, D1)}
Alias = {(A0), (A1)}
Group = {(G0)}
Addr = {(D0), (D1), (D2)}

we have the following expressions:

- Alias.address = {(D0), (D1)}
  the set of results obtained by looking up any alias in the address book;

- Group.address = {(A0), (A1)}
  the set of results obtained by looking up any group in the address book;

- address.Group = {}
  the set of names that when looked up in the address book yield groups;

- address.Alias = {(G0)}
  the set of names that when looked up in the address book yield aliases.

Joins of relations of higher arity are common too, especially the forms $x.q$ and $q.x$, where x is a scalar, and q is a multirelation.

Example. Given a particular address book b, and a ternary relation *addr* associating books, names, and addresses

b = {(B0)}
addr = {(B0, N0, D0), (B0, N1, D1), (B1, N2, D2)}

the expression $b.addr$ is the name-address mapping for book b:

b.addr = {(N0, D0), (N1, D1)}

Example. Given a time t, and a ternary relation *addr* that contains the triple $n \rightarrow a \rightarrow t$ when name n maps to address a at time t

t = {(T1)}
addr = {(N0, D0, T0), (N0, D1, T1), (N1, D2, T0), (N1, D2, T1)}

the expression $addr.t$ is the name-address mapping at time t:

addr.t = {(N0, D1), (N1, D2)}

Example. Given a relation *addr* of arity four that contains the tuple $b \rightarrow n \rightarrow a \rightarrow t$ when book b maps name n to address a at time t, and a book b and a time t

addr = {(B0, N0, D0, T0), (B0, N0, D1, T1), (B0, N1, D2, T0),
    (B0, N1, D2, T1), (B1, N2, D3, T0), (B1, N2, D4, T1)}
t = {(T1)}
b = {(B0)}

the expression $b.addr.t$ is the name-address mapping of book b at time t:

b.addr.t = {(N0, D1), (N1, D2)}

Note that $b.addr.t$ doesn't need parentheses to indicate the order in which the joins are applied. The expressions $b.(addr.t)$ and $(b.addr).t$ are equivalent: you can project onto a particular book, and then onto a particular time, or you can first select the time, and then the book.

Discussion

Is dot join associative?

No. The expressions $(a.b).c$ and $a.(b.c)$ are not always equivalent, because one may be ill-formed and the other well-formed. Because of the dropped column, the arity of a join is always one less than the sum of the arities of its arguments. If *s* and *t* are unary, and *r* is ternary, for example, the expression *t.r* will be binary, and *s.(t.r)* will be unary. The expression *s.t*, however, would have zero arity, and is thus illegal, so *(s.t). r* is likewise illegal, and is not equivalent to *s.(t.r)*.

But if two ways to parenthesize a join expression are both well formed—as in the example just above—they *will* be equivalent. So a mistake in placing parentheses won't cause a model to have an unintended meaning, and you can ignore the issue unless the type checker complains. (Thanks to Somesh Jha for pointing this out.)

Is dot join the same as a database's join?

Not quite. In relational database query languages, the join operator matches columns by name rather than position, and the matching column is not dropped. You can define a more database-like join as follows. Let *id3* be the ternary identity relation

id3 = {a, b, c: **univ** | a = b **and** b = c}

and define

p ⊙ q = p.id3.q

Then *p ⊙ q* concatenates matching tuples like dot join, but retains the matching elements like database join. It also provides a nice shorthand for restrictions (introduced in section 3.4.3.6): *s <: r* and *r :> s* can be written *s ⊙ r* and *r ⊙ s*. (Thanks to Butler Lampson for this insight.)

3.4.3.3 Box Join

The box operator *[]* is semantically identical to join, but takes its arguments in a different order, and has different precedence. The expression

e1 [e2]

has the same meaning as

e2.e1

Example. Given a relation *address* from names to addresses, and a scalar *n* representing a name, the expression *address[n]* is equivalent to *n.address*, and denotes the set of addresses that *n* is mapped to.

Dot binds more tightly than box, however, so

a.b.c [d]

is short for

d.(a.b.c)

The rationale for this operator is that it allows an syntactic distinction to be made between dereferencing a field of a composite object (with dot join) and performing an indexed lookup (with box join), even though there is no semantic distinction between the two.

Example. Given a ternary relation *addr* associating books, names, and addresses, the expression *b.addr[n]* denotes the set of addresses associated with name *n* in book *b*, and is equivalent to *n.(b.addr)*.

The choice of the box is motivated by analogy to array notation.

Example. In a model of a class *C* that has an array-valued field *f*, the result of dereferencing *x* with field *f*, and then retrieving the object at index *i* can be denoted *x.f[i]*, just as in Java, or equivalently as *i.(x.f)*.

3.4.3.4 Transpose

The *transpose* ~*r* of a binary relation *r* takes its mirror image, forming a new relation by reversing the order of atoms in each tuple.

Example. Given a relation representing an address book that maps names to the addresses they stand for

address = {(N0, D0), (N1, D0), (N2, D2)}

its transpose is the relation that maps each address to the names that stand for it:

~address = {(D0, N0), (D0, N1), (D2, N2)}

A binary relation *r* is *symmetric* if, whenever it contains the tuple *a->b*, it also contains the tuple *b->a*, or more succinctly as a relational constraint:

~r **in** r

Taking the transpose of a symmetric relation has no effect. The *symmetric closure* of *r* is the smallest relation that contains *r* and is symmetric, and is equal to *r* + ~*r*.

Examples. A relation *connects* mapping hosts to the neighbors they are connected to in a network would be symmetric if the connections were bidirectional. The transpose of a relation *wife* mapping men to their wives is the relation *husband* mapping women to their husbands, and its symmetric closure is the relation *spouse* mapping each person to his or her spouse.

Some useful facts about transpose:

· *s.~r* is equal to *r.s*, and is the image of the set *s* navigating backward through the relation *r*;

· *r.~r* is the relation that associates two atoms in the domain of the relation *r* when they map to a common element; when *r* is a function, *r.~r* is the equivalence relation that equates atoms with the same image.

· *r.~r in iden* therefore says that *r* is injective, and *~r.r in iden* says that *r* is functional.

Example. If *mother* is the relation that maps a child to its mother, the expression *mother.~mother* is the sibling relation that maps a child to its siblings (and also to itself).

Discussion

Why did you write ~r in r to say that r is symmetric?

You might have expected *~r = r* instead. The two conditions are equivalent, but I prefer the first because (1) it matches the informal statement more closely; (2) it follows the pattern of the conditions for reflexivity and transitivity; and (3) it's a good habit from an analysis perspective to write constraints in their weakest form. Admittedly, this is a bit pedantic, and it's not unreasonable to expect a definition of symmetry to be symmetric.

3.4.3.5 Transitive Closure

A binary relation is *transitive* if, whenever it contains the tuples *a->b* and *b->c*, it also contains *a->c*, or more succinctly as a relational constraint:

r.r **in** r

The *transitive closure* ^r of a binary relation *r*, or just the *closure* for short, is the smallest relation that contains *r* and is transitive. You can compute the closure by taking the relation, adding the join of the relation with itself, then adding the join of the relation with that, and so on:

^r = r + r.r + r.r.r + ...

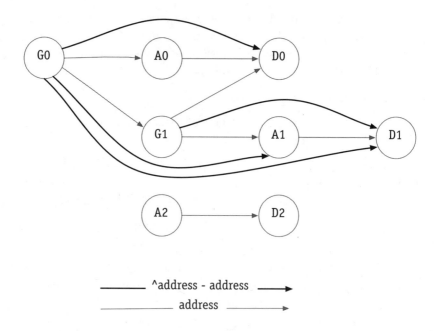

FIG. 3.9 A snapshot illustrating transitive closure of a relation: the
feint arcs represent the relation *address*; the solid arcs are those that
are added to it to form its closure ^*address*.

Example. A relation *address* representing an address book with
multiple levels (which maps aliases and groups to groups, aliases,
and addresses), and its transitive closure:

address =
   {(G0, A0), (G0, G1), (A0, D0), (G1, D0), (G1, A1), (A1, D1), (A2, D2)}
^address =
   {(G0, A0), (G0, G1), (A0, D0), (G1, D0), (G1, A1), (A1, D1), (A2, D2),
   (G0, D0), (G0, A1), (G1, D1),
   (G0, D1)}

I've broken the transitive closure into lines to indicate the contribution from the relation itself (on the first line), from its square
address.address (on the second), and from its cube *address.address.*
address (on the third). Fig. 3.9 shows the closure graphically.

Viewing a relation as a graph, the transitive closure represents reachability. Since the relation itself represents the paths that are one step
long, its square the paths that are two steps long, and so on, the closure

relates one atom to another when they are connected by a path of any length (except for zero).

A binary relation r is *reflexive* if it contains the tuple $a \rightarrow a$ for every atom a, or as a relational constraint,

iden in r

The *reflexive-transitive closure* $*r$ is the smallest relation that contains r and is both transitive and reflexive, and is obtained by adding the identity relation to the transitive closure:

$*r = {}^\wedge r + $ **iden**

From the graphical viewpoint, the reflexive-transitive closure relates one atom to another when they are connected by a path of any length, including zero.

Because *iden* relates every atom in the universe to itself (as explained in section 3.4.1 and the discussion that follows it), the reflexive-transitive closure will do so as well.

Discussion

Why does the reflexive-transitive closure associate "irrelevant" atoms?

Suppose a model has a set *Book* of books, a set *Name* of names, a set *Addr* of addresses, a book b, and a relation *addr* mapping books to their contents, with the following values:

```
Book = {(B0), (B1)}
Name = {(N0), (N1)}
Addr = {(D0), (D1)}
b = {(B0)}
addr = {(B0, N0, N1), (B0, N1, D0), (B1, N1, D1)}
```

Then the universe will contain all the atoms

univ = {(B0), (B1), (N0), (N1), (D0), (D1), (B0), (B1)}

and the identity relation will map each to itself:

iden = {(B0, B0), (B1, B1), (N0, N0), (N1, N1), (D0, D0), (D1, D1)}

The expression ${}^\wedge(b.addr)$, denoting the direct and indirect mapping of names in book b to the names and addresses reachable, will map names to names and addresses:

${}^\wedge(b.addr) = \{(N0, N1), (N1, D0), (N0, D0)\}$

The expression *(b.addr) will include the tuples of both these relations. In addition to tuples such as (N0, N0), which are expected, it will also includes tuples such as (B0, B0).

Although this seems odd, it follows naturally from the definition of reflexive-transitive closure and the identity relation. The alternative would be to have sets implicitly associated with each relation that represent the possible members of its domain and range, which would complicate the logic.

In practice this is not a problem. Closures often appear in navigation expressions, and the irrelevant self-tuples disappear in the join. For example, the names and addresses reachable in zero or more steps from a set of names *friends* would be denoted *friends.*(b.addr)*, and would not include any books, because *friends* and *Book* would be disjoint. If you need to remove the extra tuples explicitly, you can always write $s <: *r$ to restrict the closure to map only atoms in the set s.

How many iterations can it take to form the closure of a relation?

For a finite universe, transitive closure needs only a finite unwinding, limited by the length of the longest path in the graph. For some relations, the transitive closure requires very few unwindings even if the universe is large. Stanley Milgram's famous experiment in which he had residents of Kansas attempt to get letters to residents of Boston via acquaintances showed that it took on average only six steps for a letter to arrive [52]. If six steps were really enough to connect any two people, it would mean that the closure of the *knows* relation is the universal relation, and that it can be obtained in six unwindings.

3.4.3.6 Domain and Range Restrictions

The restriction operators are used to filter relations to a given domain or range. The expression $s <: r$, formed from a set s and a relation r, contains those tuples of r that start with an element in s. Similarly, $r :> s$ contains the tuples of r that end with an element in s.

Restrictions can be applied to relations of any arity of two or more, but are most often applied to binary relations.

> *Examples.* Given a relation representing a multilevel address book and sets representing the aliases, groups, and addresses
>
> address = {(G0, A0), (G0, G1), (A0, D0),
>   (G1, D0), (G1, A1), (A1, D1), (A2, D2)}

Alias = {(A0), (A1), (A2)}
Group = {(G0), (G1)}
Addr = {(D0), (D1), (D2)}

·   address :> Addr = {(A0, D0), (G1, D0), (A1, D1), (A2, D2)}
    contains the entries that map names to addresses (and not to
    other names);

·   address :> Alias = {(G0, A0), (G1, A1)}
    contains the entries that map names to aliases;

·   Group <: address = {(G0, A0), (G0, G1), (G1, D0), (G1, A1)}
    contains the entries that map groups.

Applying a restriction to a binary relation is like taking the image of a
set, but without dropping the matching elements. Put more formally, if
r is a binary relation, and s is a set, then

range (s <: r) = s.r
domain (r :> s) = r.s

The identity relation maps every atom in the universe to itself. Often,
what we want instead is a relation that maps every atom in some set s to
itself, which can be written $s <: iden$.

3.4.3.7 Override

The *override* p ++ q of relation p by relation q is like the union, except that
the tuples of q can replace the tuples of p rather than just augmenting
them. Any tuple in p that matches a tuple in q by starting with the same
element is dropped. The relations p and q can have any matching arity
of two or more.

Example. An address book might be represented by two relations,
homeAddress and *workAddress*, mapping an alias to email addresses
at home and at work:

homeAddress = {(A0, D1), (A1, D2), (A2, D3)}
workAddress = {(A0, D0), (A1, D2)}

The preferred address for an alias, which is the work address if it
exists, and otherwise the home address, is given by

homeAddress ++ workAddress = {(A0, D0), (A1, D2), (A2, D3)}

Override can be defined in terms of simpler operators. Taking the override of p by q is equivalent to taking the union of q and what's left of p
after removing the tuples that start with an element in the domain of q:

p ++ q = p - (domain (q) <: p) + q

Override is useful for modeling insertions into map datatypes, and assignment-like statements in programs.

> *Example.* Insertion of a key *k* with value *v* into a hashmap can be
> modeled by representing the value of the map before and after as
> two relations *m* and *m'* from keys to values, satisfying
>
> m' = m ++ k -> v
>
> *Example.* The environment *e* of an executing Java program can be
> viewed (simplistically) as a relation mapping variables to object
> references. The effect of an assignment
>
> x = y
>
> with a variable on both sides is
>
> e' = e ++ x -> y.e
>
> where *e* and *e'* are the values of the environment before and after
> execution. The state of the heap at any point can be represented by
> one relation for each field (that is, instance variable) of each class.
> A setter statement such as
>
> x.f = y
>
> in which *x* and *y* are variables and *f* is a field can thus be described
> by
>
> f' = f ++ x.e -> y.e
>
> where *f* and *f'* represent the values of the field *f* before and after
> execution.

Discussion

What are the operator precedences?

Operators have a standard precedence ranking so that constraints aren't
marred by masses of parentheses. The ranking follows the usual conventions: unary operators (closure, transpose) precede binary operators; product operators (such as dot and arrow) precede sum operators
(plus, minus, intersect). The details are given in appendix B. All operators associate to the left.

3.5   Constraints

We've seen how to make a constraint from two expressions using the
comparison operators *in* and =. Larger constraints are made from smaller constraints by combining them with the standard logical operators,
and by quantifying constraints that contain free variables over bindings.

3.5.1 Logical Operators

There are two forms of each logical operator: a shorthand and a verbose
form (similar to the operators used in boolean expressions in programming languages):

· **not**	!	negation
· **and**	&&	conjunction
· **or**	||	disjunction
· **implies**	=>	implication
· **else**	,	alternative
· **iff**	<=>	bi-implication

The negation symbol can be combined with comparison operators, so
a != b is equivalent to *not a = b*, for example. The shorthand and the
verbose forms are completely interchangeable, so you can write *a not =
b* as well.

The *else* operator is used with the implication operator;

> F **implies** G **else** H

is equivalent to

> (F **and** G) **or** ((**not** F) **and** H)

Implications are often nested. The common idiom

> C1 => F1 ,
> C2 => F2 ,
> C3 => F3

or equivalently

> C1 **implies** F1
> **else** C2 **implies** F2
> **else** C3 **implies** F3

says that under condition *C1*, *F1* holds, and if not, then under condition
C2, *F2* holds, and if not, under condition *C3*, *F3* holds.

Conjunctions of constraints are so common that we'll often omit the *and* operator, and wrap the entire collection of constraints in braces. So *{F G H}* is equivalent to *F and G and H*.

Sometimes, it's more natural to use a conditional expression than a conditional formula. This takes the form

    if C **then** E1 **else** E2

where *C* is a constraint, and *E1* and *E2* are expressions, and has the value of *E1* when *C* is true, and the value of *E2* otherwise.

Examples. Suppose an address book is modeled with three relations: *homeAddress* and *workAddress* mapping an alias to email addresses at home and at work, and *address* mapping an alias to the preferred address. To say that the preferred address for an alias *a* is the work address if it exists, otherwise the home address, we can write

    some a.workAddress =>
    a.address = a.workAddress ,
    a.address = a.homeAddress

or, using an if-then-else expression

    a.address =
        if some a.workAddress **then** a.workAddress **else** a.homeAddress

3.5.2 Quantification

A quantified constraint takes the form

    Q x: e | F

where *F* is a constraint that contains the variable *x*, *e* is an expression bounding *x*, and *Q* is a quantifier.

The forms of quantification in Alloy are

- **all** *x: e | F*   *F* holds for every *x* in *e*;
- **some** *x: e | F*   *F* holds for some *x* in *e*;
- **no** *x: e | F*   *F* holds for no *x* in *e*;
- **lone** *x: e | F*   *F* holds for at most one *x* in *e*;
- **one** *x: e | F*   *F* holds for exactly one *x* in *e*.

To remember what *lone* means, it might help to think of it as being short for "less than or equal to one."

Several variables can be bound in the same quantifier;

> **one** x: e, y: e | F

for example, says that there is exactly one combination of values for *x* and *y* that makes *F* true. Variables with the same bound can share a declaration, so this constraint can also be written

> **one** x, y: e | F

By using the keyword *disj* before the declaration, you can restrict the bindings only to include ones in which the bound variables are disjoint from one another, so

> **all disj** x, y: e | F

means that *F* is true for any distinct combination of values for *x* and *y*. (See subsection 3.5.3 for cases in which *x* and *y* are not scalars.)

> *Examples.* Given a set *Address* of email addresses, *Name* of names, and a relation *address* representing a multilevel address book mapping names to names and addresses,

- **some** n: Name, a: Address | a **in** n.address
  says that some name maps to some address (that is, the address book is not empty);

- **no** n: Name | n **in** n.^address
  says that no name can be reached by lookups from itself (that is, there are no cycles in the address book);

- **all** n: Name | **lone** d: Address | d **in** n.address
  says that every name maps to at most one address;

- **all** n: Name | **no disj** d, d': Address | d + d' **in** n.address
  says the same thing, but slightly differently: that for every name, there is no pair of distinct addresses that are among the results obtained by looking up the name.

Quantifiers can be applied to expressions too:

- **some** *e*   *e* has some tuples;
- **no** *e*   *e* has no tuples;
- **lone** *e*   *e* has at most one tuple;
- **one** *e*   *e* has exactly one tuple.

Note that *some e* and *no e* could be written *e != none* and *e = none* respectively, but using the quantifiers makes the constraints more readable.

Examples. Using the sets and relation from the previous example,

- **some** Name
  says that the set of names is not empty;

- **some** address
  says that the address book is not empty: there is some pair mapping a name to an address;

- **no** (address.Addr - Name)
  says that nothing is mapped to addresses except for names;

- **all** n: Name | **lone** n.address
  says that every name maps to at most one address (more succinctly than in the previous example);

- **all** n: Name | **one** n.address **or no** n.address
  says the same thing.

3.5.3 Higher-order Quantification

Quantified variables don't have to be scalars; they can be sets, or even multirelations. A logic that allows this is no longer "first order" and becomes "higher order." Alloy includes such quantifications, but they cannot always be analyzed (see subsection 5.2.2).

Examples. Higher-order quantifications are often useful for stating properties about operators:

- **all** s, t: **set univ** | s + t = t + s
  the union operator on sets is commutative;

- **all** p, q: **univ lone -> lone univ** | p.q: **univ lone -> lone univ**
  the join of two functions is a function too.

Discussion

Does Alloy allow freestanding declarations?

No. The declaration forms described in this section can be used for quantified variables, and for fields, and can be used as formulas. But top-level relation declarations are not supported, although they are unnecessary (as explained in the discussion following section 4.2.2).

When can higher-order quantifications be analyzed?

Generally, the Alloy Analyzer cannot handle formulas that involve higher-order quantifications, so their use is discouraged. But in some useful cases, higher-order quantifiers can be eliminated by a scheme known as "skolemization," which turns a quantified variable into a free variable whose value can then by found by constraint solving. See subsection 5.2.2 for more details.

What's the difference between lone p: some X | F *and* some p: lone X | F?

Novices are sometimes confused by the difference between these quantifications:

> **lone** p: **some** X | F
> **some** p: **lone** X | F

What makes these confusing is the use of the same keywords for the quantifier and the bounding expression's multiplicity. In the first case, the quantifier is *lone* (at most one), and the multiplicity is *some* (one or more), so *p* is constrained to be drawn from the nonempty subsets of *X*, and the constraint says that *F* holds for at most one such subset *p*. In the second case, the quantifier is *some*, and the multiplicity is *lone*, so the constraint says that *F* holds for some option *p*, and is equivalent to

> (**some** p: X | F) **or** (**let** p = **none** | F)

and is thus not really a higher-order quantification at all. I've never come across a need for the first, but the second is occasionally useful.

3.5.4 Let Expressions and Constraints

When an expression appears repeatedly, or is a subexpression of a larger, complicated expression, you can factor it out. The form

> **let** x = e | A

is short for *A* with each occurrence of the variable *x* replaced by the expression *e*. The body of the let, *A*, and thus the form as a whole, can be a constraint or an expression.

> *Example.* Revisiting the address book with three relations—*homeAddress* and *workAddress* mapping an alias to email addresses at home and at work, and *address* mapping an alias to the preferred address—we can say that the preferred address for an alias *a* is the work address if it exists, otherwise the home address, by writing

> > **all** a: Alias |
> >   **let** w = a.workAddress |
> >   a.address = **if some** w **then** w **else** a.homeAddress

or

all a: Alias |
  a.address =
    let w = a.workAddress |
      if some w **then** w **else** a.homeAddress

Discussion

Can let *bindings be recursive?*

No. They only provide a convenient shorthand, and don't allow recursive definitions. A variable introduced by a let on the left-hand side of a binding cannot appear on the right-hand side of the same binding, or one that precedes it in the same *let* construct.

3.5.5 Comprehensions

Comprehensions make relations from properties. The comprehension expression

$$\{x_1: e_1, x_2: e_2, ..., x_n: e_n \mid F\}$$

makes a relation with all tuples of the form $x_1 \text{->} x_2 \text{->} ... \text{->} x_n$ for which the constraint F holds, and where the value of x_i is drawn from the value of the bounding set expression e_i. Each expression e_i must denote a set, and not a relation of higher arity.

> *Examples.* In a multilevel address book represented by a relation *address* mapping names in the set *Name* to names and also to addresses in the set *Addr*,

- {n: Name | **no** n.^address & Addr}
  is the set of names that don't resolve to any actual addresses;

- {n: Name, a: Addr | n -> a **in** ^address}
  is a relation mapping names to addresses that corresponds to the multilevel lookup.

3.6   Declarations and Multiplicity Constraints

A declaration introduces a relation name. We've just seen how declarations are used in quantified constraints and comprehensions. Free-standing declarations of relation names make sense too, although we'll see in chapter 4 how, in the full Alloy language, these would instead be declared within "signatures."

The notion of multiplicity is closely tied to the notion of declaration. It's not essential in a logic, but I've included it in this chapter because it's so useful, and can be explained independently of the structuring mechanisms of Alloy.

3.6.1 Declarations

A constraint of the form

> relation-name : expression

is called a *declaration*. Its meaning is almost—a caveat soon—as if the colon were replaced by the keyword *in*, so that it becomes a simple constraint saying that the relation named on the left has a value that is a subset of the value of the *bounding expression* on the right. The bounding expression is usually formed with unary relations and the arrow operator, but any expression can be used.

> *Examples.* The *address* relation, representing a single address book, maps names to addresses:

> > address: Name -> Addr

> The *addr* relation, representing a collection of address books, maps books to names to addresses:

> > addr: Book -> Name -> Addr

> A relation *address* representing a multilevel address book maps names to names and addresses:

> > address: Name -> (Name + Addr)

The same relation can be declared in different ways, depending on how much information you want to put in the declaration.

> *Example.* A declaration saying that a relation *address* maps aliases and groups to addresses and to aliases and groups

> > address: (Alias + Group) -> (Addr + Alias + Group)

> and a stronger declaration of the same relation, saying, in addition, that aliases, unlike groups, are always mapped directly to addresses:

> > address: (Alias -> Addr) + (Group -> (Addr + Alias + Group))

Relations, not just sets, can appear on the right-hand side of declarations too.

Example. An address book might be represented with three relations, representing the home, work, and preferred addresses:

```
workAddress, homeAddress: Alias -> Addr
prefAddress: workAddress + homeAddress
```

3.6.2 Set Multiplicities

In the last subsection, I said that the meaning of a declaration

    x: e

was almost the same as the meaning of a subset constraint

    x **in** e

Now the caveat: the declaration can include *multiplicity constraints*, which are sometimes implicit. Multiplicities are expressed with the *multiplicity keywords*:

- **set**   any number
- **one**   exactly one
- **lone**   zero or one
- **some**   one or more

Note that *one, lone,* and *some* are the same keywords used for quantification.

The meaning of a declaration depends on the arity of the bounding expression. If it denotes a set (that is, is unary), it can be prefixed by a multiplicity keyword like this

    x: *m* e

which constrains the size of the set *x* according to *m*. For a set-valued bounding expression, omitting the keyword is the same as writing *one*. So if no keyword appears, the declaration makes the variable a scalar.

Examples

- RecentlyUsed: **set** Name
  says that *RecentlyUsed* is a subset of the set *Name*;

- senderAddress: Addr
  says that *senderAddress* is a scalar in the set *Addr*;

- senderName: **lone** Name
  says that *senderName* is an option: either a scalar in the set *Name*, or empty;

·   receiverAddresses: **some** Addr
    says that *receiverAddresses* is a nonempty subset of *Addr*.

The declarations of variables in quantified constraints are declarations
of exactly the same form, and follow the same rules. The only difference
is that quantifiers introduce variables that are bound within the body of
the quantified constraint; the other declarations we have seen introduce
free variables.

Example. The quantification we saw above,

> **some** n: Name, a: Address | a **in** n.address

has two declarations, binding the scalars *n* and *a*.

3.6.3 Relation Multiplicities

When the bounding expression is a relation (that is, a relation with arity
greater than one), it may not be preceded by a multiplicity keyword. But
if the bounding expression is constructed with the arrow operator, multiplicities can appear inside it. Suppose the declaration looks like this:

> r: A *m* -> *n* B

where *m* and *n* are multiplicity keywords (and where *A* and *B* are, for
now, sets). Then the relation *r* is constrained to map each member of *A*
to *n* members of *B*, and to map *m* members of *A* to each member of *B*.

Such a declaration can indicate the domain and range of the relation
(see subsection 3.2.5), and whether or not it is functional or injective
(see subsection 3.2.4):

·   r: A -> **one** B
    a function whose domain is *A*;

·   r: A **one** -> B
    an injective relation whose range is *B*;

·   r: A -> **lone** B
    a function that is partial over the domain *A*;

·   r: A **one** -> **one** B
    an injective function with domain *A* and range *B*, also called a
    bijection from *A* to *B*;

·   r: A **some** -> **some** B
    a relation with domain *A* and range *B*.

Examples. Some declarations and their meaning:

· workAddress: Alias ->**lone** Addr
The relation *workAddress* is a function that maps each member
of the set *Alias* to at most one member of the set *Addr*; each alias
represents at most one work address.

· homeAddress: Alias ->**one** Addr
Each alias represents exactly one home address.

· members: Group **lone** ->**some** Addr
An address belongs to at most one group, and a group contains at
least one address.

Multiplicities are just a shorthand, and can be replaced by standard
constraints; the multiplicity constraint in

r: A *m* ->*n* B

can be written as

all a: A | *n* a.r
all b: B | *m* r.b

but multiplicities are preferable because they are terser and easier to
read.

Example. The last declaration of the previous example

members: Group **lone** ->**some** Addr

can be replaced by

members: Group ->Addr

along with the constraints

all g: Group | **some** g.members
all a: Addr | **lone** members.a

The expressions *A* and *B* can be arbitrary expressions, and don't have
to be relation names. They also don't have to represent unary relations.
The rule is generalized simply by replacing "member" by "tuple." Thus

r: A *m* ->*n* B

says that *r* maps *m* tuples in *A* to each tuple in *B*, and maps each tuple in
A to *n* tuples in *B*.

Example. The declaration

addr: (Book ->Name) ->**lone** Addr

says that the relation *addr* associates at most one address with each address book and name pair.

3.6.4 Declaration Constraints

Declarations usually introduce new names, but they can also be used to impose constraints on relations that have already been declared, or on arbitrary expressions. In this case, the only difference between a declaration (using the colon operator) and a regular constraint (using the subset operator *in*) is that the declaration imposes multiplicity constraints—for sets, even in the absence of multiplicity keywords (because of the default multiplicity).

Example. For an address book represented by a relation *address* mapping groups and aliases to addresses

address: (Group + Alias) -> Addr

an additional declaration might constrain each alias to map to at most one address:

Alias <: address : Alias ->**lone** Addr

Declaration constraints are like any other formula, and can be combined with logical operators, placed inside the body of quantifications, and so on.

Example. Given a relation *addr* associating address books, names and addresses, the constraint that each address book is injective (that is, maps at most one name to an address) can be written

all b: Book | b.addr: Name **lone** -> Addr

3.6.5 Nested Multiplicities

Multiplicities can be nested. Suppose you have a declaration of the form

r: A -> (B m -> n C)

This means that, for each tuple in A, the corresponding tuples in B->C form a relation with the given multiplicity. In the case that A is a set, the multiplicity constraint is equivalent to

all a: A | a.r : B m -> n C

Similarly,

r: (A m -> n B) -> C

will be equivalent to

> **all** c: C | r.c : A m->n B

Examples. The declaration

> addr: Book -> (Name **lone** -> Addr)

says that, for any book, each address is associated with at most one name, and is equivalent to

> **all** b: Book | b.addr: Name **lone** -> Addr

whereas

> addr: (Book -> Name) **lone** -> Addr

says that each address is associated with at most one book/name combination. The first allows an address to have different names in different books; the second does not.

3.7   Cardinality Constraints

The operator # applied to a relation gives the number of tuples it contains, as an integer value. The following operators can be used to combine and compare integers:

+	plus
-	minus
=	equals
<	less than
>	greater than
=<	less than or equal to
>=	greater than or equal to

Positive integer literals can appear as constants.

Example. For a relation *address*

> address: (Group + Alias) -> Addr

mapping groups and aliases to addresses, the constraint that every group has more than one address associated with it can be written

> **all** g: Group | #g.address > 1

Example. Suppose an email program needs to break groups of addresses into smaller subgroups. Given a relation mapping groups to the addresses they contain,

    address: Group -> Addr

a second relation

    split: Group -> Group

might map a group to its subgroups under the constraint that no group is a subgroup of itself

no g: Group | g **in** g.split

that a group's subgroups contain all its addresses

all g: split.Group | g.address = g.split.address

and that the subgroups are disjoint

all g: Group, **disj** g1, g2: g.split | **no** g1.address & g2.address

The cardinality constraints on the division into subgroups might be that any group with more than 5 members is split up

all g: Group | #g.address > 5 **implies some** g.split

that no subgroup contains more than 5 members

all g: Group.split | #g.address =< 5

and that subgroups are of roughly equal size (differing from each other by at most one)

all g: Group, **disj** g1, g2: g.split |
        #g1.address < #g2.address **implies** #g2.address = #g1.address + 1

The expression

sum x: e | ie

denotes the integer obtained by summing the values of the integer expression *ie* for all values of the scalar *x* drawn from the set *e*.

Example. The size of a group is the sum of the sizes of its subgroups:

all g: split.Group | #g.address = (**sum** g': g.split | #g'.address)

Discussion

How does Alloy distinguish the plus of union from the plus of arithmetic?

They are easily disambiguated from the context—in fact, by parsing alone. Integers aren't atoms, so the relational operators can't be applied to integer-valued expressions. Integers can be stored within relations, using the special *Int* atoms described in section 4.8.

4: Language

A *language* for describing software abstractions is more than just a logic. You need ways to organize a model, to build larger models from smaller ones, and to factor out components that can be used more than once. There are also small syntactic details—such as shorthands for declarations—that make a language usable in practice. And finally, there's the need to communicate with an analysis tool, by indicating which analyses are to be performed.

This chapter explains the Alloy modeling language. It covers all aspects of the language, and explains them informally by way of examples. A more complete summary of Alloy is given in the reference manual, which appears in appendix B.

Alloy is a small language. Some of its features are unique to Alloy, notably *signatures* and the notion of *scope*. The rest—modules, polymorphism, parameterized functions, and so on—are standard features of most programming and modeling languages, and have been designed to be as conventional as possible.

4.1   An Example: Self-Grandpas

There's a popular song titled "I'm My Own Grandpa." Let's use Alloy to find out how this could be. Take a look at the Alloy model of fig. 4.1.

The gross structure of a model consists of

- A *module header* that gives the module its name (line 1). Modules are named as in Java: the full name of the module corresponds to its path and filename in the file system. Alloy modules have the file extension ".als" by default, so this module is stored in the file *language/grandpa1. als* relative to the working directory of the analyzer.

- Some *signature declarations*, labeled by the keyword *sig*. Each signature represents a set of atoms, and may also introduce some fields, each representing a relation.

- Some *constraint paragraphs*, labeled by the keywords *fact, fun, pred* that record various forms of constraints and expressions.

```
1   module language/grandpa1
2   abstract sig Person {
3       father: lone Man,
4       mother: lone Woman
5       }
6   sig Man extends Person {
7       wife: lone Woman
8       }
9   sig Woman extends Person {
10      husband: lone Man
11      }

12  fact {
13      no p: Person | p in p.^(mother + father)
14      wife = ~husband
15      }

16  assert NoSelfFather {
17      no m: Man | m = m.father
18      }
19  check NoSelfFather

20  fun grandpas (p: Person): set Person {
21      p.(mother + father).father
22      }
23  pred ownGrandpa (p: Person) {
24      p in grandpas (p)
25      }
26  run ownGrandpa for 4 Person
```

FIG. 4.1 A first Alloy model: Can you be your own grandpa?

· Some *assertions*, labeled by the keyword *assert*, that record properties
  that are expected to hold.

· Some *commands*, labeled by the keywords *run* and *check*, which are
  instructions to the analyzer to perform particular analyses.

The signature declarations set up a classification hierarchy. The declarations of *Man* and *Woman* say that they *extend* the signature *Person*. This
means that they represent disjoint subsets of the set *Person*: no person is
both a man and a woman. Marking *Person* as abstract says that it has no
elements of its own that do not belong to its extensions; if omitted, the
declarations would allow a person that is neither a man nor a woman.

The fields of a signature declare relations whose domain is a subset of the signature. So the field *father* declared within *Person*, for example, relates persons to men. The keyword *lone* says that a person has at most one father. Similarly, *wife*, for example, relates men to women.

A fact records a constraint that is assumed always to hold. The fact starting on line 12 says that you can't be your own ancestor (13) and that if someone is your husband, you are his wife, and vice versa (14).

An assertion, marked by the keyword *assert*, introduces a constraint that is intended to follow from the facts of the model. The command, marked *check*, tells the analyzer to find a *counterexample* to the assertion: that is, an instance that makes it false. In this case, the assertion *NoSelfFather*, which says that nobody is his own father, is valid, and no counterexamples are found.

A function defines a reusable expression. Having written the function *grandpas* (20), we can now use *grandpas (p)* to refer to *p*'s grandpas, rather than the more cumbersome expression *p.(mother + father).father*.

A predicate defines a reusable constraint. Having written the predicate *ownGrandpa* (23), we can now use *ownGrandpa (p)* to say that *p* is his own grandpa, rather than the constraint *p in grandpas (p)*.

Finally, we come to the real action. The command *run ownGrandpa for 4* (26) instructs the analyzer to attempt to find a solution to the constraint *ownGrandpa*. The phrase *for 4* is a *scope setting*: it limits the search to a universe in which each top-level set (in this case, just *Person*) contains at most four elements. When the scope setting is omitted, as in the check for *NoSelfFather*, a default scope of 3 is used.

In fact, there is no action. The analyzer finds no solution within this scope. This could mean that there is a solution in a larger scope, so we might increase the scope, by replacing 4 with 10 in the run command, for example. Again, no solution is found, and if we increase the scope further, we'll soon reach the point at which the analyzer is no longer able to exhaust the space of possibilities within a reasonable time.

Under these circumstances, we might have instead cast the predicate as an assertion:

```
assert NoSelfGrandpa {
  no p: Person | p in grandpas (p)
}
check NoSelfGrandpa for 4 Person
```

When the analyzer finds no counterexample to an assertion, as here, it reports success (as opposed to failure when a predicate is found to have no instances).

Clearly, if it is possible to be your own grandpa, something must give: either our definition of grandpa, or the constraint that you can't be your own ancestor. The first seems more plausible. Suppose we extend the grandpa notion beyond biological grandpas to include grandpas by marriage. Here's our new definition of grandpa:

```
fun grandpas (p: Person): set Person {
  let parent = mother + father + father.wife +mother.husband |
    p.parent.parent & Man
  }
```

The *let* binds *parent* to the relation that maps a person to his or her mother, father, father's wife, and mother's husband. The definition as a whole says that your grandpa is any man who is your parent's parent, where "parent" now includes stepparents.

Running *ownGrandpa*, we now get a solution, shown in fig. 4.2. There are two persons, *Woman_0* and *Man_0*, who are mother and son, and also wife and husband. This is not a solution appropriate for a popular song.

We can rule out incest by adding another fact:

```
no (wife + husband) & ^(mother + father)
```

I've written this constraint relationally. The expression *mother + father* relates children to parents; its closure relates persons to their ancestors. Finally, *no p & q* says that the relations *p* and *q* share no tuples, so the constraint as a whole says that no person has a spouse who is also an ancestor.

Now running *ownGrandpa* again, we get a more socially acceptable solution, shown in fig. 4.3. There are two couples, in which the wife in each is the mother of the husband in the other. The person who is his own grandpa, *p*, achieved this by having his stepson marry his mother.

The final version of the model, incorporating the new definition of grandpa, and with the constraints ruling out incest, is given in fig. 4.4. I've split the facts into separate paragraphs to show that it's usually a good idea to group constraints according to their role or origin, and to give them suggestive names.

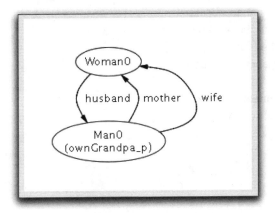

FIG. 4.2 An inappropriate solution to *ownGrandpa*.

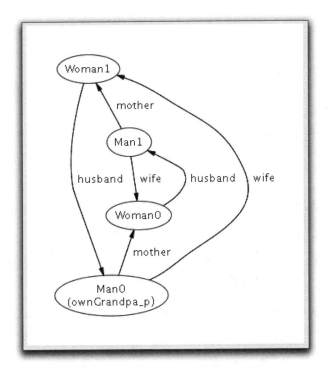

FIG. 4.3 Another solution to *ownGrandpa*.

```
module language/grandpa2
abstract sig Person {
  father: lone Man,
  mother: lone Woman
  }
sig Man extends Person {
  wife: lone Woman
  }
sig Woman extends Person {
  husband: lone Man
  }

fact Biology {
  no p: Person | p in p.^(mother + father)
  }
fact Terminology {
  wife = ~husband
  }
fact SocialConvention {
  no (wife + husband) & ^(mother + father)
  }

assert NoSelfFather {
  no m: Man | m = m.father
  }
check NoSelfFather

fun grandpas (p: Person): set Person {
  let parent = mother + father + father.wife +mother.husband |
    p.parent.parent & Man
  }
pred ownGrandpa (p: Man) {
  p in grandpas (p)
  }
run ownGrandpa for 4 Person
```

FIG. 4.4 Self-grandpas revisited.

Discussion

Where does the song "I'm My Own Grandpa" come from?

It was originally a skit written by Dwight Latham and Moe Jaffe for their radio show in the 1930's. Dwight Latham credited the idea to a book of anecdotes by Mark Twain. They later expanded it into a song, which was recorded in 1948 by "Lonzo and Oscar" (Ken Marvin and Rollin Sullivan), and became a hit. You can find the text of the song, in Lonzo and Oscar's 1948 version, along with a recording of it being sung, at *http://www.wwco.com/gean/grandpa*. The song's scenario is not identical to the one Alloy found, by the way: instead of having his stepson marry his mother, the self-grandpa has his stepdaughter marry his father.

How do you construct relational formulas?

To the novice, the relational style can be hard to grasp. But it becomes quite natural when you're comfortable with it. I find it helpful to think about sets of arrows rather than atoms and their relationships. For example, to construct a formula such as

no (wife + husband) & ^(mother + father)

from the *SocialConvention* fact of 4.4, my thinking would go as follows. The constraint to be expressed is that no person should marry a parent, grandparent, and so on. This says that certain relationships are prohibited—some arrows should not exist—so the constraint will have the form *no e* for some expression *e*. The prohibited relationship involves being both a spouse *and* a parent or grandparent, and so on. This conjunction suggests taking the *intersection* of two relations: there should not be an arrow belonging to both. Now we need to express the two relations. Being a spouse means being a wife *or* a husband; that tells us to take the *union* of the relations wife and *husband*. The "so on" in "being a parent or grandparent, and so on" suggests applying transitive closure to the parent relation. A parent is a mother *or* a father, indicating another union. Putting all this together gives the desired formula.

To increase your confidence that a constraint has the meaning you intended, you can check an assertion that it is equivalent to a different formulation. In this case, for example, you might compare the relational formulation to one in a navigational style:

```
pred SocialConvention () {
    no (wife + husband) & ^(mother + father)
}

pred SocialConvention' () {
    let parent = mother + father {
        no m: Man | some m.wife and m.wife in m.*parent.mother
        no w: Woman |
            some w.husband and w.husband in w.*parent.father
    }
}

assert Same {
    SocialConvention () iff SocialConvention'()
}
check Same
```

If the two formulations are not equivalent (within the scope), a counterexample will be generated showing a family that satisfies one and not
the other.

*Is there really a difference between running a predicate and checking an
assertion?*

From an analysis perspective, there's no fundamental difference between
assertions and predicates. Running a predicate involves searching for
an instance of its constraint; checking an assertion involves searching
for an instance of the negation of its constraint. So, checking an assertion with a constraint C is equivalent to running a predicate with the
constraint *not C*.

But this blurs a vital methodological distinction, and in the design of Alloy I thought it was important to be able to factor out those properties
conjectured to follow from the rest. This idea of recording redundan-
cies explicitly in a model, and marking them as such, is due to John Guttag and Jim Horning and was part of the Larch language [22].

*If the Alloy Analyzer finds no counterexample to an assertion, does that
mean it is valid?*

Not necessarily. It's possible that there's a counterexample in a larger
scope. But, in practice, as you increase the scope, the chance that a
counterexample remains does decrease. So you get some assurance, but
not in any absolute sense.

4.2 Signatures and Fields

Now that you've seen at least one example in full, and have a rough idea of how an Alloy model is organized, it's time to look at the details of the language. The rest of this chapter assumes you already understand the logic of chapter 3, and concentrates on the larger structure in which constraints are placed.

4.2.1 Signatures

A *signature* introduces a set of atoms. The declaration

```
sig A {}
```

introduces a set named *A*. A signature is actually more than just a set, because—as we'll say in later sections—it can include declarations of relations, and can introduce a new type implicitly. But it's convenient to use the term "signature" loosely to refer both to this larger structure and to the set associated with it, so we'll talk, for example, of the "elements of the signature," meaning the atoms contained in the set.

A set can be introduced as a subset of another set; thus

```
sig A1 extends A {}
```

introduces a set named *A1* that is a subset of *A*. The signature *A1* is an *extension* or *subsignature* of *A*. A signature such as *A* that is declared independently of any other is a *top-level* signature. The extensions of a signature are mutually disjoint, as are top-level signatures. So given the declarations

```
sig A {}
sig B {}
sig A1 extends A {}
sig A2 extends A {}
```

we can infer that *A* and *B* are disjoint, and *A1* and *A2* are disjoint (but not that *A = A1 + A2*).

An *abstract* signature has no elements except those belonging to its extensions. So if we write

```
abstract sig A {}
sig A1 extends A {}
sig A2 extends A {}
```

for example, we have introduced three sets with the implicit constraints

    A1 **in** A
    A2 **in** A

because *A1* and *A2* extend *A*, and

    A **in** A1 + A2

because *A* is abstract. So

    A = A1 + A2

and *A1* and *A2* partition *A*.

The effect of a collection of signature declarations, some top-level, and some as extensions, is thus to introduce a classification hierarchy. With the addition of the constant *univ*, the universal set, which can be viewed as an implicit abstract signature that all top-level signatures extend, this hierarchy takes the form of a tree, with *univ* at its root, the top-level signatures one level down, then their extensions, and so on. This tree gives a primary classification to all atoms which is exploited in the type system (see section 4.4).

Sometimes other, orthogonal, classifications are needed. To express these, you can declare subset signatures, such as

    sig A3 **in** A {}

which introduces a set *A3* that is a subset of *A*. Subset signatures, unlike extension signatures, are not necessarily mutually disjoint, so if you introduce a second subset

    sig A4 **in** A {}

then *A3* and *A4* may intersect, unless constrained not to.

A signature can be declared as a subset of a union of sets; given

    sig C **in** A + B {}

every element of *C* belongs to *A* or to *B*. The union expression can list any number of sets, but union is the only operator that can appear in a signature declaration in this way.

Finally, a multiplicity keyword placed before a signature declaration constrains the number of elements in the signature's set; thus

    m **sig** A {}

says that *A* has *m* elements. Declaring an abstract signature with scalar extensions introduces an enumeration, so

```
abstract sig T {}
one sig A, B, C extends T {}
```

declares a set *T* with three elements, *A*, *B*, and *C*.

Example. A classification of targets in an address book into names and addresses, with names further classified into aliases and groups:

```
abstract sig Target {}
abstract sig Name extends Target {}
sig Alias, Group extends Name {}
sig Addr extends Target {}
```

*Example.*A set of pixels, each of which is red, green, or blue:

```
abstract sig Pixel {}
sig Red, Green, Blue extends Pixel {}
```

Example. An enumeration of traffic light colors:

```
abstract sig Color {}
one sig Red, Yellow, Green extends Color {}
```

Example. A file system whose objects are classified as files or directories, with aliases that are treated as files, and temporary objects, which may be files or directories:

```
abstract sig Object {}
sig File, Dir extends Object {}
sig Alias extends File {}
sig Temp in Object {}
```

Example. The same file system, described without making the set of objects explicit, and with an explicit root directory:

```
sig File {}
sig Dir {}
one sig Root extends Dir {}
sig Alias extends File {}
sig Temp in File + Dir {}
```

Example. A classification of teas, first by country of origin and then by variety:

```
sig Tea {}
sig IndiaTea, ChinaTea extends Tea {}
sig Assam, Darjeeling extends IndiaTea {}
sig Keemun, Lapsang extends ChinaTea {}
```

Example. A classification of teas that includes Earl Grey teas, which may be China or India teas:

```
sig Tea {}
sig IndiaTea, ChinaTea extends Tea {}
sig EarlGrey in ChinaTea + IndiaTea {}
```

Discussion

Does Alloy have multiple inheritance?

Yes. Alloy can express multiple inheritance, but not entirely by declarations—some explicit facts are needed. For example, you can't say that Jasmine tea is both flavored *and* a China tea by declarations alone; one of these relationships must be stated explicitly as a fact. You might write, for example,

```
sig Tea {}
sig ChinaTea extends Tea {}
sig FlavoredTea in Tea {}
sig JasmineTea extends ChinaTea {}
fact {JasmineTea in FlavoredTea}
```

which will have the desired effect.

Unions in declarations shouldn't be confused with multiple inheritance. The declaration

```
sig EarlGrey in ChinaTea + IndiaTea {}
```

says that Earl Grey is a China tea *or* an India tea. And it doesn't express uncertainty about the country of origin of Earl Grey tea. The signature *EarlGrey* represents a set—the set of all Earl Grey teas—so the declaration says that each *member* of that set is either a China tea or an India tea.

Do singleton signatures correspond to atoms?

Singleton signatures, marked by the keyword *one*, represent singleton sets— sets that contain a single element. In an instance, such a set will correspond to a single atom. But it's a mistake to think of singletons as fundamentally different from other sets. In some modeling notations, a model that includes singletons is viewed as a kind of hybrid model/instance. This is unnecessary. The difference between a model and an instance is that a model represents a set of instances, and so, in a model, a singleton set isn't bound to a particular atom, but could represent different atoms in different instances.

For example, a model of a file system that declares a singleton for the root of the file system describes the collection of all possible file systems, each with its own root. The roots of the different file systems can be different atoms. When we use the term *Root* in the file system model, we mean whatever atom is the root of the file system being described, which can vary from file system to file system.

4.2.2 Basic Field Declarations

Relations are declared as fields of signatures. Writing

   sig A {f: e}

introduces a relation *f* whose domain is *A*, and whose range is given by the expression *e*, as if a fact included the declaration constraint

   f: A -> e

This constraint can be written equivalently as

   all this: A | **this**.f : e

saying that if we had a particular element *this* in the set *A*, the set denoted by *this.f* would be a subset of *e*.

The second constraint is a better way to understand the declaration, because it gives the right meaning when multiplicity symbols are added (see section 3.6). For a set *e*, the declaration

   sig A {f: *m* e}

adds the constraint

   all this: A | **this**.f : *m* e

which says that, for any *this* in *A*, *this.f* has *m* elements drawn from the set *e*.

So

> **sig** A {f: **one** e}
> **sig** A {f: **some** e}
> **sig** A {f: **lone** e}
> **sig** A {f: **set** e}

say that *this.f* has one, at least one, at most one, and any number of elements from *e*. The default keyword, if omitted, is *one*, so

> **sig** A {f: e}
> **sig** A {f: **one** e}

are equivalent.

If the expression *e* denotes a relation (that is, its arity is two or more), it may include multiplicity keywords within it. The same rule applies; the declaration

> **sig** A {f: e1 *m* -> *n* e2}

for example, gives the constraint

> **all this**: A | **this**.f : e1 *m* -> *n* e2

which is interpreted according to the standard multiplicity rules (explained in section 3.6).

Example. A collection of teas, each with a single country of origin:

> **sig** Tea {origin: Country}
> **sig** Country {}

Example. A file system in which each directory contains any number of objects, and each alias points to exactly one object:

> **abstract sig** Object {}
> **sig** Directory **extends** Object {contents: **set** Object}
> **one sig** Root **extends** Directory {}
> **sig** File **extends** Object {}
> **sig** Alias **extends** File {to: Object}

Example. A collection of weather forecasts, each of which has a field *weather* associating every city with exactly one weather condition:

> **sig** Forecast {weather: City -> **one** Weather}
> **sig** City, Weather {}
> **one sig** Rainy, Sunny, Cloudy **extends** Weather {}

Example. A collection of names in an address book, with a field *address* that associates each name with at most one address or name:

```
sig Name {address: lone Addr + Name}
sig Addr {}
```

Example. A collection of address books, with a field *addr* associating each book with a partial function from names to addresses and names:

```
sig Book {
    addr: Name -> lone (Addr + Name)
    }
sig Name {}
sig Addr {}
```

Example. A collection of traffic lights, each of which shows some combination of colors at a given time:

```
sig TrafficLight {
    color: Color some -> Time
    }
abstract sig Color {}
one sig Red, Green, Yellow extends Color {}
sig Time
```

It become tedious to describe a signature *S* as "a collection of elements of *S*," so from now on, I'll refer to the elements of a signature in the singular—as "an *S*". Just remember that a signature represents potentially any number of elements.

Discussion

Must all relations be declared as fields?

Yes: there are no top-level relation declarations in Alloy. If you want to declare some relations that don't belong naturally to any existing signatures, you can simply declare them as fields of a singleton signature. In a file system model, for example, a relation from names to objects that models the results of a lookup might be declared as:

```
one sig Globals {
    lookup: Name -> Object
    }
```

and then referred to as *Globals.lookup.*

4.2.3 Grouping Fields

Fields can be grouped together so that they share a declaration expression. The keywords *disj* and *part* indicate that the group of fields are mutually disjoint, or form a partition. So the declaration

> **sig** A {**disj** f, g: e}

implies the constraint

> **all this:** A | **no this.**f & **this.**g

and

> **sig** A {**part** f, g: e}

implies the same constraint, and additionally

> **all this:** A | e **in this.**f + **this.**g

Example. A cat has three names:

> **sig** Cat {**disj** daily, peculiar, ineffable: Name}
> **sig** Name {}

which are distinct from each other: for any cat *c*, *c.daily*, *c.peculiar*, and *c.ineffable* are three different names.

Example. A cat regards all cats that aren't friends as enemies:

> **sig** Cat {**part** friends, enemies: **set** Cat}

Example. A traffic junction has one light (conceptually) in each direction, which is assigned a single color in a given state:

> **sig** Junction {northSouth, eastWest: LightState}
> **sig** LightState {color: Light -> **one** Color}
> **sig** Color, Light {}

4.2.4 Dependent Declarations

A field declaration's bounding expression can be any Alloy expression, with one restriction. If the expression appears in a declaration of a field of a signature *X*, the only fields it can mention are those declared previously in *X* itself, or in one of the signatures of *X*'s supertypes.

Example. A cat's three names, made distinct in another way:

> **sig** Cat {
>   daily: Name,
>   peculiar: Name - daily,
>   ineffable: Name - (daily + peculiar) }
> **sig** Name {}

Example. An address book with three mappings from names to addresses: one for home addresses, one for work addresses, and one for the default, which is either the home address or the work address:

```
sig Book {
    homeAddress, workAddress: Name -> lone Addr,
    address: homeAddress + workAddress
    }
sig Name, Addr {}
```

The declaration of *address* allows it to map a name to both home and work address; to limit it to one, an additional constraint would be added (in a signature fact, subsection 4.5.1, for example).

Example. A radio station that owns a set of frequencies for different locations:

```
sig RadioStation {owns: set Freq, freq: Location -> one owns}
sig Freq, Location {}
```

Example. A zoom lens with a maximum aperture on its telephoto setting that must be one of its possible aperture settings:

```
sig Lens {apertures: set FStop}
sig ZoomLens extends Lens {maxTeleAperture: apertures}
sig FStop {}
```

The constraint implicit in dependent declarations is slightly more elaborate than for simple declarations in which only signatures appear in the bounding expression. For

```
sig A {f: e}
```

the constraint is

```
all this: A | this.f in e'
```

where *e'* is just like *e*, but has each field reference expanded. Every field that appears in the expression *e* is regarded as a dereferencing of *this*, so each occurrence of a field *g* is replaced by the expression *this.g*.

Example. The constraint arising from

```
sig Lens {apertures: set FStop}
sig ZoomLens extends Lens {maxTeleAperture: apertures}
sig FStop {}
```

is

```
all this: ZoomLens | this.maxTeleAperture in this.apertures
```

Discussion

Why can't dependent declarations mention arbitrary fields?

The limitation makes models easier to typecheck, and perhaps also easier to read. They do rule out some useful cases. For example, we might want to describe a radio station whose frequency is one permitted by the class it belongs to as

```
sig RadioStation {class: StationClass, freq: class.band}
sig StationClass {band: set Freq}
sig Freq {}
```

but this is illegal. If mutual dependence were permitted, there could be fields without unique types. For example, a declaration of a person whose surname is one of the parents' surnames

```
sig Person {surname: parents.surname, parents: set Person}
```

leaves the type of *surname* unconstrained. In all these cases, however, the constraint can be added after the declaration, as explained in subsection 4.5.1. The radio station example can be written

```
sig RadioStation {class: StationClass, freq: Freq}
    {freq in class.band}
sig StationClass {band: set Freq}
sig Freq {}
```

and the surname example

```
sig Name {}
sig Person {surname: Name, parents: set Person}
    {surname in parents.surname}
```

Can dependent declarations get confusing?

Yes. A common mistake arises with closure. Suppose you want to specify a peer-to-peer network in which each peer has a set of friends it's connected to directly, and a community of peers reachable from its friends. This attempt at a signature declaration

```
sig Peer {
    friends: set Peer,
    community: set *friends
    }
```

will be rejected, because the mention of *friends* in the declaration of *community* is expanded to *this.friends*, which is a set, and not a binary relation. You might be tempted to write

```
sig Peer {
    friends: set Peer,
    community: *@friends
}
```

using the special symbol @ to prevent expansion (see subsection 4.5.1). This will be accepted, but it doesn't mean what you might expect. The expression *@friends* denotes a binary relation, so *community* will be a ternary relation! The correct way is to use the reserved word *this* to refer to the particular peer:

```
sig Peer {
    friends: set Peer,
    community: set this.*@friends
}
```

resulting in the implicit constraint

all this: Peer | **this**.community **in this**.*friends

The lesson is not to try so hard to squeeze all constraints into declarations, and to write an explicit constraint instead:

```
sig Peer {friends, community: set Peer}
fact {community in *friends}
```

4.3 Model Diagrams

A *model diagram* declares some sets and binary relations, and imposes some basic constraints on them. A diagram is a good way to convey the outline of a model, but diagrams aren't expressive enough to include detailed constraints. Some people like to start with diagrams, and then move to text; others prefer to start with text and use diagrams as illustrations. The Alloy Analyzer can generate a model diagram from an Alloy textual model; you can use this feature to help understand large models, or to watch a model grow as you add new signatures.

Appendix D summarizes the diagrammatic notation.

4.3.1 Multiplicity Symbols

In a diagram, symbols are used instead of multiplicity keywords:

* *   any number
* !   exactly one
* ? zero or one
* +   one or more

The default multiplicity is always *, so if no multiplicity symbols are used, there are no implicit multiplicity constraints. You can attach multiplicities to a set (as a suffix to the label of a box) and to relations (as prefixes and suffixes of labels on arrows).

4.3.2 Boxes and Arrows

Each box represents a set of atoms. Boxes are connected in two ways. *Fat arrows*, which have large, unfilled triangles as their arrowhead, denote subset relationships and are used to express the classification hierarchy. *Thin arrows*, which have small, filled triangles as their arrowhead, represent relations.

As shown in fig. 4.5, a box without an outgoing fat arrow corresponds to a top-level signature. A box labeled *A1* with a fat arrow connecting it to a box labeled *A* corresponds to a signature *A1* declared as an extension of *A*. Labeling the fat arrow with the keyword *in* results in a subset signature rather than an extension. For an extension, you can also explicitly label a fat arrow with the keyword *extends*.

You can mark a set as *abstract* (either by writing the keyword in the box, or by italicizing the name) to indicate that it contains no elements except those contained by its extending subsets.

A multiplicity symbol following the label of a box constrains the number of elements in the set, as if the corresponding multiplicity keyword had been written before the signature declaration. The default multiplicity being *, there is no implicit constraint if omitted. A useful convention is to draw a set with multiplicity *!* or *?* as an oval rather than a rectangle.

As shown in fig. 4.6, a line with a thin arrow from set *A* to set *B* denotes a relation whose domain is contained in *A* and whose range is contained in *B*. The label gives the name of the relation. The label can include multiplicity symbols; a label of the form

$$m \, R \, n$$

on an arc from *A* to *B* is like declaring a relation

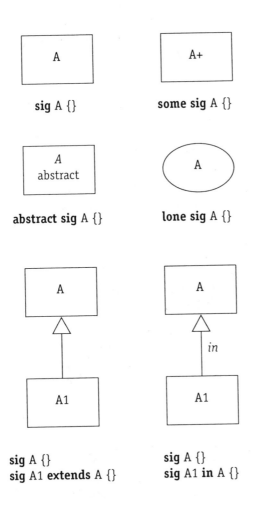

FIG. 4.5 Examples of set boxes and subset relationships,
with their corresponding Alloy text.

R: A *m->n* B

with multiplicity keywords replacing multiplicity symbols.

An arc can have several labels. This is one reason that it's convenient to make the multiplicity symbols part of the label and not write them as annotations on the ends of the arc: two relations with the same domain and range can share the same arc even if they have different multiplicities.

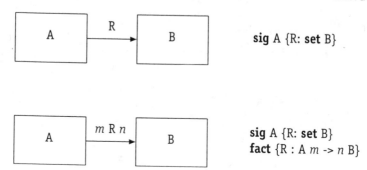

4.3.3 Expressions and Higher-Arity Relations

You can show any expression that denotes a set or a binary relation in a model diagram. Just use the expression as the label of the box or arrow instead of a set or relation name.

A relation whose arity is greater than two cannot be shown directly. But you can usually say everything you need to say by creating one or more arcs and labeling them with appropriate expressions. For example, suppose you have a relation

    R: A -> B -> C

You might show this as an arc from *B* to *C* labeled *A.R*; or from *A* to *B* labeled *R.C*.

To show the multiplicity of a relation like *R*, however, what you often want is instead to show an archetypal expression such as *a.R*, where *a* is a scalar in the set *A*. Labeling a relation arc

    all v: be | e

means that the constraints implicit in the arc (due its source and target sets and multiplicities) hold for the expression *e*, with *v* ranging over the set given by *be*. So, for example, an arc labeled

    all a: A | a.R !

(consisting of such a label combined with a multiplicity marking) from *B* to *C* says that *a.R* is a function that maps every *B* to one *C*, for every *a*, as if you'd written in textual for

    all a: A | a.R : B -> **one** C

In practice, the bound is almost always over a named set, and this notation is a bit clumsy. So as a convenient shorthand, a variable that ranges over the set S is written instead as <S>. For the last example, then, we'd write the label just as <A>.R.

Examples. Fig. 4.7 shows some examples of Alloy models and corresponding diagrams.

Discussion

Why doesn't the diagrammatic notation map more directly to the textual notation?

There is a fundamental difference between Alloy's textual and diagrammatic forms. The diagrammatic notation is flat; each relation belongs no more to its source than its target. It thus makes sense to mark multiplicities at both ends. The textual notation, on the other hand, bundles relations into signatures. It encourages viewing relations as fields of an object, and the syntax doesn't allow you to give multiplicities for the elements of the signature itself. For example, the declaration

sig S {r: **lone** T}

says that r is a partial function—that is, it maps each S to at most one T—but it doesn't say anything about how many members of S map to each T. You can add an explicit declaration formula, such as

fact {r : S **lone** -> **lone** T}

which makes the transpose of r a function too, but you can't express this in the declaration itself. The diagrammatic form doesn't suffer from this asymmetry.

An exact correspondence between textual and diagrammatic forms was a design goal of an earlier version of Alloy [33], but was lost when signatures were introduced.

Why don't you use UML's diagram syntax?

UML's syntax has the advantage of familiarity to many people. But our syntax has a more direct mapping to the Alloy textual language, and it's also easier to draw without specialized tools (since it uses only standard shapes, and doesn't require an arc to carry labels at different positions).

A common convention is to draw a shared fat arrowhead for subsets that are disjoint, with a separate arrow for each orthogonal classification. This is fine when working with drawings alone, but if you want to

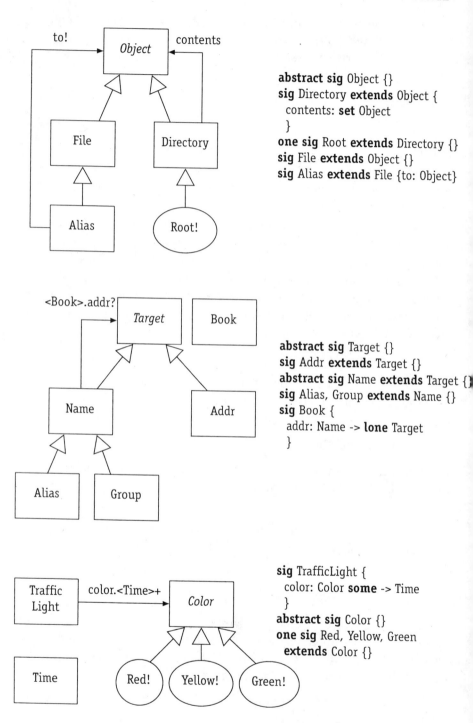

```
abstract sig Object {}
sig Directory extends Object {
  contents: set Object
  }
one sig Root extends Directory {}
sig File extends Object {}
sig Alias extends File {to: Object}
```

```
abstract sig Target {}
sig Addr extends Target {}
abstract sig Name extends Target {}
sig Alias, Group extends Name {}
sig Book {
  addr: Name -> lone Target
  }
```

```
sig TrafficLight {
  color: Color some -> Time
  }
abstract sig Color {}
one sig Red, Yellow, Green
  extends Color {}
```

FIG. 4.7 Textual models and corresponding model diagrams.

convert such a diagram to Alloy's textual notation, you'll need to iden-
tify one of the classifications as primary, so that expressions can be giv-
en unique types. The secondary classification will have to be expressed
with subset arrows labeled *in*, and its disjointness properties will have
to recorded explicitly as facts.

Why is set *the default multiplicity in diagrams?*

A diagrammatic notation should be *monotonic*: as you embellish it, you
are adding and not removing constraints. Otherwise, if you stop along
the way, the diagram you have is incorrect, because it says things you
did not intend to say. It's rare to write a textual model and omit all the
multiplicities, but with a diagram it's common to sketch the gross structure first and then flesh it out with details. Some diagrammatic notations violate this principle, for example by using a regular line-end for
a multiplicity of "exactly one," and a more elaborate line-end for weaker
multiplicities.

4.4   Types and Type Checking

Alloy's type system has two functions. First, it allows the analyzer to
catch errors before any serious analysis is performed. The essential idea
is that an expression is erroneous if it can be shown to be redundant,
using types alone. This notion of error, although unconventional, is in
practice a reasonable match to intuition; it accepts and rejects expressions much as you'd expect. Second, the type system is used to resolve
overloading. When different signatures have fields with the same name,
the type of an expression is used to determine which field of a given
name is meant.

4.4.1 Basic Types

Types are associated implicitly with signatures. A *basic type* is introduced for each top-level signature and for each extension signature
(that is, a signature that *extends* another signature). When signature *A1*
extends signature *A*, the type associated with *A1* is a *subtype* of the type
associated with *A*.

A subset signature does not have its own type, but acquires its parent's
type. If declared as a subset of a union of signatures, its type is the union
of the types of its parents. Unions are explained in the next subsection.

Two basic types are said to *overlap* if one is a subtype of the other.

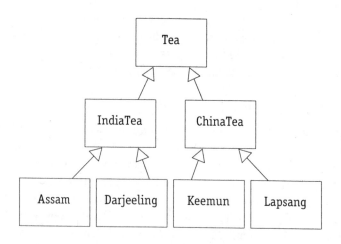

FIG. 4.8 Type hierarchy for teas.

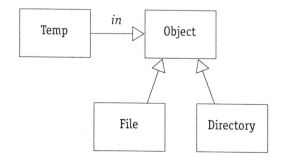

FIG. 4.9 Type hierarchy for a file system.

Example. The declarations

sig Tea {}
sig IndiaTea, ChinaTea **extends** Tea {}
sig Assam, Darjeeling **extends** IndiaTea {}
sig Keemun, Lapsang **extends** ChinaTea {}

result in the subtype hierarchy of fig. 4.8.

Example. The declaration of *Temp* in

```
sig Object {}
sig File, Directory extends Object {}
sig Temp in Object {}
```

results in the hierarchy of fig. 4.9. The set *Temp* does not have its own type; its elements belong to the type *Object*. The types *File* and *Object* overlap (because there are atoms that are both files and objects), but the types *File* and *Directory* do not.

4.4.2 Relational Types

Every expression has a *relational type*, consisting of a union of products:

$$
\begin{aligned}
& A_1 \texttt{->} B_1 \texttt{->} \ldots \\
+\ & A_2 \texttt{->} B_2 \texttt{->} \ldots \\
+\ & \ldots
\end{aligned}
$$

where each of the A_i, B_i, and so on, is a basic type. Each product term must have as many basic types as the arity of the relation. A binary relation's type, for example, will look like this:

$$A_1 \texttt{->} B_1 + A_2 \texttt{->} B_2 + \ldots$$

and a set's type like this:

$$A_1 + A_2 + \ldots$$

Note that the type of an expression is itself just an Alloy expression. Types are inferred automatically so that the value of the type always contains the value of the expression; that is, it's an *overapproximation*. This means that if two types have an empty intersection, the expressions they were obtained from must also have an empty intersection.

Types are determined as follows:

First, the hierarchy of basic types is obtained from the signature declarations.

Example. The signature declarations

```
abstract sig Object {}
sig Directory extends Object {}
one sig Root extends Directory {}
sig File extends Object {}
sig Alias extends File {}
sig Temp in Object {}
```

result in the basic types *Object*, *File*, *Alias*, *Directory*, and *Root*, with *File* and *Directory* subtypes of *Object*, *Alias* a subtype of *File*, and *Root* a subtype of *Directory*. The signature *Temp* is given the type *Object*.

Second, each field is given a type, by typing the bounding expression on the right-hand side of the declaration.

Example. The fields *to* and *contents* in

> **sig** Directory **extends** Object {contents: **set** Object}
> **sig** Alias **extends** File {to: Object}

are given the types *Alias -> Object* and *Directory -> Object* respectively.

Third, the constraints of the model are examined, and a type is inferred for each expression, using the types of signatures and fields, and the types of quantified variables (which are inferred from the declarations just like the types of fields).

Example. In the constraint

> **all** d: Directory - Root | **some** d.~contents

the quantified variable *d* is given the type *Directory*, and then *d.~contents* is given the type *Directory* also.

Determining the type of an expression is straightforward. For each relational operator, there's a corresponding rule. The rule for dot join, for example, is

> If the type of p contains a product $P_1 -> \ldots -> P_n$,
> and the type of q contains a product $Q_1 -> Q_2 -> \ldots -> Q_m$,
> and the basic types P_n and Q_1 overlap,
> then the type of $p.q$ includes the product $P_1 -> \ldots -> P_{n-1} -> Q_2 -> \ldots -> Q_m$

Note that this rule has the same form as the semantic rule for join itself. This isn't surprising, since the type is just an approximation of the value, computed in the same way, but more crudely.

4.4.3 Type Errors

There are two kinds of type error. First, since our logic assumes that all relations have a fixed arity, it is illegal to form expressions that would give relations of mixed arity.

Examples. Given the declarations

> **sig** Tea {origin: Country}
> **sig** Country {}

the expression *origin + Country* would be illegal, since *origin* has arity two, and *Country* has arity one.

Second, an expression is illegal if it can be shown, from the declarations alone, to be redundant, or to contain a redundant subexpression. A common and simple case is when an expression is redundant because it is equal to the empty relation.

Examples. In the context of our file system

```
sig Object {}
sig Directory extends Object {contents: set Object}
sig File extends Object {}
sig Alias extends File {to: Object}
```

the following expressions are ill-typed:

- *Directory & Alias*, the set of objects that are both directories and aliases, which must be empty, because these signatures are disjoint;

- *Alias.contents*, the contents of aliases, because *contents* is declared to map only directories, and no directory is an alias, so this expression likewise can be shown to be empty.

The type checker reasons only about types; it doesn't distinguish the signatures themselves from other expressions of the same type.

Example. The expression *Alias - Object*, the set of aliases that aren't objects, denotes the empty set, but the type checker will not reject it, because an expression of the form *A - O* where *A* has type *Alias* and *O* has type *Object* might not be empty.

In this type system, the subtype hierarchy is used primarily to determine whether types are disjoint. The asymmetry that you'd expect if you're familiar with subtypes in programming languages is not present. In particular, the typing of an expression of the form *s.r* where *s* is a set and *r* is a relation only requires *s* and the domain of *r* to overlap.

Examples. There are four possible relationships between a set and a relation combined by dot:

- Exact match: *Directory.contents* is well-typed.
- Subtype: *Root.contents* is well-typed.
- Supertype: *Object.contents* is well-typed.
- Disjoint: *File.contents* is ill-typed.

Only the disjoint case is rejected, because it's the only one that always results in the empty set. Note that any of the other combinations *may* also result in an empty set, so distinguishing them doesn't make much sense.

Disjointness of subexpressions doesn't always imply redundancy. The arguments of a union expression can certainly be—and often are—disjoint.

> *Example.* Even though the expression *File & Directory* is not well-typed, the expression *File + Directory* is. It might be used in a version of the file system in which no signature were declared for the set of all objects:
>
>   sig Directory extends Object {contents: set File + Directory}
>   sig File {}
>   sig Alias {to: File + Directory}

A more subtle case of a type error due to redundancy arises when an expression is not equal to the empty relation, but can be replaced by it without affecting the meaning of an enclosing expression.

> *Example.* The expression *(Directory + Alias).contents* is ill-typed, because aliases do not have contents; the mention of *Alias* is redundant, and the expression could have been written equivalently as *Directory.contents*.

> *Example.* The expression *Directory - Alias* is ill-typed, because no directory is an alias, so the mention of *Alias* is redundant. The expression *Directory in Alias* is ill-typed for a similar reason; it could have been written equivalently as *no Directory*.

Discussion

Does the type checker ever issue false alarms?

No. Whenever you get a type error, there is some real redundancy in your model that you will almost certainly want to eliminate. As we've noted, types are just relational expressions of a particular form, and for any expression e, its type expression Te will always denote a larger relation—that is, one containing at least the same tuples and maybe more. This is what makes type checking sound. When checking an intersection expression, for example, if the resulting type is empty, the relation represented by the expression must be empty—and therefore an error.

On the other hand, the type checker offers no guarantees. Traditional type systems for programming languages are the other way round: they guarantee no type errors will arise at runtime, but complain about programs that will never in fact go wrong. In modeling, there's no analogy to runtime failures, so it's not clear what guarantees would be useful.

Why does Alloy let you apply fields to supertypes?

Applying a field declared in a subtype to an expression that is known only to belong to the supertype might have an empty result. But since the result is not always empty, the Alloy type checker doesn't forbid it, or require some kind of cast. The rationale is that even applying a field of the subtype itself might have an empty result, so there is no additional benefit to be gained from the burden of casts.

In an object-oriented programming language, things are very different. If an expression is known to evaluate to an object of some class, then any method declared in that class can be invoked successfully. The type system can therefore make a guarantee, in such a situation, that there will be no problem of invoking a method that is not declared. In a modeling language like Alloy, however, the issue is navigating through relations, not calling methods, and because relations can be partial, there is never a guarantee that the result will be nonempty. Moreover, an empty result is not necessarily an error: that's why the Alloy type system only rules out expressions that are *always* empty rather than those that are *sometimes* empty.

Where can I find out more about the type system?

The type system of Alloy is described in detail, with justifications of its design, in a research paper [14]. An important property of the Alloy language is that types are not required to give meaning to a model; the paper explains how this is done with a simple extension of the semantics to allow mixed-arity relations, and to treat unresolved fields as unions of their possible resolvents.

4.4.4 Field Overloading

A signature defines a local namespace for its declarations, so you can use the same field name in different signatures, and each occurrence will refer to a different field. The only restriction is that if two signatures share a field name, they mustn't overlap (that is, potentially share elements, by one being a subtype of the other).

Field references are resolved automatically. When a field name appears that could refer to multiple fields, the types of the candidate fields are used to determine which field is meant. If more than one field is possible, an error is reported.

Example. Consider adding a field *contents* to the *File* signature of our file system model, mapping a file to a set of blocks:

sig Object, Block {}
sig Directory **extends** Object {contents: **set** Object}
sig File **extends** Object {contents: **set** Block}

The occurrence of the field name *contents* in the constraint

all f: File | **some** f.contents

is trivially resolved, because if it were to refer to the field of *Directory*, the expression *f.contents* would be empty. On the other hand, the occurrence in

all o: Object | **some** o.contents

is not resolved, and the constraint is rejected.

Example. Both singers and radio stations have bands:

sig Singer {band: Band}
sig RadioStation {band: **set** Freq}
sig Band, Freq {}

To say that radio stations don't have overlapping (frequency) bands, and that all (singing) bands have at least one singer, we can write, without ambiguity,

no disj s, s': RadioStation | **some** s.band & s'.band
all b: Band | **some** b.~band

Note how, in the first constraint, the field is resolved using the first column of the relation, and in the second, using the second column of the relation.

Resolution of overloading exploits the entire context in which a field reference appears, and there are no syntactic constraints on how the field must appear.

Example. The last constraint of the example above can be written in any of these forms:

all b: Band | **some** b.~band
all b: Band | **some** band.b
all b: Band | **some** s: Singer | s->b **in** band

Example. More subtly, given the declarations

sig Object, Block {}
sig Directory **extends** Object {contents: **set** Object}
sig File **extends** Object {contents: **set** Block}

the occurrence of *contents* in this constraint

no o: Object | o **in** o.contents

is resolved to the field of *Directory*. If it were to refer to the field in *File*, the expression *o.contents* would have type *Block*. Then, since *o* has the type *Object*, and the types *Object* and *Block* are disjoint, the constraint *o in o.contents* would be vacuously false.

Occasionally, an overloaded field name can't be resolved, so you need to disambiguate the name by elaborating the expression in which it appears (without changing the meaning). A simple way to do this that always works is to use the domain restriction operator, writing $S <: f$ for the field f appearing in signature S.

Example. A ring of network nodes, each linked by a relation *next* to its successor, and holding a value that changes over time:

sig Node {next: Node, value: Value **one** -> Time}
sig Time {next: Time}
sig Value {}

To say that nodes form a ring, we can write

fact {**all** n: Node | Node **in** n.^next}

The time steps are ordered with a relation also called *next*. To say that this relation is acyclic, we might try writing

fact {**no** ^next & **iden**}

but this will be rejected, because the reference to *next* is ambiguous. To fix it, we can write

no ^(Time <: next) & **iden**

(although in practice, the ordering of time steps is a common idiom for which you'd use a library module instead.)

Discussion

Can fields be declared in subset signatures?

Yes, they can. Remember, though, that when you extend a signature using the *in* keyword, the extensions are not subtypes, and need not be disjoint. According to the no-overlapping rule, they therefore can't share field names. Even if you happen to know that they are in fact disjoint (because of some fact you've written), the type checker won't know and will reject your model. For example,

> **sig** Name, Thing {}
> **sig** Man **in** Thing {name: Name}
> **sig** Island **in** Thing {name: Name}

is illegal, even if you add the fact

> **fact** {**no** Man & Island}

Why can't overlapping signatures share field names?

The consequence of this rule is that two fields with the same name must always differ in the type of their first column. So fields with the same name always have different types, and there is some context in which they might be distinguished. If the same name could be used for fields in two overlapping signatures, a more complicated rule would be required, and the standard trick using domain restriction to resolve field references would not always work.

How does Alloy's treatment of overloading relate to Java's?

Resolving of overloading is used in languages like Java to allow the names of fields and methods within a class to be chosen without regard for the names chosen in other classes. But the resolving mechanism is usually much simpler.

In Java, for example, field references can be overloaded, but they either stand for self-references (that is, *f*, being short for *this.f*), or follow a dot (as in *x.f*). In the former case, they resolve by default to fields of the class in which they appear. In the latter, they are resolved using the type of the expression preceding the dot. There's no transpose operator—you can't navigate backward.

In Alloy, we want to be able to write an expression *x.f* in the equivalent form *f.~x*, and to write *x.(f + g)* in place of *x.f* and *x.g*. This demands a more flexible overloading scheme, which doesn't rely on any particular syntactic form. Alloy's mechanism for resolution therefore relies not only on the field's type and arity but also on the full context in which it appears.

Is the domain restriction operator a special casting operator?

We saw that if you want the *f* field of type signature *S*, you can always write *S* <: *f* and be sure there will be no ambiguity. The domain restriction operator <: might seem to be a kind of cast. But don't be misled into thinking that there's anything special happening here. You could equally well write *(S->univ) & f* instead of *S* <: *f* (at least as far as overloading goes—it's hardly an attractive form!).

This is an important consequence of the design of Alloy's type system [14]: it is *implicit* and adds no syntax of its own to the language. In fact, Alloy can be regarded as an untyped language. Overloading doesn't actually have to be resolved to understand the meaning of a constraint. Each field name is taken to be a union of all the fields it might refer to. When the name is unambiguous, the union will actually be equivalent to the resolved field. So you don't need to know anything about types to read an Alloy model, but you do need to know a little in order to write them.

4.5   Facts, Predicates, Functions, and Assertions

The constraints of a model are organized into *paragraphs*. Assumptions are placed in *fact* paragraphs; implications to be checked are placed in *assertions*; constraints to be used in different contexts are packaged as *predicates*; and reusable expressions are packaged as *functions*.

4.5.1   Facts

Constraints that are assumed always to hold are recorded as *facts*. A model can have any number of facts, each a paragraph of its own, labeled by the keyword *fact*, and consisting of a collection of constraints. The order in which facts appear, and the order of constraints within a fact, is immaterial. You can give a fact a unique mnemonic name.

Example. Radio stations with nonoverlapping frequency bands:

```
sig RadioStation {band: set Freq}
fact NoOverlapping {
    no disj s, s': RadioStation | some s.band & s'.band
    }
```

Example. A file system that has no directory cycles, and in which each object is reachable from the root, and has at most one parent:

```
sig Object {}
sig Directory extends Object {contents: set Object}
one sig Root extends Directory {}
sig File extends Object {}
fact {
    no d: Directory | d in d.^contents,
    Object in Root.*contents
    all o: Object | lone o.~contents
    }
```

Example. A traffic light system (model diagram in fig. 4.10), in which, in every state, some light at each junction must show red:

```
sig LightState {color: Light -> one Color}
sig Light {}
abstract sig Color {}
one sig Red, Yellow, Green extends Color {}
sig Junction {lights: set Light}
fact {
    all s: LightState, j: Junction |
        some s.color.Red & j.lights
    }
```

Many facts are constraints that apply to each element of a signature's set. These can be recorded more succinctly as *signature facts*. A constraint immediately following a signature is implicitly quantified over its elements, and each field reference is implicitly dereferenced, just like fields mentioned in field declarations. So the signature fact *F* in

```
sig A {...}  {F}
```

is equivalent to writing

```
sig A {...}
fact {all this: A | F'}
```

where F' is just like *F*, but has each mention of a field *g* appearing in *A* or one of its supertypes replaced by *this.g*.

Example. A network with hosts and links, none of which connects a host to itself:

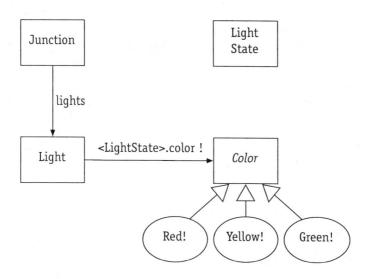

FIG. 4.10 Model diagram for a traffic light system.

```
sig Host {}
sig Link {from, to: Host}
fact {all x: Link | x.from != x.to}
```

can be expressed more succinctly as

```
sig Host {}
sig Link {from, to: Host} {from != to}
```

To prevent a field name from being expanded, you can prefix it with the symbol @.

Example. A network in which each link has a corresponding link in the other direction:

```
sig Host {}
sig Link {from, to: Host}
    {some x: Link | x.@from = to and x.@to = from}
```

This signature fact is short for

```
all this: Link |
    some x: Link |
        x.from = this.to and x.to = this.from
```

Without the @ symbols, it would instead be short for

all this: Link |
   some x: Link |
     x.(**this**.from) = **this**.to **and** x.(**this**.to) = **this**.from

which doesn't even typecheck.

The constraint implicit in a field declaration can be understood by treating the declaration as a formula that appears as a signature fact.

Example. The declarations

```
sig Book {
    homeAddress, workAddress: Name -> Addr,
    address: homeAddress + workAddress
    }
sig Name, Addr {}
```

can be written equivalently as

```
sig Book {
    homeAddress, workAddress, address: Name -> Addr }
    {
    address: homeAddress + workAddress
    }
sig Name, Addr {}
```

Accordingly, you can use the keyword *this* and the symbol @ in bounding expressions of declarations, although this is rarely necessary.

Discussion

Are signature facts like class invariants in an object-oriented language?

Yes, often they play the same role: to express constraints about individual members of a set. But signature facts are more expressive, because fields in Alloy can be "navigated" in any direction (so you can talk about objects that point to this object), and because of the ability to quantify in arbitrary ways. For the link examples, the first ("no link connects a host to itself") is like a class invariant, but the second ("every link has a corresponding backlink") is not.

In fact, it's good practice to limit the use of signature facts to those constraints that only apply to elements of the signature set. The implicit quantification in signature facts can have unexpected consequences otherwise, especially if you don't mention any field of the signature. Perhaps the most egregious and baffling example is this:

sig A {} {**some** A}

You may be surprised that there are instances of this model in which A has no elements. Expanding the fact reveals what's going on; the constraint

all this: A | **some** A

is vacuously true when A is empty, irrespective of the body of the quantification. The lesson is to write the intended constraint in a freestanding fact instead:

sig A {}
fact {**some** A}

where it now has the desired meaning (that A is nonempty), or to write it equivalently as

some sig A {}

4.5.2 Functions and Predicates

Often, there are constraints that you don't want to record as facts. You might want to analyze the model with a constraint included and excluded; check whether a constraint follows from some other constraints; or declare a constraint so it can be reused in different contexts. Predicates package expressions for such purposes. Functions package expressions for reuse.

A *function* is a named expression, with zero or more declarations for arguments, and a declaration expression for the result. When the function is used, an expression must be provided for each argument; its meaning is just the function's expression, with each argument replaced by its instantiating expression.

> *Example.* A function defining the ways in which a traffic light may change color:

```
abstract sig Color {}
one sig Red, Yellow, Green extends Color {}
fun colorSequence (): Color -> Color {
    Color <: iden + Red -> Green + Green -> Yellow + Yellow -> Red
    }
```

A *predicate* is a named constraint, with zero or more declarations for arguments. When the predicate is used, an expression must be provided for each argument; its meaning is just the predicate's constraint with each argument replaced by its instantiating expression.

Example. A predicate constraining a junction so that all lights but one at most are showing red:

```
sig Light {}
sig LightState {color: Light -> one Color}
sig Junction {lights: set Light}

fun redLights (s: LightState): set Light {s.color.Red}
pred mostlyRed (s: LightState, j: Junction) {
  lone j.lights - redLights(s)
  }
```

A predicate can be used to represent an *operation*, which describes a set of state transitions, by constraining the relationship between pre- and poststates.

Example. A rule describing how lights at a junction may change color, in which s and s' denote the before and after states respectively:

```
1    pred trans (s, s': LightState, j: Junction) {
2      lone x: j.lights | s.color[x] != s'.color[x]
3      all x: j.lights |
4        let step = s.color[x]-> s'.color[x] {
5          step in colorSequence ()
6          step in Red -> (Color - Red) => j.lights in redLights(s)
7        }
8    }
```

The constraints of this operation say that at most one light changes (2), and that, for each light at the junction, the lights operate in sequence (5), and if one turns from red to another color, then all the others were showing red (6).

This operation illustrates *nondeterminism*. How the colors change for the set of traffic lights in a junction is constrained, but it isn't fully determined. The predicate allows all the lights to remain the same color, and it doesn't say which light changes when all the lights are red. Now if this operation can be shown to be safe, we know that any operation that resolves these choices in accordance with the given constraints is also safe.

Alloy has a shorthand similar to the "receiver" convention of object-oriented programming languages, for functions or predicates whose first argument is a scalar. Rather than writing

pred f (x: X, y: Y, ...) {... x ...}

you can write

pred X::f (y: Y, ...) {... **this** ...}

with an implicit first argument referred to by the keyword *this* (and similarly for functions). Whether or not the predicate or function is declared in this way, it can be used in the form

x::f (y, ...)

where *x* is taken as the first argument, *y* as the second, and so on.

Example. The function and predicate defined above

```
fun redLights (s: LightState): set Light {s.color.Red}
pred mostlyRed (s: LightState, j: Junction) {
    lone j.lights - redLights(s)
    }
```

can be written equivalently as

```
fun LightState::redLights (): set Light {s.color.Red}
pred LightState::mostlyRed (j: Junction) {
    lone j.lights - s::redLights()
    }
```

and the invocation expressions *s::mostlyRed (j)* and *mostlyRed (s, j)* and equivalent, however the predicate *mostlyRed* is declared.

Discussion

How do you decide whether to use a predicate or a fact?

Recall that a predicate only holds when invoked; a fact always holds. The general rule is therefore that assumptions that always hold go in facts, but other constraints go in predicates. But this rule is a bit naive. First of all, you can package constraints as predicates and then include the predicates in facts. Second, you can actually dispense with facts altogether, and insert what would have been facts as predicates throughout. So the choice is more subtle.

Because facts are global, they are very convenient. A constraint written as a fact in just one place applies everywhere, assumed in every predicate and assertion. The downside is a loss of control. Perhaps you want to check an assertion without that constraint. You can of course simply comment it out in the fact paragraph while checking that particular assertion. But that's clumsy; if there are two assertions and you want to check one with and one without the constraint, you'll need to be commenting and uncommenting the fact as you perform the analysis.

For this reason, a more verbose style is appealing, in which there are very few facts, or none at all, and constraints are repeated in every context in which they apply. By packaging the repeated constraints as predicates, you only need to repeat the name of the predicate, and not the constraint itself. For small models, it's convenient to use facts because they make the model more succinct and are easily turned into predicates. For large models, this more sophisticated approach often works best.

When is the receiver syntax used in practice?

Its benefit comes when you have an expression involving a sequence of function applications. Then, instead of a nested expression such as

h (g (f (x, arg1), arg2), arg3)

in which the function names appear in reverse order of their application, amid a mass of parentheses, you can write

x::f(arg1)::g(arg2)::h(arg3)

How are predicates and functions typechecked?

In the obvious way. When checking the body of a predicate or function, the type checker assumes the formal parameters have the types declared. When checking an invocation, the checker determines whether the type of each actual argument and the type of the corresponding formal argument overlap. If they are disjoint, an error is reported.

4.5.3 Assertions

An *assertion* is a constraint that is intended to follow from the facts of the model. The analyzer checks assertions. If an assertion does not follow from the facts, then either a design flaw has been exposed, or a misformulation. Even assertions that do follow are useful to record, both because they express properties in a different way, and because they act like regression tests, so that if an error is introduced later, it may be detected by checking assertions.

Examples. For a file system in which every object is reachable from the root directory,

```
abstract sig Object {}
sig Directory extends Object {contents: set Object}
one sig Root extends Directory {}
sig File extends Object {}
fact {
    Object in Root.*contents
    }
```

a valid assertion that every object except the root is in some directory:

```
assert SomeDir {
    all o: Object - Root | some contents.o
    }
```

an invalid assertion that no object contains the root directory:

```
assert RootTop {
    no o: Object | Root in o.contents
    }
```

and a valid assertion that every file belongs to some directory:

```
assert FileInDir {
    all f: File | some contents.f
    }
```

Assertions can be entirely self-contained, without depending on any facts, implicit or explicit, and can be declared in a model without any signatures either. In this case, the assertion is a logical conjecture, intended to be a tautology. Such assertions can be used to check mathematical properties of operators, or to experiment with different ways to phrase a constraint.

Example. Assertions claiming that dot is associative for binary relations (correctly), and that union and difference can be manipulated like plus and minus in arithmetic (wrongly):

```
assert DotAssociative {
    all p, q, r: univ->univ | (p.q).r = p.(q.r)
    }
assert BadUnionRule {
    all p, q, r: univ->univ | p = q+r  iff p-q = r
    }
```

Assertions are often written using functions and predicates.

> *Example.* The traffic light model of fig. 4.11 includes an assertion *Safe* claiming that a key safety property is preserved by the transitions: that if, at a junction, all but one light is red before the transition, then all but one light is red after.

Discussion

What are assertions used for in practice?

Typically, assertions play two different roles. Some express mundane properties that aren't interesting in their own right; they're written purely to detect flaws in the model. It's surprising how effective even a few such assertions can be in uncovering subtle flaws.

Take our traffic light system, for example. We might believe that we've specified the system to a degree of detail that ensures that it's deterministic: that is, every state has at most one successor. Determinism, in this case, isn't in itself an interesting property, but by checking it, we'll find holes in the model—places in which detail is missing.

Other assertions express truly essential properties, and are sometimes more fundamental than the facts of the model. I've often found that the development of the right assertions for a design gives me a completely different view of what it's all about that is much clearer and simpler than the view I started with.

In the traffic light system, for example, there are properties that are fundamental to its working and which motivate the entire design: for example, that the lights properly guard the vehicles passing through, by never showing more than one green light at a time.

Must assertions have names?

Like facts, assertions need not be named. But to check an assertion, you need to refer to it in a command, so it's rare to leave it anonymous.

Can a model have assertions but no facts?

A model can have assertions without any explicit facts (as the example *language/theorems* demonstrated). Even in the absence of explicit facts, there are usually facts implicit in the declarations of signatures.

```
module language/lights

abstract sig Color {}
one sig Red, Yellow, Green extends Color {}
fun colorSequence (): Color -> Color {
    Color <: iden + Red -> Green + Green -> Yellow + Yellow -> Red
    }

sig Light {}
sig LightState {color: Light -> one Color}
sig Junction {lights: set Light}

fun redLights (s: LightState): set Light {s.color.Red}
pred mostlyRed (s: LightState, j: Junction) {
    lone j.lights - redLights(s)
    }

pred trans (s, s': LightState, j: Junction) {
    lone x: j.lights | s.color[x] != s'.color[x]
    all x: j.lights |
        let step = s.color[x] -> s'.color[x] {
            step in colorSequence ()
            step in Red -> (Color - Red) => j.lights in redLights(s)
        }
    }

assert Safe {
    all s, s': LightState, j: Junction |
        mostlyRed (s, j) and trans (s, s', j) => mostlyRed (s', j)
    }
check Safe
```

FIG. 4.11 Traffic light model, with safety assertion.

4.6 Commands and Scope

To analyze a model, you write a *command* and instruct the tool to execute it. A *run* command tells the tool to search for an instance of a
predicate. A *check* command tells it to search for a counterexample of
an assertion.

In addition to naming the predicate or assertion, you may also give a
scope that bounds the size of the instances or counterexamples that will

be considered. If you omit the scope, the tool will use the default scope in which each top-level signature is limited to three elements.

Examples. The command

    check Safe

in fig. 4.11 checks the safety of the traffic light system, by considering all transitions involving at most three light states, three junctions, three lights, and three colors.

For the same model, the command

    run trans

instructs the analyzer to find an example of a traffic light transition, using the same scope.

To specify a scope explicitly, you can give a bound for each signature that corresponds to a basic type. You can give bounds on top-level signatures, or on extension signatures, or even on a mixture of the two, so long as whenever a signature has been given a bound, the bounds of its parent and of any other extensions of the same parent can be determined.

Examples. Given these declarations of a file system

    abstract sig Object {}
    sig Directory **extends** Object {}
    sig File **extends** Object {}
    sig Alias **extends** File {}

and an assertion *A*, the following commands are well formed:

    check A **for** 5 Object
    check A **for** 4 Directory, 3 File
    check A **for** 5 Object, 3 Directory
    check A **for** 3 Directory, 3 Alias, 5 File

but this command is ill-formed

    check A **for** 3 Directory, 3 Alias

because it leaves the bound on *File* unspecified.

You can set a default scope explicitly, and you can mix a specified default scope with explicit bounds for particular types, which override and augment the default scope.

Examples. The command

> **check** A **for** 5

places a bound of 5 on all top-level types (in this case just *Object*). The command

> **check** A **for** 5 **but** 3 Directory

additionally places a bound of three on *Directory*, and a bound of two on *File* by implication.

Whenever a signature's size is determined by declarations, that size will be used as an implicit override.

Example. Given the declarations of fig. 4.11, a command such as

> **check** Safe **for** 2

will limit the signatures *Junction*, *Light* and *LightState* to two atoms each, but will assign a size of exactly three to *Color*.

Keep in mind that a scope declaration only gives an upper bound on the size of each set. If you want to prescribe the exact size, you can use the keyword *exactly*.

Example. The command

> **check** A **for exactly** 3 Directory, **exactly** 3 Alias, 5 File

limits *File* to at most 5 elements, but requires that *Directory* and *Alias* have exactly 3 elements each.

Discussion

Is the scope determined by the size of the instances in the actual system?

Not usually. Occasionally, there is a resource bound in the actual system that influences the choice of scope. In an analysis we performed of a proton therapy installation, for example, there were exactly three treatment rooms, so it made sense to limit the corresponding set to three elements.

But more typically the scope is determined purely by analysis concerns: an estimate of the size of instance that will be needed to find flaws (and which will still allow tractable search). For example, you might check a file system in a scope of 10 because you believe that's sufficient to catch almost all design flaws: that any bad scenario can most likely be illustrated in a file system with ten objects. The power of the analysis derives from the fact that there are a huge number of possible file systems containing ten objects, and your model will be checked for each of them. But of course you don't intend the model itself to have such a limitation: a file system that can only hold ten objects would not be very useful.

Why must the scope be specified repeatedly in each command?

Separating scope settings from the model proper is a significant language design decision. It prevents the model itself from being polluted by analysis concerns, and allows the same model to be analyzed under different scopes. The notion of scope is not unique to Alloy, but it tends to be handled less systematically in other tools. Many model checkers either hardwire the scope, or use global constants. A typical description of a traffic light system would limit the number of traffic lights at a junction, and all analyses would be performed within this same limit. Worse, the model will often hardwire a particular configuration. A model with two traffic lights would not cover the case in which there is only one.

4.7   Modules and Polymorphism

Alloy has a simple module system that allows you to split a model among several modules, and make use of predefined libraries. Modules correspond one-to-one with files. Every analysis is applied to a single module; any other modules containing relevant model fragments must be explicitly imported.

Each module has a path name that must match the path of its corresponding file in the file system. Paths are interpreted with respect to a collection of root directories, given as preferences in the tool.

4.7.1 Module Declarations and Imports

The first line of every module is a *module header* of the form

> **module** *modulePathName*

Every module that is used must have an explicit *import* immediately following the header, whose simplest form is

> **open** *modulePathName*

> *Examples.* A module that defines a predicate true of relations that are acyclic:

> **module** library/graphs
> **pred** Acyclic (r: **univ**->**univ**) {**no** ^r & **iden**}

and two uses, one in a model of a family:

```
module family
open library/graphs
sig Person {parents: set Person}
fact {Acyclic (parents)}
```

and one in a model of a file system:

```
module fileSystem
open library/graphs
sig Object {}
sig Directory extends Object {contents: set Object}
fact {Acyclic (contents)}
```

Modules have their own namespaces. A name clash between components of different modules can be resolved by referring to components with *qualified names*. A signature, predicate or function X in the module with path name p has the qualified name p/X. Even if an unqualified name would be unambiguous, the qualified name may still be used.

Example. A module that refers to the imported predicate Acyclic using a qualified name to avoid a clash with a predicate of the same name in the importing module:

```
module family
open library/graphs
sig Person {parents: set Person}
pred Acyclic () {library/graphs/Acyclic (parents)}
```

When path names get long, you can declare an *alias* for an imported module

```
open modulePathName as alias
```

and refer to its components using the alias as a qualifier instead of the path name.

Example. The same module, using an alias to shorten the reference to the imported predicate *Acyclic*:

```
module family
open library/graphs as g
sig Person {parents: set Person}
pred Acyclic () {g/Acyclic (parents)}
```

4.7.2 Parametric Modules

A module can be *parameterized* by one or more signature parameters, given as a list of identifiers in brackets after the module name. Any importing module must then instantiate each parameter with the name of a signature. Parameterization is just a syntactic mechanism; the effect of instantiating a module is just like importing a copy of the module with the instantiating signature names substituted for the parameters throughout.

Example. A parameterized module

> **module** library/graphs [t]
> **pred** Acyclic (r: t -> t) {**no** ^r & **iden**}

and two modules that use it

> **module** family
> **open** library/graphs [Person]
> **sig** Person {parents: **set** Person}
> **fact** {Acyclic (parents)}

> **module** fileSystem
> **open** library/graphs [Object]
> **sig** Object {}
> **sig** Directory **extends** Object {contents: **set** Object}
> **fact** {Acyclic (contents)}

The most common use of parameterized modules is for generic data structures, such as orderings, queues, lists, and trees. The type parameters represent the types of the elements held in the data structure.

Example. A parameterized list module:

> **module** library/list [t]
> **sig** List {}
> **sig** NonEmptyList **extends** List {next: List, element: t}
> **fact** Canonical {
>   **no disj** p, p': List | p.next = p'.next **and** p.element = p'.element
>   }
> **fun** List::first (): t {**this**.element}
> **fun** List::rest (): List {**this**.next}
> **fun** List::addFront (e: t): List {
>   {p: List | p.next = **this and** p.element = e}
>   }

Any module declared with parameters could have been declared instead without them, using *univ*. The advantage of parameters is that they allow stronger type checking; the disadvantage is that they require a separate instantiation for each use.

Discussion

When are module aliases useful?

Aliases are most useful when a parameterized module is imported more than once with different instantiations of its parameters, in which case the names of components will always need to be qualified. For example, we might have a resource allocation module parameterized by resources and the users they are allocated to:

> **module** general/resourceAllocation [user, resource]
>
> ...
>
> **pred** Allocate (...) {...}

and used in a model of a train system:

> **module** trainSystem
> **open** general/resourceAllocation [Train, Track]
>   **as** trainResource
> **open** general/resourceAllocation [Track, Current]
>   **as** trackResource

A name such as *general/resourceAllocation[Train, Track]/Allocate* now becomes *trainResource/Allocate* using the alias.

Can signature extensions cross module boundaries?

Yes. An importing module can extend a signature declared in an imported module, and vice versa. Here, for example, is a module that adds a *name* field to a signature:

> **module** named [t]
> **sig** named_t **extends** t {name: Name}
> **fact** {**all disj** a, b: t | a.name != b.name}
> **fact** {t = named_t}

Now if we write

> **open** named [S]

for any signature S, any element x of S will now have a distinct name *x.name*.

4.8   Integers and Arithmetic

Section 3.7 introduced expressions with integer values. Recall that #*e* is
an integer representing the number of tuples in the relation denoted by
e, and that such expressions can be combined with addition and subtraction, and compared.

> *Examples.* A hand is "three of a kind" if it consists of three cards,
> all of the same suit:

```
sig Card {suit: Suit}
sig Suit {}
pred ThreeOfAKind (hand: set Card) {
    #hand.suit = 1 and #hand = 3
    }
```

You may wonder whether integers can appear as atoms in relations. Integers themselves are not atoms, but associated with each *integer value*
there is an *integer atom* that holds that integer value, allowing the integer effectively to be included in a relation.

For an integer-valued expression *e*, the expression *Int e* denotes the integer atom holding the integer value of *e*. Given an expression *e* denoting
a set of integer atoms, the integer-valued expression *int e* denotes the
sum of the integer values of those atoms. The keyword *Int* represents
the set of all integer atoms.

From a typechecking perspective, there is a type *int* associated with integer-valued expressions, and a type *Int* representing sets of integer atoms. You can think of *Int* as a predefined signature, like *univ*. The special
operators can then be given these types:

```
int: Int -> int
Int: int -> Int
```

> *Example.* A weighted graph, in which a field *adj* maps each node
> to its adjacent nodes and their weights, with a constraint that self-
> connections have zero weight:

```
sig Node {
    adj: Node -> lone Int
    }
fact {
    all n: Node |
        let w = n.adj[n] |
            some w => int w = 0
    }
```

Discussion

Why leave integers to the end?

Integers are actually not very useful. If you think you need them, think again; there is often a more abstract description that matches the problem better. Just because integers appear in the problem domain does not mean that they should be modeled as such. To figure out whether integers are necessary, ask yourself what properties are actually relied upon. For example, a communication protocol that numbers its messages may rely only on the numbers being distinct; or it may rely on them increasing; or perhaps even being totally ordered. In none of these cases should integers be used. Of course, if you have a heavily numerical problem, you're likely to need integers (and more), but then Alloy is probably not suitable anyway.

Does Alloy have a multiplication operator?

No, it doesn't. Fortunately, it's rarely needed in structural models. The kinds of model that need multiplication tend to be heavily numerical, and not well suited to Alloy anyway.

How are integers scoped in Alloy?

In scope specifications, a setting for *Int* limits the number of Int atoms, whereas a setting for *int* gives the maximum bit-width for integers. For example, a command that includes the scope

   3 **Int**, 6 **int**

results in a search limited to at most three *Int* atoms, and involving integers from -31 to $+31$.

Is Alloy's Int *like Java's* Integer?

Yes. The distinction between *Int* and *int* in Alloy is very similar to Java's distinction between primitive integer values and Integer objects. It has a different purpose though. If integer values were treated as atoms, we would need an atom for every possible integer value within the scope, which would make the analysis less tractable. The distinction could be hidden syntactically, with implicit coercions between *Int* and *int*, but then we wouldn't be able to overload the + and - operators.

Are integer objects unique to the values they carry?

Yes. The following assertion is valid:

assert UniqueInts {**all** i, j: **Int** | **int** i = **int** j => i = j}

What about booleans? Is there no boolean type in Alloy?

Alloy has no boolean type. At first sight, this is very strange, especially for a language based on first-order logic. Formulas, of course, do have boolean values, but expressions never do. To see why not, suppose Alloy had a boolean type that could be used in declarations such as

sig Phone {offhook, ringing: boolean}

The motivation for such a type would be to allow us to write constraints like this:

all p: Phone | p.offhook => **not** p.ringing

But now we run into trouble. A term like *p.ringing* will in general denote a *set* of booleans. So what will be the value of *not p.ringing* when the set contains zero booleans, or more than one? There is no good way out of this. Perhaps you could reject such expressions, and only allow constraints, like the one above, in which they don't appear? This is not easy, because it involves reasoning about the domains of functions. Or perhaps you could extend the interpretation of the standard logical operators over sets of boolean values?

These problems are just a particular case of the old problem of partial functions and their application, which are avoided in Alloy by offering only relational image, and no function application (see the discussion in subsection 3.4.3). Admitting a boolean type would reintroduce all that complexity, because the boolean expressions involve function applications, for little benefit.

If you really want booleans, you can define a boolean type of your own:

```
module booleans
sig Boolean {}
one sig True, False extends Boolean {}
```

and now you can write the above constraint as

```
module phones
open booleans
sig Phone {offhook, ringing: Boolean}
fact {all p: Phone | p.offhook = True => not p.ringing = True}
```

and, if you're a real glutton for punishment, you could define extended versions of the logical operators too, such as this version of negation, which gives *Not e* as false when *e* is not a scalar:

```
...
    fun Boolean::Not (): Boolean {if this = False then True else False}
..
```

and now you can write things like

```
...
    fact {all p: Phone | Implies (p.offhook, Not (p.ringing))}
```

In fact, the Alloy library includes such a module. It's useful when boolean values must be closely modeled, for example in reasoning about code. But for design modeling, this is the wrong approach. The way to classify objects is not to associate them with boolean values using attributes, but to declare subtypes:

```
sig Phone {calling: set Phone}
sig Offhook, Ringing extends Phone {}
```

Now the constraint that an offhook phone is not ringing is implicit in the declarations. For a dynamic classification, you could associate with each attribute the set of times at which it holds:

```
sig Phone {
    calling: Phone -> Time,
    offhook, ringing: set Time
    }
```

and the constraint now becomes

```
all t: Time | no offhook.t & ringing.t
```

Using set operators, constraints are more succinct than they would have been with boolean attributes, without any of the complications.

5: Analysis

The first principle is that you must not fool yourself, and you are the easiest person to fool.—Richard P. Feynman

Analysis brings software abstractions to life in three ways. First, it encourages you as you explore, by giving you concrete examples that reinforce intuition and suggest new scenarios. Second, it keeps you honest, by helping you to check as you go along that what you write down means what you think it means. And third, it can reveal subtle flaws that you might not have discovered until much later (or not at all).

This chapter explains the form of analysis that underlies Alloy, and discusses its power and limitations. The key idea is the specification of a *scope*, which bounds the sizes of the signatures, and *exhaustive search* within the scope for *examples* or *counterexamples*.

5.1 Scope-Complete Analysis

5.1.1 Instance Finding and Undecidability Compromises

Checking an assertion and running a predicate reduce to the same analysis problem: finding some assignment of relations to variables that makes a constraint true. So rather than referring to both problems, we'll refer just to the problem of checking assertions.

Alloy's relational logic is undecidable. This means that it is impossible to build an automatic tool that can tell you, with perfect reliability, whether an assertion is valid—that is, holds for every possible assignment. Some compromise is therefore necessary.

The traditional compromise is embodied in *theorem proving*. An automatic theorem prover attempts to construct a proof that an assertion holds. If it succeeds, the assertion is valid. If it fails, however, the assertion may be valid or invalid. Unfortunately, it can be hard to tell whether the failure to verify the assertion was due to a faulty assertion, to limitations of the prover itself, or to a lack of appropriate guidance from the user.

The analysis underlying Alloy, *instance finding*, makes a different compromise. Rather than attempting to construct a proof that an assertion holds, it looks for a *refutation,* by checking the assertion against a huge set of test cases, each being a possible assignment of relations to variables. If the assertion is found not to hold for a particular case, that case is reported as a *counterexample.* If no counterexample is found, it's still possible that the assertion does not hold, and has a counterexample that is larger than any of the test cases considered.

This compromise is a better match for lightweight modeling. Since the analysis is applied repeatedly and incrementally throughout the development of an abstraction, it will most often be presented with *invalid* assertions. Instance finding is well suited to analyzing invalid assertions because it generates counterexamples, which can usually be easily traced back to the problem in the description, and because invalid assertions tend to be analyzed much more quickly than valid ones (since a valid assertion requires the entire space of possible instances to be covered, whereas, for an invalid assertion, the analysis can stop when the first instance has been found).

5.1.2 The Notion of Scope

To make instance finding feasible, a *scope* is defined that limits the size of instances considered. The analysis effectively examines every instance within the scope, and an invalid assertion will only slip through unrefuted if its smallest counterexample is outside the scope.

You might think that a good strategy would be for the analyzer to start with a small scope and increment it automatically until either a counterexample has been found or some preset time limit has been exceeded. But this presupposes a scope that is just a number. A richer notion of scope turns out to be more useful, in which each signature is bounded separately, under the user's control. For example, an analysis of a railway switching operation may call for a scope of only two states (the before and after states), and only one junction, but a larger number of track segments and trains.

The scope thus defines a multidimensional space of test cases, each dimension corresponding to the bound on a particular signature. Even a small scope usually defines a huge space. In the default scope of 3, for example, which assigns a bound of three to each signature, each binary relation contributes 9 bits to the state (since each three elements of the domain may or may not be associated with each three elements of the range)—that is, a factor of 512. So a tiny model with only four relations has a space of over a billion cases.

5.1.3 The Small Scope Hypothesis

Isn't instance finding just testing? In a sense it is: the assertion is checked against a finite set of cases that occupies only an infinitessimally small proportion of the space of possible cases. Dijkstra's dictum [13]

> *Program testing can be used to show the presence of bugs, but never to show their absence*

applies also to instance finding. But the weakness of testing goes beyond its inability to show the absence of bugs; it can't usually show their presence either. Most bugs in code elude testing, and the challenge in writing test suites is to catch more of the bugs that are there, not to show that no bugs remain (which is a very different, and even harder, problem).

Instance finding has far more extensive coverage than traditional testing, so it tends to be much more effective at finding bugs. In short:

> *Most bugs have small counterexamples.*

That is, if an assertion is invalid, it probably has a small counterexample. I call this the "small scope hypothesis," and it has an encouraging implication: if you examine *all* small cases, you're likely to find a counterexample.

Discussion

What role do theorem provers have in analyzing software abstractions?

Theorem provers and instance finders play complementary roles. Once the Alloy Analyzer has failed to find a counterexample to an assertion, you could use a theorem prover to prove that the assertion holds in all scopes. Completing a proof with the aid of a theorem prover usually demands an effort an order of magnitude greater than the modeling effort that preceded it, so for most applications, it's not cost-effective. For checking safety-critical abstractions, however, the additional assurance obtained from proof may be worthwhile.

Does analysis depend on having perfect assertions?

Some people assume that, without assertions that capture some platonic "higher-level specification," analysis is not worthwhile. On the contrary, even simple forms of analysis are beneficial. Simple simulation predicates often generate surprising scenarios, and formulating basic sanity checks as assertions can expose deep errors. Of course, if you can express the critical properties of a software design with assertions, then you can use analysis to check them, and a lack of counterexamples is more significant.

Is the primary purpose of analysis to expose subtle bugs?

The case for formal methods is often based on the prospect of catching subtle bugs that elude testing. But in practice the less glamorous analyses that are applied repeatedly during the development of an abstraction, and which keep the formal model in line with the designer's intent, are far more important. Software, unlike hardware, rarely fails because of a single tiny but debilitating flaw. In almost all cases, software fails because of poor abstractions that lead to a proliferation of bugs, one of which happens to cause the failure.

What makes the logic undecidable?

First-order logic is undecidable, unless some severe restrictions are placed on the constraints that can be written. For example, you can restrict the logic to "monadic" predicates (that is, predicates with only a single argument), which in a relational setting eliminates relations, leaving only sets and scalars. Alternatively, you can restrict how quantifiers are used, for example allowing only certain "prefix" patterns in which all quantifiers appear at the start of an assertion in a particular pattern of existential and universal quantifiers. Eliminating quantifiers wouldn't make our logic decidable, however, because the relational calculus, consisting of only binary relations and our relational operators (notably, dot join) is undecidable. In short, there appears to be no practical logic that's rich enough to capture software abstractions that is still decidable.

For a gentle introduction to the notion of undecidability, see chapter 8 of David Harel's book [25]. For a comprehensive treatment of the decidability of first-order logic and its variants, see [6], which includes a nice classification that is available also online in a short paper [20].

Why the term "instance"?

In standard mathematical terminology, an instance of a constraint is called a "model," and a tool that finds models is a "model finder." But the word "model" is so heavily overloaded that it seemed best to avoid it.

Is the idea of scope new?

A technique known as "model checking" was developed in the 1980's for analyzing protocols and hardware designs that could be expressed as finite state machines. The technique was so effective that it was soon applied to unbounded systems, by constructing a description that artificially (and often somewhat arbitrarily) made the system finite. In fact, this process is now seen as so fundamental to model checking that people have come to think that this is what the word "model" refers to in its name: a finite model of an infinite system. (The word was actually intended in its mathematical sense, that the analysis checks whether the state machine is a "model" of a temporal logic formula.) So the idea of searching within finite bounds, relying—at least implicitly—on the small scope hypothesis to find bugs, is not new.

What is perhaps new to Alloy is the separation of the scope specification from the model proper, and the ability to adjust the scope in a fine-grained manner. The separation prevents the model from being polluted with analysis concerns, and makes it easy to run different analyses with different scopes without adjusting the model itself. The fine-grained control goes beyond static configuration parameters (such as the number of processes in a network) to bounds on dynamically allocated data (such as the number of messages in a queue, or the number of objects in a heap).

What use is a design that only works in a small scope?

This question exposes a common misunderstanding of the notion of scope. Of course a system that only worked when each type had no more than a small number of elements would be useless. The point of the small scope hypothesis is that systems that fail on large instances almost always would fail on small ones with similar properties, even if such small instances don't occur in practice. So by checking all small instances, we are effectively checking for large ones too.

What about resource allocation limits?

Implementations often have built-in resource allocation limits that cause failures when crossed. This would seem to contradict the small scope hypothesis, because the failures only occur on huge instances that exceed the allocation limits. Abstractions don't have these issues, though, because resource allocation is either factored out, or represented more abstractly, either by a parameter in the model which can be set arbitrarily low, or by nondeterministic behavior.

Can you prove the small scope hypothesis?

No—that's why I call it a hypothesis. It makes a claim about the assertions that arise in practice, not the space of all possible assertions. One can construct an invalid assertion whose smallest counterexample is just beyond any given scope. Fortunately, inadvertent errors are rarely so devious in practice. It's important to bear in mind, nevertheless, that instance finding is an incomplete analysis, and sometimes the scope needed to find a bug is larger than intuition would suggest.

If there were a scope large enough to find a counterexample to any invalid assertion, or even a way to compute a large enough scope on an assertion-by-assertion basis, it would be possible—in principle at least—to determine whether or not an assertion is valid. This would contradict the undecidability of the logic, so it cannot be done. Nevertheless, there are subsets of first-order logic that have a "small model theorem," which allows a sufficient scope to be determined from the structure of an assertion: an example relevant to modeling is the theory of set-valued fields [45].

5.2   Instances, Examples, and Counterexamples

5.2.1   Analysis Constraints and Variables

When you run a predicate or check an assertion, the analyzer searches for an *instance* of an *analysis constraint*: an assignment of values to the variables of the constraint for which the constraint evaluates to true.

In the case of a predicate, the analysis constraint is the predicate's constraint conjoined with the facts of the model—both the explicit facts appearing in *fact* paragraphs, and the facts that are implicit in declarations. An instance is an *example*: a scenario in which both the facts and the predicate hold.

In the case of an assertion, the analysis constraint is the negation of the assertion's constraint conjoined with the facts of the model. An instance is a *counterexample*: a scenario in which the facts hold but the assertion does not (or, equivalently, a scenario in which the assertion fails to follow from the facts).

The variables that are assigned in an instance comprise

- the sets associated with the signatures;
- the relations associated with the fields;
- and, for a predicate, its arguments.

```
module analysis/addressBook

abstract sig Target {}
sig Addr extends Target {}
sig Name extends Target {}
sig Book {addr: Name -> Target}

fact Acyclic {all b: Book | no n: Name | n in n.^(b.addr)}
pred add (b, b': Book, n: Name, t: Target) {
   b'.addr = b.addr + n -> t
   }
run add for 3 but 2 Book
fun lookup (b: Book, n: Name): set Addr {n.^(b.addr) & Addr}

assert addLocal {
   all b,b': Book, n,n': Name, t: Target |
     add (b,b',n,t) and n != n' => lookup (b,n') = lookup (b',n')
   }
check addLocal for 3 but 2 Book
```

FIG. 5.1 An address book example.

Example. As a running example, we'll use a version of the address book taken from chapter 2, shown in fig. 5.1, which has the merit of including every basic language construct. Each address book *b* has a mapping *b.addr* from names not only to addresses, but also to names (thus allowing multiple levels of indirection). The signature *Target* is declared for the purpose of this generalization. The fact says that these indirections never form cycles. The *add* operation simply adds a mapping from a name to a target. The *lookup* function returns the set of addresses reachable from the name—that is, the leaves of the tree. Finally, the assertion *addLocal* makes the (incorrect) claim that an addition for a name *n* only affects lookups for *n* itself.

For the command *run add*, the analysis variables are:

· the signatures *Target*, *Addr*, *Name*, and *Book*;
· the field *addr*; and
· the four arguments to the *add* predicate: *b*, *b'*, *n*, and *t*.

The analysis constraint is the conjunction of the constraints implicit in the signatures

Name **in** Target
Addr **in** Target
no Name & Addr
Target **in** Name + Addr
no Book & Target

the constraints implicit in field and argument declarations

addr : Book -> Name -> Target
b: Book
n: Name
t: Target

the explicit facts, in this case just *Acyclic*

all b: Book | **no** n: Name | n **in** n.^(b.addr)

and the body of the predicate being run

b'.addr = b.addr + n -> t

Here is the first sample instance generated by running the command, being the case in which a name/address pair is added that is already present:

Target = {(Addr_0), (Name_0)}
Addr = {(Addr_0)}
Name = {(Name_0)}
Book = {(Book_0), (Book_1)}
addr = {(Book_0, Name_0, Addr_0), (Book_1, Name_0, Addr_0)}
b = {(Book_0)}
b' = {(Book_0)}
n = {(Name_0)}
t = {(Addr_0)}

For consistency, I've used the format of chapter 3, in which the elements of sets were parenthesized to remind the reader that, from a semantic perspective, sets are represented in Alloy as relations. The Alloy Analyzer's textual output has a more conventional (and slightly friendlier) format that uses the declarations of relations to determine how they should be formatted. Fig. 5.2 shows three forms of output offered by the analyzer: this textual form, a tree form, and the diagrammatic form.

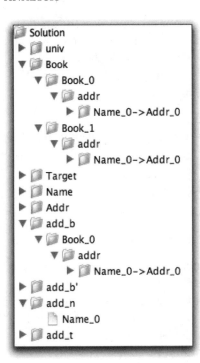

module alloy/lang/univ
sig univ = {Addr_0, Book_0, Book_1, Name_0}
module analysis/addressBook
sig Target extends univ = {Addr_0, Name_0}
sig Addr extends Target = {Addr_0}
sig Name extends Target = {Name_0}
sig Book extends univ = {Book_0, Book_1}
  addr: analysis/addressBook/Name
    -> analysis/addressBook/Target =
    {Book_0 -> Name_0 -> Addr_0,
     Book_1 -> Name_0 -> Addr_0}
Skolem constants
add_b = Book_0
add_b' = Book_0
add_n = Name_0
add_t = Addr_0

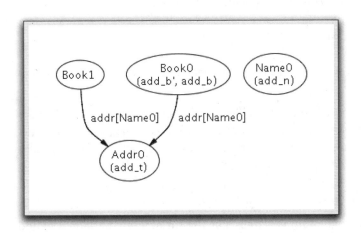

FIG. 5.2 A generated instance for the *run* command of fig. 5.1, as shown by the Alloy Analyzer in tree form (above left), textual form (above right) and diagram form (below).

For the command *check addLocal*, the variables include the signatures and the field *addr*, but no predicate arguments. The analysis constraint is the conjunction of the constraints implicit in signature and field declarations, and the explicit fact, as before, and additionally, the negation of the assertion

> **some** b,b': Book, n,n': Name, a: Addr |
>   add (b,b',n,a) **and** n != n' **and not** lookup (b,n') = lookup (b',n')

which becomes

> **some** b,b': Book, n,n': Name, a: Addr |
>   b'.addr = b.addr + n->t
>   **and** n != n'
>   **and not** n.^(b.addr) & Addr = n'.^(b'.addr) & Addr

when the predicate *add* and the function *lookup* are expanded. A counterexample to this assertion is shown graphically in Fig. 5.3 in three different views produced by making different visualization selections in the Alloy Analyzer, and using the projection facility as described in section 3.3. Note the labels that indicate which atoms are the witnesses for the quantified variables: *addLocal_b*, for example, is the witness for the variable *b* of *addLocal*. These are *skolem constants* explained in subsection 5.2.2.

Discussion

Aren't multiple values of a variable needed to handle pre- and post-states?

No, no, no! In the variables for the analysis of *addLocal*, b and b' are distinct variables; as far as the analyzer is concerned, they have no more in common than any other pair of variables, even though they happen to represent the before and after values of an address book.

So variables don't actually vary?

That's right. Our variables, like the variables in mathematics and physics (and unlike variables in an imperative program), only vary in the sense that they can be assigned a variety of values. It's standard practice in engineering to use different names to describe phenomena at different points in time; it's what makes reasoning by algebraic manipulation possible. In computer science, the use of distinct names for describing pre- and poststates goes back at least to the use of auxiliary variables in Hoare logic.

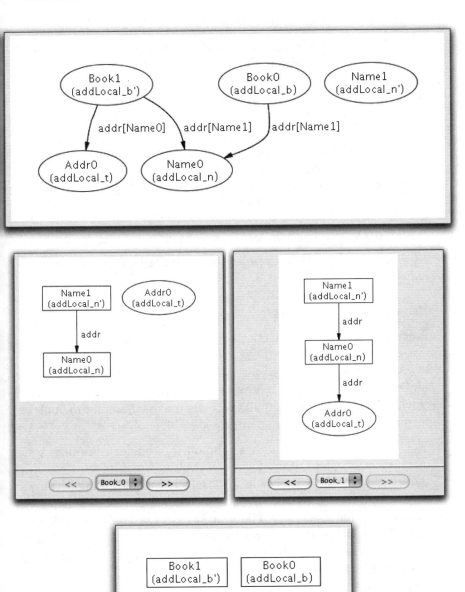

FIG. 5.3 A generated instance for the *check* command of fig. 5.1,
as shown by the Alloy Analyzer in diagram form
with the default visualization settings (top),
projected onto the set *Book* (middle),
and with just *Book* atoms showing (bottom).

Why aren't there primed variables for the poststate values of fields too?

That approach is taken by most modeling languages, especially Z [65]. The approach we've taken in this book is more like the approach taken in physics, in which a time-varying phenomenon is modeled as a function from times to values. The *addr* field, for example, can be viewed as a function with a value *x.addr* for each book *x*. The multiple address books might represent distinct books at a given time, or — as in this case—the same book at different times. In the leader election and hotel locking examples of chapter 6, time is made fully explicit, and a time-varying state component is modeled by a field *f* with times in the last column, so that *f.t* represents the value at time *t*.

Is Alloy the first language to use this approach?

No. The approach was pioneered by John McCarthy in his *situation calculus* [51].

How does the analysis work?

Every analysis involves solving a constraint: either finding an instance (for a *run* command) or finding a counterexample (for a *check*). The Alloy Analyzer is therefore a constraint solver for the Alloy logic. In its implementation, however, it is more of a compiler, because, rather than solving the constraint directly, it translates the constraint into a boolean formula and solves it using an off-the-shelf SAT solver.

SAT stands for "satisfiability": a solution to a boolean formula is an assignment of values to the formula's boolean variables that "satisfies" the formula. In the last decade, SAT solver technology has advanced dramatically, and a state-of-the-art SAT solver can often solve a formula containing thousands of boolean variables and millions of clauses. The Alloy Analyzer is bundled with several SAT solvers, the fastest of which are Chaff [55] and Berkmin [19], and a preference setting lets you choose which is used.

The translation into a boolean formula is conceptually very simple. Think about a particular value of a binary relation *r* from a set *A* to a set *B*. This value can be represented as an adjacency matrix of 0's and 1's, with a 1 in row *i* and column *j* when the *ith* element of *A* is mapped to the *jth* element of *B*. So the space of all possible values of *r* can be represented by a matrix not of boolean *values* but of boolean *variables*. A variable $r_{i,j}$ is placed in each position of the matrix. The dimensions of these matrices are determined by the scope; if the scope bounds *A* by

3 and B by 4, for example, r will be a 3×4 matrix containing 12 boolean variables, and having 2^{12} possible values.

Now, for each relational expression, a matrix is created whose elements are boolean expressions. For example, the expression corresponding to $p + q$ for binary relations p and q would have the expression $p_{i,j} \vee q_{i,j}$ in row i and column j, because A_i is related by $p+q$ to B_j when it is related by p or by q. For each relational formula, a boolean formula is created. For example, the formula corresponding to p *in* q would be the conjunction of $p_{i,j} \Rightarrow q_{i,j}$ over all values of i and j, because p *in* q holds if whenever p relates A_i to B_j, then q does also.

The resulting boolean formula is passed to the SAT solver. If it finds no solution, the Alloy Analyzer just reports that no instance or counterexample has been found. If it does find a solution, the solution is mapped back into an instance. If the variable $r_{i,j}$ is true, for example, the tuple relating the *ith* element of A to the *jth* element of B will be included in the value of the relation r.

In performing the translation from the Alloy logic to a boolean formula, the Alloy Analyzer applies a variety of optimizations. The most significant and interesting of these is *symmetry breaking*. Because atoms are uninterpreted (see section 3.2), every Alloy model has a natural symmetry: you can take any instance of a command and create another one by permuting the atoms. This means that when an analysis constraint has a solution, it actually has a whole set of solutions corresponding to all the ways in which the atoms of the solution can be permuted. Conceptually, we can divide the space of assignments (possible solutions) into equivalence classes, with two assignments belonging to the same class if one can be permuted into the other. The solver need then only look at one assignment in each equivalence class. Since there are very many permutations, the equivalence classes are very large, and restricting the search in this way can dramatically improve its performance.

In fact, the Alloy Analyzer influences the search only indirectly. It generates symmetry-breaking constraints from the model, and conjoins them to the analysis constraint. If they were perfect, these constraints would rule out all but one assignment in each equivalence class, but that turns out to require very large symmetry-breaking constraints, which would overload the solver and actually damage performance. The analyzer therefore generates a much smaller constraint, which breaks only some of the symmetries, but in practice eliminates a very high proportion (over 99%) of the assignments.

The simplest case of symmetry breaking applies when a model uses *util/ordering*. This library module is used to impose an ordering on a signature, and declares a relation *next* over the signature being ordered. Since the atoms that are being ordered are interchangeable, they can be ordered in their natural lexical order without any loss of generality. This is why ordering a signature *S* with *util/ordering* will always order its elements *S0, S1, S2*, etc., which is good not only for performance (since other orders aren't considered) but also for visualization.

The idea of writing models in a relational logic and using a constraint solver to analyze them was first developed for a predecessor of Alloy called Nitpick [35]. Nitpick's tool worked by enumerating entire relation values, and had a rather elaborate symmetry-breaking scheme [34, 36]. A scheme for solving Nitpick formulas by reduction to satisfiability was not very successful [11], because it used a BDD to represent the boolean formula—a data structure that had worked very well in other areas but was not a good match to relational logic.

The basic scheme of translation of Alloy to SAT was developed in 1997 [31, 32], and worked much better, largely due to a switch (suggested by Greg Nelson) from BDD's to SAT. The algorithms in the current version of the Alloy Analyzer were developed primarily by Ilya Shlyakhter [64], in particular this symmetry breaking scheme [63], and an optimization for detecting opportunities for sharing in the generated formula.

5.2.2 Skolemization

If the analysis constraint contains an existential quantifier, the analyzer can often (depending on the exact form of the constraint) provide a *witness*: a value for the quantified variable that makes the body of the existentially quantified formula true. This is done by extending the set of variables bound in the instance to include the quantified variables, using a transformation known as *skolemization*.

Let's start by seeing how an existential quantifier is handled without skolemization. Suppose our analysis constraint has the form

some x: S | F

where *S* is a signature and *F* is some arbitrary constraint in which *x* appears. If the signature *S* is assigned a bound of *k* by the scope, it can be represented by atoms

$$S_1, S_2, ..., S_k$$

and the quantification can be expanded to

F [S_0/x] **or** F [S_1/x] **or** ... **or** F [S_n/x]

where F [S_i/x] is the constraint F, with S_i substituted for x. Note that the variable x does not appear explicitly in this new constraint, so when an instance is generated, it may not be clear which disjunct is true.

Skolemization takes the original analysis constraint, and instead of expanding the quantifier, replaces the bound variable by a free variable, giving

(sx: S) **and** F [sx/x]

where *sx* is a new free variable. It's easy to see that this new analysis constraint will have an instance whenever the old one does, but it will be a more helpful one, because it will assign a value to *sx*.

There's nothing magical about skolemization. A free variable in the analysis constraint—such as a signature or relation—is treated by the constraint solver as if it were existentially quantified. Skolemization is simply making implicit an explicit existential quantification.

Example. The analysis constraint for the *check addLocal* command of fig. 5.1 includes

some b,b': Book, n,n': Name, a: Addr |
add (b,b',n,a) **and** n != n'
and not lookup (b,n') = lookup (b',n')

which can be skolemized to

b: Book **and** b': Book **and** n: Name **and** n': Name **and** a: Addr
and add (b,b',n,a) **and** n != n'
and not lookup (b,n') = lookup (b',n')

As noted in section 5.2.1, the counterexample to *addLocal* (shown in fig. 5.2) includes the following bindings of skolem constants:

addLocal_b = Book_0
addLocal_b' = Book_1
addLocal_n = Name_0
addLocal_n' = Name_1
addLocal_t = Addr_0

The skolem constants are named by prefixing the corresponding variables names with the names of the predicates or functions in which they appear (and with an additional index if a name is used more than once in the same lexical scope.)

The existential quantifier need not be outermost. Suppose the analysis constraint takes the form

>   **all** x: S | **some** y: T | F

where S and T are signatures, and F again is some arbitrary constraint. This can be skolemized to

>   (sy: S -> **one** T) **and** (**all** x: S | F [x.sy/y])

where F [x.sy/y] is the constraint F, but with each occurrence of y replaced by the expression x.sy.

This is more complicated, but the intuition is still straightforward. If the original constraint has an instance, then there is a value for y that makes F true for each value of x. This value of y can be regarded as being obtained by applying a function sy to the appropriate value of x, so the quantification over y can be eliminated by introducing such a function as a variable whose value is to be determined.

>   *Example.* The analysis constraint for the *run* command in this model

>   ```
>   sig Name, Address {}
>   sig Book {addr: Name -> Address}
>   pred show () {
>       all b: Book | some n: Name | some b.addr[n]
>       }
>   run show for 3
>   ```

>   can be skolemized to

>   (sn: Book -> **one** Name) **and** (**all** b: Book | **some** b.addr [b.sn])

>   whose instances will include a variable *sn* that's a relation showing, for each book *b*, a witness of a name *b.sn* that it maps.

Skolemization can be applied not only to scalars but also to sets and relations. Nothing in the arguments above required the existentially quantified variables to be scalars. In the simple case of an outermost quantifier, the introduced variable becomes a set or relation. In the case of an inner quantifier, the introduced variable is no longer a function, but a relation (to obtain a set), or a multirelation (to obtain a relation).

Example. The analysis constraint for

```
assert BadUnionRule {
    all s, t, u: set univ | s = t + u  iff s - t = u
    }
check BadUnionRule
```

skolemizes, after negation, to

ss: **set univ and**
st: **set univ and**
su: **set univ and**
not (ss = st + su **iff** ss - st = su)

and gives counterexamples that show witnesses for the bound variables, such as

ss = {(U0)}
st = {(U0)}
su = {(U0)}

Discussion

What are the advantages of skolemization?

It has three advantages. First, it causes witnesses to be generated for bound variables, as explained and illustrated in the previous section. Second, it allows many higher-order quantifications—such as that of the assertion *BadUnionRule*—to be analyzed that would otherwise not be analyzable at all. Third, it tends to improve the performance of the analysis even for first-order quantifications, because the unfolding associated with existential quantifiers grows constraints dramatically.

5.3 Unbounded Universal Quantifiers

This section explains an important and subtle limitation of finite instance finding. Fortunately, it doesn't arise very often in practice, and it leads to the presence of surprising counterexamples, rather than surprising omissions (which would be far worse).

The problem arises when a signature is intended to represent all possible values of a composite structure. This contradicts the semantics of Alloy, in which a signature denotes just some set of values. The contradiction only becomes apparent when universal quantification is used in a particular way.

5.3.1 Generator Axioms and Exploding Scopes

Suppose, for example, we want to check that sets are closed under union—that is, the union of any two sets is also a set. We can represent a set as an object by declaring the signature

```
sig Set {
    elements: set Element
    }
```

along with a signature for the elements

```
sig Element {}
```

Now we can write an assertion saying that, for any pair of sets *s0* and *s1*, a set *s2* exists that contains the elements of both:

```
assert Closed {
    all s0, s1: Set | some s2: Set |
        s2.elements = s0.elements + s1.elements
    }
```

Running this in a default scope of 3

```
check Closed
```

gives counterexamples such as

```
Set = {(S0), (S1)}
Element = {(E0), (E1)}
s0 = {(S0)}
s1 = {(S1)}
elements = {(S0, E0), (S1, E1)}
```

in which *s0* is the atom *S0* containing *E0*, *s1* is the atom *S1* containing *E1*, and there is no *Set* atom containing both elements.

What went wrong? Roughly speaking, the analyzer found a counterexample that didn't populate the signature *Set* with enough values; it's missing a *Set* atom, *S2*, say, that's mapped by *elements* to *E0* and *E1*.

To remedy all such problems, we could add a *generator axiom* forcing *Set* to be fully populated, for example as a structural induction saying that there is a set with no elements, and for each set and each element, there is a set with the element added:

```
fact SetGenerator {
    some s: Set | no s.elements
    all s: Set, e: Element |
        some s': Set | s'.elements = s.elements + e
}
```

Now we have a different problem, though: the scope explodes. If there are k atoms in *Element*, there must be 2^k atoms in *Set*. Or, to put it differently, if we specify a scope that bounds *Set* by k, only instances in which there are at most $\log k$ atoms in *Element* will be considered. In this tiny example, it's still possible to do some useful analysis: a scope of 4 elements and 16 sets should be sufficient to analyze some interesting assertions.

But suppose that instead of sets, our model involved graphs:

```
sig Graph {
    adj: Node -> Node
}
```

There are $2^{k \times k}$ distinct graphs over k nodes. So to consider graphs of three nodes, the scope should bound *Graph* by 512.

Worse, in some cases, the generator axiom would require an infinite number of atoms for the composite. A model of lists, for example, might declare signatures for empty and nonempty lists

```
abstract sig List {}
one sig EmptyList extends List {}
sig NonEmptyList extends List {
    element: Element,
    rest: List
}
```

and then force the existence of all possible lists with a generator axiom such as

```
fact ListGenerator {
    all l: List, e: Element |
        some l': List | l'.rest = l and l'.element = e
}
```

Unless *Element* is empty, this axiom makes the model effectively inconsistent—since the only possible instances would be infinite. Any assertion becomes valid, including patently false ones, such as

```
assert {all l: List | not l = l}
```

Discussion

In the set example, why did you declare Element*?*

The *Set* signature could have been declared with elements arbitrarily drawn from the universe of atoms

sig Set {elements: **set univ**}

but this would allow sets to contain sets, introducing an orthogonal complication. Another (better) option would have been to make the declaration polymorphic in the element signature:

module analysis/paramSets [t]
sig Set {elements: **set** t}

Why introduce a signature for sets?

The assertion that sets are closed under union can be written

assert {
all s0, s1: **set univ** | **some** s2: **set univ** | s2 = s0 + s1
}

avoiding the need to introduce signatures at all. But the example was intended to illustrate composite structures in general, of which sets are just a particularly simple example, and other structures (such as lists and sequences) are not built into Alloy the way sets and relations are. Incidentally, even with the assertion in this form, the analysis doesn't scale well, because the analyzer has to 'ground out' the inner quantifier, causing the same explosion as the generator axiom.

Are recursively defined lists common in Alloy models?

Not as common as you might expect, particularly if you've been influenced by functional programming languages such as Lisp, ML, and Haskell, in which the list is the primary data structure. In Alloy, lists include extraneous structure (the atoms representing the sublists), so their use often indicates a failure of abstraction, especially when the ordering of the elements is not relevant, and a simple set should have been used instead.

List-like structures are useful occasionally, however; a path name in a file system, for example, can be represented as a prefix and a directory or filename, with the prefix defined recursively like the tail of a list.

When an ordering is required, a simple relation suffices if duplicates are not permitted; otherwise, a sequence modeled as a signature with a field mapping indexes to elements

```
sig Seq {
    element: Index -> lone Element
    }
```

is better than a recursive list because it introduces less extraneous structure.

Universal quantifiers over such sequences can suffer from the same problems as lists. The Alloy library includes a sequence module with a predicate that forces the existence of all sequences up to a given length (namely, the scope of *Index*). This predicate must obviously be used with care to avoid scope explosion. There's no predicate for forcing all possible sequences to exist, because that would introduce a contradiction.

5.3.2 Omitting the Generator Axiom

You might wonder, given the depressing picture painted in the last section, why Alloy is ever useful! There are three reasons why the problem of generator axioms rarely arises in practice:

- The motivation for generator axioms in some other languages is to ensure that every expression denotes a value. Because relations are closed under all their operators by definition, no explicit generator axioms are needed, and every relational expression in Alloy has a value.

- Generator axioms are needed for mathematical objects, but most signatures denote objects in the problem domain. In a model of a file system, for example, you wouldn't expect a generator axiom over the signature representing directories, saying that a directory exists for every possible combination of contents.

- Even when a generator axiom is appropriate, it can often be omitted. So long as every universal quantifier is bounded, and only certain expression forms are used, the analyzer will give the same results whether or not the generator axiom is included. This is the *bounded-universal rule*.

"Bounded" means that the quantified variable's bounding expression doesn't mention the names of generated signatures (those signatures for which we would have liked to write a generator axiom). The allowed expression forms exclude relational transpose, and use dot joins only with a set on the left and a relation on the right. These restrictions ensure that universally quantified constraints can look only "inside" structures—into the sublists of a list, for example, or the subtrees of a tree—and thus can't tell whether or not the generator axiom has been applied.

Example. The analysis constraint in the problematic example from the previous subsection

```
sig Set {
  elements: set Element
  }
assert Closed {
  all s0, s1: Set | some s2: Set |
    s2.elements = s0.elements + s1.elements
  }
```

after negation becomes

```
some s0, s1: Set |
  all s2: Set |
    not s2.elements = s0.elements + s1.elements
```

which is not in bounded-universal form, because the quantification of *s2* isn't bounded. Checking this assertion therefore might (and actually does) result in spurious counterexamples that would not be present if a generator axiom for *Set* were added.

Example. In contrast, suppose we formulate an assertion in the same model saying that union of sets is commutative:

```
sig Set {
  elements: set Element
  }
assert UnionCommutative {
  all s0, s1, s2: Set |
    s0.elements + s1.elements = s2.elements
    implies s1.elements + s0.elements = s2.elements
  }
```

The analysis constraint is

```
some s0, s1, s2: Set |
  s0.elements + s1.elements = s2.elements
  and not s1.elements + s0.elements = s2.elements
```

which *is* in bounded-universal form, since it contains no universal quantifiers. Checking this assertion will not produce spurious counterexamples; it has its intended meaning even in the absence of the generator axiom.

Perhaps the most serious consequence of this issue is that assertions about preconditions, in which the precondition is asserted to be at least as weak as some property, cannot generally be checked.

The declarative style of description is very powerful, but it has a downside: inadvertent overconstraint. A specification of an operation that is intended to constrain only the values of the poststate may unintentionally constrain the prestate and arguments too, so that the operation is not "total" and cannot be applied in some contexts. To mitigate this risk, you might think you could assert that, for every prestate, there is at least one poststate that the operation's constraint admits. Unfortunately, assertions in this form are not in the bounded universal category, and thus may produce spurious counterexamples.

Example. Take the *add* operation of an address book

```
sig Name, Addr {}
sig Book {
  addr: Name -> Addr
  }
pred add (b, b': Book, n: Name, a: Addr) {
  b'.addr = b.addr + n -> a
  }
```

and consider checking the following assertion:

```
assert AddTotal {
  all b: Book, n: Name, a: Addr |
    some b': Book | add (b, b', n, a)
  }
check AddTotal
```

You might think this is valid, since every map can be extended with a new pair. In contrast, if instead the field *addr* were declared as

```
addr: Name -> lone Addr
```

so that at most one address can be associated with a name, you would no longer expect the operation to be total, because, if presented with a new address for an existing name, it would not be possible to extend the address book without violating the multiplicity constraint.

Indeed, in this second case, the assertion would be invalid. Surprisingly, it's invalid in the first case too, and the analyzer will generate a counterexample such as

```
b = {(B0)}
n = {(N0}
a = {(A0)}
addr = {(B0, N0, A1)}
```

in which there is no *Book* to bind to *b'* that will satisfy the operation constraint.

The problem is that, for the assertion to have its intended meaning, we need to ensure that all possible *Book* structures exist. Adding an axiom to this effect is not practical, because for a scope of 3 for *Name* and *Addr*, it would require a scope of 512 for *Book*! Omitting the axiom is not acceptable either, because the assertion, which reduces to

all b': Book | **not** b'.addr = b.addr + n -> a

is not a bounded-universal formula.

Discussion

Does the bounded-universal rule allow an infinite model to be analyzed by considering only finite cases?

Yes, that's exactly what it allows. It's not that surprising, however, since the properties that fall in the bounded-universal category only "look downward" into a finite part of an infinite instance.

Does that mean that a check in a finite scope applies automatically to the infinite case?

No. It means that, if there is a counterexample to an assertion, then there is a finite one in *some* scope. You can still miss a counterexample because the scope is too small. For the example just discussed, it means that checking the assertions in all finite scopes covers the case of an imaginary analysis in which the generator axiom is included and the scope is infinite. So, in short, it means that omitting the axiom and not considering the infinite scope case doesn't make it any more likely that counterexamples will be missed.

Can't a universal quantifier be converted into an existential one by adding negations?

No. The bounded-universal rule assumes that the formula is in a normal form in which all quantifiers are outermost, and are not negated. A research paper presents the rule in more detail and proves its soundness in a general setting of algebraic datatypes and first-order logic [44].

5.4 Scope Selection and Monotonicity

The scope sets a bound on the size of each of the top-level signatures, and, optionally, on subsignatures too (see section 4.6). An instance is *within a scope* if each signature constrained by the scope has no more elements than its associated bound permits.

To perform an analysis, the analyzer considers all candidate instances within the scope. Of course, the number of candidates is usually so large that an explicit enumeration would be infeasible. The analysis therefore uses pruning techniques to rule out whole sets of candidate cases at once. If it finds no instance, it is guaranteed that none exists within that scope, although there might be one in a larger scope.

5.4.1 Selecting a Scope

Selecting an appropriate scope can demand some careful thought. In most cases, it makes sense to start with the default scope, which was chosen to give a space small enough for analysis to terminate quickly, but large enough to include interesting instances.

If an instance is found, it may immediately serve its purpose: for an assertion, to expose a problem, or, for a predicate, to demonstrate consistency, and illustrate an expected (or unexpected) case. But it may appear to be more complicated than necessary, and before trying to assimilate it, you may want to repeat the analysis on a smaller scope, which will usually yield a smaller, and more intelligible, example.

If no instance is found, you may want to increase the scope in order to obtain greater confidence that there is indeed no instance—that the assertion being checked is valid or the predicate being run is inconsistent. The larger the scope, the more confidence is warranted, but the longer the analysis will take. At some point, the analysis becomes intolerably slow. If it's an analysis whose results are critical, you may want to set it aside and run it overnight, perhaps on a larger machine. Often, however, a terminating analysis can be achieved in a few minutes for a scope that gives adequate confidence.

What scope suffices to give adequate confidence? With experience, you'll develop a sense of the relationship between constraint complexity and appropriate scope, and, for a particular model, you'll discover how large the scope must be to include known important cases. In the meantime, here are some rough guidelines:

· Ensure that a signature's bound is enough to accommodate any constants you've declared belonging to it.

  Example. An analysis constraint involving a path in a graph

      some disj start, end: Node | ...

  requires *Node* to have at least two elements, to accommodate the skolem variables *start* and *end*.

· Whenever possible, when you want to constrain the size of a set, you should use signature multiplicity declarations, because the analyzer uses multiplicities to generate warnings when the scope setting and signature declarations are mutually inconsistent, or to override the default scope when called for.

  Example. If you write

      sig Color {}
      one sig Red, Green, Blue **extends** Color {}
      pred show () {}
      run show **for** 2

  you'll get a compilation error telling you that the scope of 2 for *Color* is too low, because the subsignature declarations require it to have at least three children. If you'd written instead

      abstract sig Color {}
      sig Red, Green, Blue **extends** Color {}
      fact {**one** Red **and one** Green **and one** Blue}
      pred show () {}
      run show **for** 2

  you'd get no error or warning message, and would need to execute the command to discover that the model is inconsistent.

· If all relevant values of a signature are explicitly named as variables, there's no point setting a scope for that signature that is larger than the number of variables.

Example. Running the *add* operation of our address book

```
sig Name, Address {}
sig Alias, Group extends Name {}
sig Book {addr: Name -> Address}
pred add (b, b': Book, n: Name, a: Address) {
    b'.addr = b.addr + n -> a
    }
run add for 3 but 2 Book
```

requires no more than two books. On the other hand, analyses of the *show* predicate for this graph model

```
sig Node {adj: Node}
fact {all n, n': Node | n' in n.*adj}
pred show () {some Node}
run show for 3
```

should not be limited to two nodes, because the variables n and n' are universally quantified over all nodes.

If an instance is expected to form a structure of a known shape, then properties of that shape can suggest constraints on the scope setting.

Example. A model of a railway might declare signatures for connection points and track segments:

```
sig Point {}
sig Segment {from, to: Point}
```

To include the case of a junction at a connection point, it seems likely that we'll need at least three segments, and therefore at least four points in total: one for the junction, and one for the other end of each segment.

5.4.2 Scope Monotonicity

A scope specifies an upper bound on the size of a signature, not its exact size. This gives the analysis a property called *scope monotonicity*, which says simply that if an analysis constraint has an instance in some scope, then it also has an instance in any larger scope.

Scope monotonicity is very important in practice, because it means that if an assertion appears to be valid in a scope (that is, has no counterexamples), you don't gain anything by repeating the analysis in smaller scopes.

The *exactly* keyword (explained in section 4.6) lets you specify that a signature has some exact number of elements, and its use therefore violates scope monotonicity. It should be used with great care. In simulation, it provides an easy way to force a more interesting instance to be generated, but in checking, its use is not recommended.

Discussion

How big a scope is feasible in practice?

On a modestly equipped machine (say, a 1 GHz PowerMac with 1 GB of memory), using the latest version of the Alloy Analyzer (2005), with a model containing up to about 20 signatures and 20 or 30 fields, an analysis in a scope of 5 to 10 is usually possible. During the incremental development of a model, analyses in a scope of 3 usually suffice, and terminate in less than a minute.

Isn't a signature a Cartesian product? Doesn't that explode the scope?

Many signatures (but not all) are introduced as a way of forming tuples. For example, the signature

sig Coord {x: X, y: Y}

might be used to represent coordinates in a two-dimensional space. If the signatures X and Y have sizes *scope(X)* and *scope(Y)* respectively, there will need to be at least *scope(X)* × *scope(Y)* values of *Coord* to represent all possible pairs.

You might think that this should determine the scope of *Coord*, and if indeed this were the case, almost no analysis would be feasible. The misunderstanding here is that the scope does not constrain the size of the set of *possible* values. Rather it constrains the size of the set of values that can appear in the instance. If an assertion being checked had a counterexample involving only one coordinate, it would be found in a scope of 1, irrespective of how many possible values the combination of fields of *Coord* can take. Similarly, if the analysis constraint involved the intersection of two straight lines, a scope of 5 may suffice for *Coord*, since it would include enough coordinates for the endpoints of the lines and their intersection.

This difference between the set of values a structure *may* take and the set that appears in an instance is the essence of the discussion of section 5.3.

Is a scope of zero possible?

Yes, a scope setting of zero is permitted, and is not necessarily nonsense. The command

    run P **for** 0

asks whether there is an instance of *P* in which the universe is empty. In practice, this is rare: every file system has at least a root, for example. But it is a good design principle to make as few assumptions as possible about sets being nonempty. For example, a client-server system should be able to handle the case in which there are no clients.

Often, this question, of whether or not sets can be empty, exposes fundamental issues in the design. Most text layout programs, for example, assume that the style sheet includes at least one style. It would be possible to design a layout program in which not all paragraphs have styles, and a style sheet could then be empty. This would make it easier to handle the case of deleting a style: the program could simply retain all the formatting of the paragraph but assign no style to it.

6: Examples

This chapter contains four examples, each chosen to illustrate a different kind of application:

- The first analyzes a well-known distributed algorithm for leader election; it shows how to model local actions and check global properties, using an idiom based on traces in which steps are modeled as predicates.

- The second is about recodable locks on hotel room doors. It's given in two forms: first, using the same trace idiom, and second, using a variant in which steps are modeled using explicit events. This example is more interesting methodologically than the first, because it's not purely algorithmic: it involves making assumptions about the behavior of other actors in the environment of the system (namely the guests who check in and out).

- The third has a very different flavor, and is more typical of the kind of modeling that software engineers do in practice. It explores the interaction between two simple features of a program for viewing media assets (such as photographs), and shows how design subtleties can be exposed by thinking about simple algebraic properties.

- The fourth and final example illustrates the application of Alloy to a textbook problem: justifying the correctness of a memory implementation using abstraction functions. It shows how Alloy can automate a familiar analysis.

6.1 Leader Election in a Ring

Many distributed protocols require one process to play the role of a leader, coordinating the others. Assigning the leader in advance is not feasible, so some mechanism is needed by which a collection of communicating processes running the same program can "elect" a leader on the fly.

We'll consider the case in which the processes form a ring. Since the communication topology is symmetric, we must look elsewhere for an asymmetry to exploit. We'll assume that processes have unique identifiers that are totally ordered; these might, for example, be the serial numbers (the so-called MAC ID's) of the network cards of the machines on which they are running. The leader will be the process with the largest identifier.

A simple and well-known protocol [8] has the processes pass their identifiers as Tokens around the ring in some direction (say clockwise). Each process examines each identifier it receives. If the identifier is less than its own identifier, it consumes the token. If the identifier is greater than its own, it passes the token on. If the identifier equals its own identifier, it knows the token must have passed all the way around the ring, so it elects itself leader.

When modeling a distributed algorithm, you want to make as few assumptions as possible about communications and scheduling. Obviously, the algorithm must work for all interleavings of process executions, since the processes run concurrently. Ideally, it should also work when messages are buffered between processes, reordered, or even dropped.

Rather than modeling explicit message buffers between the processes, we'll give each process a pool of tokens. In one step, a token can be taken from the pool of one process and moved to the pool of its successor in the ring. We'll make arbitrary the selection of the token (to model reordering), as well as the selection of which processes are involved in a given step (to model concurrency). Message delivery will be reliable, but it would be easy to modify the model to allow messages to be dropped.

6.1.1 Topology and State Components

The complete model is shown in figs. 6.1 and 6.2, with a model diagram in fig. 6.3. Let's examine it bit by bit. First, we name the module and import the library module for total ordering, applying it to a signature that will be used to represent time steps, and to a signature representing the processes in the ring:

> **module** examples/ringElection
> **open** util/ordering[Time] **as** TO
> **open** util/ordering[Process] **as** PO

A special notion of process identifier isn't needed; the atom representing the process will serve also as its identifier.

We declare a signature representing moments in time:

> **sig** Time {}

```
module examples/ringElection
open util/ordering[Time] as TO
open util/ordering[Process] as PO

sig Time {}
sig Process {
    succ: Process,
    toSend: Process -> Time,
    elected: set Time
    }
fact Ring {all p: Process | Process in p.^succ}

pred init (t: Time) {all p: Process | p.toSend.t = p}

pred step (t, t': Time, p: Process) {
    let from = p.toSend, to = p.succ.toSend |
        some id: from.t {
            from.t' = from.t - id
            to.t' = to.t + (id - PO/prevs(p.succ))
            }
        }
pred skip (t, t': Time, p: Process) {p.toSend.t = p.toSend.t'}

fact Traces {
    init (TO/first ())
    all t: Time - TO/last() | let t' = TO/next (t) |
            all p: Process |
                step (t, t', p) or step (t, t', succ.p) or skip (t, t', p)
    }

fact DefineElected {
    no elected.TO/first()
    all t: Time - TO/first()|
        elected.t =
            {p: Process | p in p.toSend.t - p.toSend.(TO/prev(t))}
    }

assert AtMostOneElected {lone elected.Time}
check AtMostOneElected for 3 Process, 7 Time
```

FIG. 6.1 Leader election in a ring, part 1.

```
pred progress () {
    all t: Time - TO/last() | let t' = TO/next (t) |
        some Process.toSend.t =>
            some p: Process | not skip (t, t', p)
    }
assert AtLeastOneElected {
    progress () => some Elected.Time
    }

pred looplessPath () {no disj t, t': Time | toSend.t = toSend.t'}
run looplessPath for 13 Time, 3 Process
```

FIG. 6.2 Leader election in a ring, part 2.

Each process has a successor process (its neighbor to one side in the ring), a pool of process identifiers to be sent along around the ring, and a set of times at which it regards itself elected as leader:

```
sig Process {
    succ: Process,
    toSend: Process -> Time,
    elected: set Time
    }
```

The *Time* signature doesn't appear in the declaration of the *succ* field, since the topology is static. Adding a *Time* column to a relation makes it dynamic. Without the *Time* column, the field *toSend* would just model a relation between processes, with *p.toSend* denoting a set of processes. With the addition of the *Time* column, *p.toSend* becomes a relation, and *p.toSend.t* is a set of processes associated with *p* at time *t*. Without the *Time* column, *elected* would be a set of processes; with it, *elected* becomes a relation, and *elected.t* is the set of processes that are elected leader at time *t* (and *p.elected* the set of times at which process *p* is elected).

The processes are to form a ring. The declaration of *succ* ensures that each process has exactly one successor, so all we need to add is the constraint that all processes are reachable from any process by following *succ* repeatedly:

```
fact Ring {all p: Process | Process in p.^succ}
```

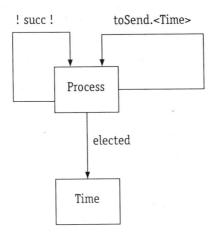

FIG. 6.3 Model diagram for leader election.

Discussion

Why import a library module for a concept as simple as an ordering?

It's always good to take standard notions and factor them out into libraries: it lowers the cognitive load of understanding a model when it uses standard vocabulary and concepts, and it reduces the risk of making mistakes—it's possible to get even a simple ordering wrong. In this case, there is also a performance advantage, since the symmetry breaking that is applied to *util/ordering* is hardwired into the implementation of the analyzer, and relies on a property of orderings that could not be inferred easily from the text of the library module.

Why does time appear explicitly in field declarations?

The alternative would be to include the notion of mutable fields in Alloy. This would complicated the language, and would tie the user to one particular idiom. When time instants appear in relations like any other atoms, the whole repertoire of relational operators can be applied. As we'll see, for example, the expression *elected.Time* represents the set of processes that are elected at any time. Declaration constraints can be used too, to express dynamic properties:

    elected in Process lone -> Time

says that at most one process is elected at any time, and

>   toSend: (Process **lone** -> Process) -> Time

says that, at any time, each process identifier resides in the sending pool of at most one process.

Why place the Time *signature at the end of a field declaration?*

At first, it might seem more natural to place the *Time* column at the beginning of a field's declaration expression, so that *toSend*, for example, would be declared as

>   **sig** Process {toSend: Time -> Process}

rather than as

>   **sig** Process {toSend: Process -> Time}

In most cases, the only difference would be in the position of the arguments of joins: the processes in the pool of process *p* at time *t* would be *p.toSend[t]* (or *t.(p.toSend)*) for the first, and *p.toSend.t* for the second. But note that in the first version, since *toSend* is a ternary relation with *Process* in the first column, the *Time* column appears in the *middle* rather than at the end. This becomes an inconvenience when you write expressions with the relational operators.

If the second declaration form is used, the expression *toSend.t* denotes a relation from *Process* to *Process* that maps *p* to *q* when *p* holds the identifier of *q* in its pool at time *t*. This makes it easy to write constraints such as

>   toSend.t = Process <: **iden**

which says that the relation is the identity on processes (and is in fact the initialization condition we'll see in subsection 6.1.2). Similarly, if the ring topology had been dynamic

>   **sig** Process {succ: Process -> Time}

the condition that it be acyclic could easily be extended from

>   **fact** Ring {**all** p: Process | Process **in** p.^succ}

as currently written, for the model in which *succ* has no *Time* column, to

>   **fact** Ring {**all** t: Time, p: Process | Process **in** p.^(succ.t)}

Had the form of declaration in which the *Time* column appears in the middle been used instead, these constraints could not have been written so conveniently.

In short, then, the issue is whether the *Time* column appears on the outside of the relation or in the middle. If it occurs in the middle, you can't write a simple join expression to denote the value of the relation at a given time *t*. Instead of *succ.t*, for example, you'd have to write something like

    {p, q: Process | p->t->q in succ}

Why not place the Time *signature first in a relation?*

A better question, therefore, is why the *Time* column was written *last* rather than *first*. Indeed, in this model, it would have made little difference had we written

    sig Process {succ: Process}
    sig Time {
       toSend: Process ->Process,
       elected: set Process
       }

in place of

    sig Time {
    sig Process {
       succ: Process,
       toSend: Process ->Time,
       elected: set Time
       }

In general, however, the difference is more significant. The first is reminiscent of object-oriented programming: it packages together all the static and dynamic aspects of a single object, and it allows objects to be classified using signature extension. The second is the idiom used in most traditional modeling languages (such as Z and VDM), in which there is a global state—and in fact the name *State* would be more appropriate than *Time* in this case. Its advantage is that it separates static and dynamic aspects more cleanly, and supports a style of modeling (common in Z) in which the state is grown incrementally. This second idiom is used in the media asset example of section 6.3.

6.1.2 Protocol Dynamics

The protocol itself is described in three stages. First, we record the initial condition—that each process is ready to send only its own identifier:

```
pred init (t: Time) {
    all p: Process | p.toSend.t = p
    }
```

Second, we describe the allowed state transitions. In a given step, an arbitrary identifier (*id*) is chosen from the pool associated with a process (*from*) and moved to the pool associated with its successor (*to*):

```
pred step (t, t': Time, p: Process) {
    let from = p.toSend, to = p.succ.toSend |
        some id: from.t {
            from.t' = from.t - id
            to.t' = to.t + (id - P0/prevs(p.succ))
            }
    }
```

The expression *id - P0/prevs(p.succ)* removes from the singleton set containing the identifier *id* the set of all identifiers that precede *p.succ*. This models the consumption of tokens: if the identifier in the token is greater than the identifier of the receiving process, it is placed in the pool for forwarding; otherwise, it's dropped. Don't get confused by the two distinct orderings here: the ordering of processes around the ring and the ordering of identifiers. The expression *p.succ* denotes the identifier successor of *p* in the ring; applying the function *P0/prevs* then gives the set of process identifiers that precede it in the space of identifiers.

Third, we describe the designation of elected processes. At the first moment in time, no processes are elected; at other times, the set of processes elected is the set of processes that just received their own identifiers:

```
fact DefineElected {
    no elected.T0/first()
    all t: Time - T0/first()|
        elected.t = {p: Process | p in p.toSend.t - p.toSend.(T0/prev(t))}
    }
```

We might have treated *elected* like the token pool, initializing it within *init* and updating it in *step*. Defining it this way, however, gives a cleaner separation of concerns, and avoids the need for frame conditions.

Discussion

Why isn't the notion of election sticky?

You might have noticed that the definition of election makes a process elected only at the time instant at which it receives its own identifier. At the next time instant, it will no longer be deemed elected. If you don't like this, you can change the model so that election is "sticky," and a process stays elected once elected.

It's not just a question of dropping the second term in the comprehension, by the way, so that the definition of election reads

elected.t = {p: Process | p **in** p.toSend.t}

rather than

elected.t = {p: Process | p **in** p.toSend.t - p.toSend.(TO/prev(t))}

If you're not sure why, try running the commands in the Alloy Analyzer and see what happens.

6.1.3 Introducing Traces

There are two properties we'd like to check: that at most one leader gets elected, and that some leader is eventually elected. We could use Alloy to automate a traditional inductive analysis. For the first property, we'd formulate an invariant, and use Alloy to check that the invariant implies the property, and is maintained at every step. For the second property, we'd find some integer metric, and use Alloy to check that it decreases in each step, and that reaching zero implies election.

Instead, we'll take an approach that requires less insight, and allows the properties to be checked directly. An instance of the model so far involves a set of states. By adding a single fact, we can form these states into an execution trace. We can then formulate assertions directly about traces. If an assertion is invalid, a counterexample will be a trace showing how it is violated.

Here is the trace constraint:

```
fact Traces {
    init (TO/first ())
    all t: Time - TO/last() | let t' = TO/next (t) |
        all p: Process |
            step (t, t', p) or step (t, t', succ.p) or skip (t, t', p)
}
```

It says that the initial condition holds for the first moment in time, and that for any subsequent time, each process *p* either takes a step, or its predecessor *succ.p* takes a step, or it does nothing. Doing nothing is modeled as an operation:

```
pred skip (t, t': Time, p: Process) {
    p.toSend.t = p.toSend.t'
    }
```

Discussion

Why does the trace constraint allow a predecessor to take a step?

The trace constraint gives three possibilities for a process *p*:

step (t, t', p) **or** step (t, t', succ.p) **or** skip (t, t', p)

When a process *p* takes a step from time *t* to time *t'*, the predicate *step (t, t', p)* holds. This means that an identifier moves from the pool of *p* to the pool of its successor process. The successor process therefore experiences a state change also. Its state change is described by the same *step* predicate, but applied to its predecessor. Without the second predicate invocation, it would not be possible to satisfy the constraint, because the successor process would either have to skip, or to be the source of a token transfer itself, neither of which is compatible with being a target of a token transfer. The *run* command would catch this error, and report an inconsistency.

Alternatively, I could have written a simpler trace constraint

some p: Process |
    step (t, t', p) **and all** p': Process - (p + p.succ) | skip (t, t', p)

saying that in each step a process makes a move, and there is no state change at any other process except for this process and its successor. The disadvantage of this formulation is that it only allows one process pair to take a move at once. The implicit concurrency of the original version, aside from being more general, also has the advantage that it allows more to happen in shorter traces, so that analyses in a smaller scope are more meaningful.

Why must an operation take two time arguments?

Given that the *step* and *skip* operations are always applied to a time instant and its successor, you may wonder why they don't declare a single argument *t*, and then define *t'* as *T0/next(t)* inside the body of the predicate. The motivation here is separation of concerns: it seems better to commit the model to the traces idiom in only one small place rather than in every operation, so that a change to a different idiom would be easy.

6.1.4 Dynamic Analysis

It's good to start with a simple simulation, to check that the model isn't overconstrained. For example, we might ask to see an execution in which some process gets elected:

```
pred show () {
  some elected
  }
run show for 3 Process, 4 Time
```

We've picked a scope of three processes—the smallest interesting ring— and four times, because the leader's token will have to go all the way around, so there must be at least one more time instant than processes. A sample trace generated by the analyzer is shown in fig. 6.4: the identifier of process *P2* goes all the way round, before any other identifiers have been sent.

Having established that the model is at least consistent, we might move on to checking some properties. The purpose of the protocol is to reach a state in which exactly one leader is elected. When possible, it's best to split a property into subproperties and check them individually. This makes it easier to diagnose what went wrong if a property doesn't hold. So we'll consider two properties separately: that there be *at most* and *at least* one elected process.

Here is an assertion claiming that there is at most one elected process:

```
assert AtMostOneElected {
  lone elected.Time
  }
check AtMostOneElected for 3 Process but 7 Time
```

The expression *elected.Time* denotes the set of processes elected at any time, so the assertion says not only that there is at most one process elected at any time, which could have been written

```
all t: Time | lone elected.t
```

but, more strongly, that the election doesn't change from one process to another. The scope in this assertion limits the analysis to a ring of 3

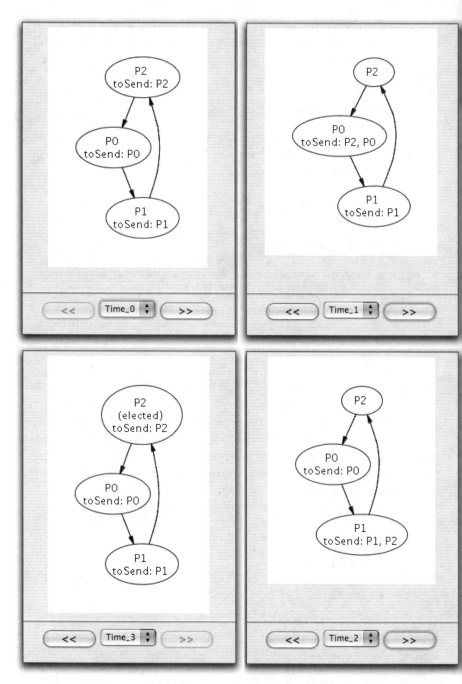

FIG. 6.4 A sample trace for ring election: the initial state is
in the panel at the top left; execution proceeds through the
panels clockwise.

processes and 7 time instants. The *AtMostOneElected* assertion is valid, and no counterexamples are found.

Here is the assertion claiming that there is at least one elected process:

```
assert AtLeastOneElected {
    some t: Time | some elected.t
    }
check AtLeastOneElected for 3 but 7 Time
```

This second assertion is invalid; it has a counterexample in which nothing happens at all. The problem is including the *skip* operation, which allows every process to skip in every step!

To fix this problem, we can force progress by insisting that whenever some process has a nonempty identifier pool, some process (not necessarily the same one) must make a move. We write this as a predicate

```
pred progress () {
    all t: Time - TO/last() |
        let t' = TO/next (t) |
            some Process.toSend.t =>
                some p: Process | not skip (t, t', p)
    }
```

and then condition the assertion on this predicate holding:

```
assert AtLeastOneElected {
    progress () => some Elected.Time
    }
check AtLeastOneElected for 3 Process, 7 Time
```

The scope of 7 time instants is actually the smallest that is guaranteed to produce a leader. To find this scope, I simply started with a smaller scope and increased it until no counterexample was generated for the assertion.

Discussion

Are the processes always placed in the ring in the order of their process identifiers?

No. They appear in that order in fig. 6.4 because of the Alloy Analyzer's symmetry-breaking optimization (see the discussion following section 5.2.1). Since atoms are interchangeable, you can take any instance (or counterexample) of a command and create another one by permuting the atoms. A mathematician would say "there is no loss of generality" in ordering the processes around the ring *P0, P1, P2*, etc., because the description of the scheme never refers to particular atoms.

The analyzer exploits this to reduce the search, by imposing a constraint on *succ*. The same trick is used in the ordering relation of the module *util/ordering*: this is why time instants in traces always come out in order. If the model explicitly compared the two relations, it would no longer be valid to break symmetry in both cases, so the analyzer will back off, and no longer include the symmetry-breaking constraint on *succ*. To see this, add

```
fact DifferentOrder {
    all p: Process | p.succ != P0/next(p)
}
```

and the simulation will show a ring in which the identifiers appear out of order.

How can AtLeastOneElected *be valid? Doesn't the scope allow shorter traces?*

The symmetry breaking associated with the ordering module (mentioned in the discussion following subsection 6.1.1) actually forces the ordered set to contain the maximum number of atoms the scope permits. So our two commands have the same effect they would have if written with an exact scope:

```
check AtMostOneElected for exactly 3 Process, exactly 7 Time
check AtLeastOneElected for exactly 3 Process, exactly 7 Time
```

Is this a violation of scope monotonicity? If so, does it matter?

Yes, it is a violation, and yes, it matters (at least in some respects). For checking *AtLeastOneElected*, the exact scope is necessary for the signature *Time*; this kind of eventuality property is never scope monotonic. For checking *AtMostOneElected*, on the other hand, the exact scope is not desirable, because it's conceivable that there are bad traces (in which two processes get elected) that cannot be extended to the full length required by the scope. Unfortunately, it's not possible to check that this doesn't happen (see section 5.3).

Another undesirable consequence of the exact scope, this time for both commands, is that it forces an exact number of processes in the ring. It would be easy, however, to adjust the model so that analysis in a scope of k considers all rings with up to k processes, by introducing a subsignature like this:

```
sig Process {}
sig RingProcess extends Process {
    succ: RingProcess,
    toSend: RingProcess -> Time,
    elected: set Time
    }
fact Ring {all p: RingProcess | RingProcess in p.^succ}
```

thereby imposing the multiplicity constraint of *succ* and the fact *ring* only on the subset of processes that appear in the ring.

6.1.5 Computing Machine Diameter

Exhaustive analysis within a scope is justified by the small scope hypothesis, and usually seems like a reasonable way to catch most bugs. For example, if this protocol has no counterexamples for rings of size five, it seems unlikely to be harboring a bug. But the bounding of traces seems less compelling.

For the *AtLeastOneElected* assertion, we're looking for witnesses to election, so increasing the trace length won't result in new counterexamples. For the *AtMostOneElected* assertion, however, we may reasonably worry that we're missing a bug that is manifested only in a longer trace than the ones the analysis considered.

One question we might ask about the sufficiency of the scope is whether we consider traces long enough to cover all reachable states. If so, we can rest assured that no bugs are missed because of inadequate trace length when analyzing an assertion such as *AtMostOneElected*, since the assertion is a claim about states, and every reachable state will be considered.

The *diameter* of a state machine is the maximum distance of a state from an initial state, where the distance between two states is the smallest number of execution steps that can take you from one to the other. In general, calculating the diameter of a modeled state machine is not possible using Alloy. But often we can find an upper bound.

Here's how it works. We write a predicate whose instances are *loopless paths*—traces in which a given state is visited at most once. The behavior of our protocol depends only on the identifier pools, so we'll regard two time instants in a trace as having equivalent states when their pools are equal:

```
pred looplessPath () {
    no disj t, t': Time | toSend.t = toSend.t'
}
```

Now we simply ask for an instance of this predicate for increasing trace lengths. Running the command

run looplessPath **for** 3 Process, 12 Time

produces a solution, but

run looplessPath **for** 3 Process, 13 Time

does not. So there is no trace involving 13 time instants that has no loop in it. We can therefore conclude that a scope of 12 for *Time* is sufficient to reach all states of the protocol for a three-node ring. In other words, for a scope of 3 for *Process*, there is nothing to be gained by increasing the scope for *Time* further: with respect to *Time*, the analysis is complete.

Discussion

How does the expressiveness of Alloy's trace assertions compare to temporal logics?

Since the instances of the model are traces, the assertions are comparable to linear temporal logic (LTL) rather than computation tree logic (CTL), which would require instances that are tree structures. For software

Any LTL property can easily be expressed in first-order logic, as demonstrated by the reduction of LTL to satisfiability known as "bounded model checking" [5]. First-order logic is more expressive than temporal logics, although the additional power—at least for the temporal aspects doesn't seem necessary.

The filtering of traces to those satisfying the progress property is a classic example of a class of properties known as "fairness properties" that are not expressible in CTL. In general, LTL seems better suited to describing temporal properties of software than CTL.

How does Alloy compare to model checkers for this kind of analysis?

Model checkers are generally capable of exhausting an entire state space. In an Alloy trace analysis, only traces of bounded length are considered, and the bound is generally small. An upper bound on the diameter can sometimes be obtained, as explained, for small systems. The Alloy approach is therefore less capable of establishing the absence of bugs, but when there is a bug, it may be more rapidly found by Alloy's SAT-based analysis than by model checking, because of the depth-first nature of SAT solving.

The machine description language of most model checkers is very low-level, so describing a protocol such as this tends to be much more challenging. Unlike Alloy, model checkers depend on the topology of processes being fixed, and cannot perform analyses for arbitrary topologies.

Also, although Zohar Manna and Amir Pnueli's pioneering formulation of linear temporal logic [50] included a non-temporal quantifier, it seems to have been omitted from many model checkers. This means that you cannot express relationships between the values of state components at different points in time—for example, that an operation increments a counter, or leaves some state component unchanged.

6.2   Hotel Room Locking

Most hotels now issue disposable room keys; when you check out, you can take your key with you. How, then, can the hotel prevent you from reentering your room after it has been assigned to someone else? The trick is *recodable locks*, which have been in use in hotels since the 1980's, initially in mechanical form, but now almost always electronic.

The idea is that the hotel issues a new key to the next occupant, which recodes the lock, so that previous keys will no longer work. The lock is a simple, stand-alone unit (usually battery-powered), with a memory holding the current key combination. A hardware device, such as a feedback shift register, generates a sequence of pseudorandom numbers. The lock is opened either by the current key combination, or by its successor; if a key with the successor is inserted, the successor is made to be the current combination, so that the old combination will no longer be accepted.

This scheme requires no communication between the front desk and the door locks. By synchronizing the front desk and the door locks initially, and by using the same pseudorandom generator, the front desk can keep its records of the current combinations in step with the doors themselves.

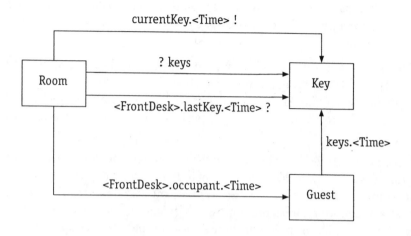

FIG. 6.5 Model diagram for the hotel locking system.

6.2.1 State Components and Key Ordering

Let's model and analyze this scheme. We'll use the same idiom as in the leader election example, adding a time atom in the last column of a relation to make it time-dependent, and ordering time atoms into traces. To represent the key generators, we'll posit a single global ordering on keys, with the room locks holding disjoint subsets of the keys. Here's the module header:

```
module examples/hotel
open util/ordering[Time] as TO
open util/ordering[Key] as KO
```

We declare signatures for the keys and the time instants:

```
sig Key {}
sig Time {}
```

The signature *Key* refers to the key combinations; we'll use the term *card* to refer to the physical key that a guest inserts into a lock.

Each room has a set of keys, and a current key at a given time:

```
sig Room {
    keys: set Key,
    currentKey: keys one -> Time
    }
```

No key belongs to more than one room lock:

```
fact DisjointKeySets {
    Room <: keys : Room lone -> Key
    }
```

The front desk is modeled as a singleton signature. Its purpose is simply to group together two relations: *lastKey*, mapping a room to the last key combination that was issued for that room, and *occupant*, mapping a room to the guests that have been assigned to it:

```
one sig FrontDesk {
    lastKey: (Room -> lone Key) -> Time,
    occupant: (Room -> Guest) -> Time
    }
```

The multiplicity constraint of *lone* in *lastKey* is to accommodate the state prior to initialization in which rooms do not yet have keys associated with them. This looseness is not in fact necessary, since the initialization will be imposed on the very first state, but it's always wise to err on the side of underconstraint.

A guest holds a set of keys at a given time:

```
sig Guest {
    keys: Key -> Time
    }
```

A model diagram for the declarations we've written is shown in fig.6.5.

The fundamental operation of the recodable locks is the generation of the successor key. We can model this as a simple function that, given a key k and a set of keys ks, finds the smallest key (under the global ordering) that follows k and belongs to ks:

```
fun nextKey (k: Key, ks: set Key): set Key {
    K0/min (K0/nexts (k) & ks)
    }
```

Discussion

How does the constraint in DisjointKeySets *have its claimed meaning?*

The constraint

```
Room <: keys : Room lone -> Key
```

is a "declaration constraint" (see subsection 3.6.4) saying that the *keys* field mapping rooms to their keys is injective. The expression on the left denotes the *keys* relation of the *Room* signature (see subsection 4.4.4); without the restriction to *Room*, it can be confused with the field in *Guest* of the same name. The multiplicity keyword *lone* in the declaration expression on the right says that at most one room is mapped to each key.

6.2.2 Hotel Operations

The dynamic behavior is described by operations for each of the interactions between the guests and hotel staff and the system.

In the initial state, no guests hold keys, the roster at the front desk shows no rooms as occupied, and the record of each room's key at the front desk is synchronized with the current combination of the lock itself:

```
pred init (t: Time) {
    no Guest.keys.t
    no FrontDesk.occupant.t
    all r: Room | FrontDesk.lastKey.t [r] = r.currentKey.t
    }
```

This initialization is nontrivial to implement. It is the only operation that requires communication between the locks and the front desk. In practice, it could be done by using a special card to reset each lock.

The successful entry of a guest into a room is described by this operation:

```
1  pred entry (t, t': Time, g: Guest, r: Room, k: Key) {
2      k in g.keys.t
3      let ck = r.currentKey |
4         (k = ck.t and ck.t' = ck.t) or
5         (k = nextKey(ck.t, r.keys) and ck.t' = k)
6      noRoomChangeExcept (t, t', r)
7      noGuestChangeExcept (t, t', none)
8      noFrontDeskChange (t, t')
9      }
```

The operation consists of a precondition (that the key used to open the lock be one of the keys the guest is holding, line 2), a postcondition (that the key on the card either matches the lock's current key, and the lock is unchanged, or matches its successor, in which case the lock is advanced, lines 4 and 5), and some frame conditions (that there are no changes to the state of another room, or to the set of keys held by guests, or to the records at the front desk, lines 6 to 8).

Here are the frame conditions:

```
pred noFrontDeskChange (t, t': Time) {
    FrontDesk.lastKey.t = FrontDesk.lastKey.t'
    FrontDesk.occupant.t = FrontDesk.occupant.t'
    }

pred noRoomChangeExcept (t, t': Time, rs: set Room) {
    all r: Room - rs | r.currentKey.t = r.currentKey.t'
    }

pred noGuestChangeExcept (t, t': Time, gs: set Guest) {
    all g: Guest - gs | g.keys.t = g.keys.t'
    }
```

Finally, there are operations for checking in and checking out. Checking out is simpler; it just requires that the room be occupied by that guest, and then records it as empty:

```
pred checkout (t, t': Time, g: Guest) {
    let occ = FrontDesk.occupant {
        some occ.t.g
        occ.t' = occ.t - Room -> g
        }
    FrontDesk.lastKey.t = FrontDesk.lastKey.t'
    noRoomChangeExcept (t, t', none)
    noGuestChangeExcept (t, t', none)
    }
```

Checking in is more interesting:

```
1   pred checkin (t, t': Time, g: Guest, r: Room, k: Key) {
2       g.keys.t' = g.keys.t + k
3       let occ = FrontDesk.occupant {
4           no occ.t [r]
5           occ.t' = occ.t + r -> g
6           }
7       let lk = FrontDesk.lastKey {
8           lk.t' = lk.t ++ r -> k
9           k = nextKey (lk.t [r], r.keys)
10          }
11      noRoomChangeExcept (t, t', none)
12      noGuestChangeExcept (t, t', g)
13      }
```

It requires that the room have no current occupant (4), and its effect is to deliver the key to the guest (2), record the guest as the new occupant of the room (5), and to update the front desk record of the room's last key (8). The new key is the successor of the last key in the sequence associated with the room's lock (9).

Finally, as in the leader election example, we add a fact ensuring that instances of the model will be traces, namely that the initialization holds in the first time instant, and that any pair of consecutive time instants are related by an entry, a checkin or a checkout:

```
fact Traces {
    init (TO/first ())
    all t: Time - TO/last() | let t' = TO/next (t) |
        some g: Guest, r: Room, k: Key |
            entry (t, t', g, r, k)
            or checkin (t, t', g, r, k)
            or checkout (t, t', g)
}
```

Discussion

Where is the case handled in which a guest is denied access to a room?

Nowhere. It's ruled out by the precondition of the *entry* operation. Since our goal is to check for unauthorized access, there's no need to model it. If we were interested, for example, in how locks audit successful and failed attempts at access, we would want to include it.

Why is the precondition in checkin *distributed throughout the operation?*

An operation's constraints can be separated into pre- and postconditions, or they can be organized around state components. I chose the latter approach here, because it avoids repeating the *let* statements or extending their scope.

6.2.3 Analysis

We'd like to check that no unauthorized entries can occur. Here is an attempt at an assertion to this effect:

```
assert NoBadEntry {
    all t: Time, r: Room, g: Guest, k: Key | let t' = TO/next(t) |
        let o = FrontDesk.occupant.t [r] |
            entry (t, t', g, r, k) and some o => g in o
}
```

It says that if guest g enters room r at time t, and the front desk records r as occupied, then g is a recorded occupant of r.

To check the assertion, we issue a command such as

check NoBadEntry **for** 3 **but** 2 Room, 2 Guest, 5 Time

Initially, it's good to start with a small scope, to get feedback as rapidly as possible. In this command, the default scope is set to 3, which in this command bounds only *Key*, the bounds on the other types being given as exceptions. Since it seemed likely that a problem would be exposed with only two guests and their rooms, the scope assigns only 2 to *Guest* and *Room*. A bound of 5 was chosen for *Time*, because at least 4 time instants are needed to execute each operation just once.

This analysis generates a counterexample, shown in fig. 6.6, correspond to the following scenario:

· Initially, the current key of *Room0* is *K0*, which is also reflected in the front desk's record.

· *Guest0* checks in to *Room0* and receives key *K1*, and the occupancy roster at the front desk is updated accordingly.

· *Guest0* checks out, and the occupancy roster is cleared.

· *Guest1* checks in to *Room0* and receives key *K2*; the occupancy roster at the front desk is updated accordingly; and *K2* is recorded as the last key assigned to *Room0*.

· *Guest0* presents *K1* to the lock of *Room0*, and is admitted.

The problem is that the lock isn't recoded until the new guest inserts the card with the new key. So a previous occupant can enter the room not only after checking out but even after a new guest has checked in.

Denial of unauthorized entry can only be guaranteed, therefore, on the assumption that there is no intervening event between a guest checking in and entering the room. This assumption can be added as a fact:

```
fact NoIntervening {
    all t: Time - TO/last() | let t' = TO/next (t), t" = TO/next(t') |
        all g: Guest, r: Room, k: Key |
            checkin (t, t', g, r, k) => (entry (t', t", g, r, k) or no t")
}
```

It says that if a checkin occurs at any time t except for the last time in a trace, then either it is followed immediately by an entry, or there is

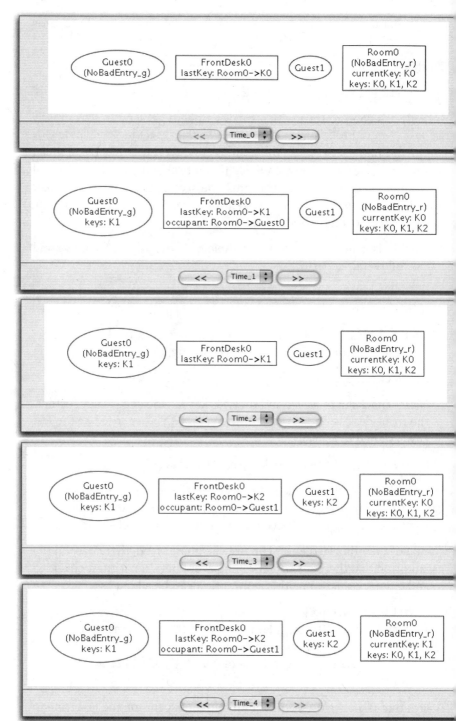

FIG. 6.6 A sample trace showing unauthorized entry.

no subsequent time step (because the checkin is the last event in the trace).

With this fact included, there is now no counterexample. To gain greater confidence, we increase the scope first to 7 time instants and 3 rooms and guests:

> **check** NoBadEntry **for** 3 **but** 3 Room, 3 Guest, 7 Time

which terminates without a counterexample in about 2 seconds (on a 2.5GHz PowerBook G5), and then to 9 time instants and 5 keys:

> **check** NoBadEntry **for** 5 **but** 3 Room, 3 Guest, 9 Time

which terminates without a counterexample in just under a minute.

The full model is shown in figs. 6.7–6.9.

Discussion

Does your fix require that the new occupant be dragged to the room immediately after checkin?

No. The added fact merely records an assumption about the world. If the assumption is false, the security guarantee is undermined.

Why does the BadEntry *assertion have the extra hypothesis that the room be occupied?*

The purpose of the locking scheme is to protect occupants from each other, not to protect the hotel from its occupants. If you remove that hypothesis, the analyzer will generate a counterexample in which a guest checks out, and then immediately reenters the room.

Isn't the essence of the problem that an occupant doesn't really take ownership of a room until entering it for the first time?

Absolutely. This idea could be expressed more elegantly perhaps in the following way. Rather than using the front desk's occupancy roster, the notion of occupancy would be *defined* in terms of that first entry, in the same way that election is defined in the leader election protocol. There would then be no need for the additional assumption.

Isn't this problem rather messy?

Yes. It's representative of most problems involving requirements that are situated in the real world, and can't be handled effectively by the

```
module examples/hotel
open util/ordering[Time] as TO
open util/ordering[Key] as KO

sig Key, Time {}

sig Room {
   keys: set Key,
   currentKey: keys one -> Time
   }
fact DisjointKeySets {
   Room <: keys : Room lone -> Key
   }

one sig FrontDesk {
   lastKey: (Room -> lone Key) -> Time,
   occupant: (Room -> Guest) -> Time
   }

sig Guest {
   keys: Key -> Time
   }

fun nextKey (k: Key, ks: set Key): set Key {
   KO/min (KO/nexts (k) & ks)
   }

pred init (t: Time) {
   no Guest.keys.t
   no FrontDesk.occupant.t
   all r: Room | FrontDesk.lastKey.t [r] = r.currentKey.t
   }

pred entry (t, t': Time, g: Guest, r: Room, k: Key) {
   k in g.keys.t
   let ck = r.currentKey |
      (k = ck.t and ck.t' = ck.t) or
      (k = nextKey(ck.t, r.keys) and ck.t' = k)
   noRoomChangeExcept (t, t', r)
   noGuestChangeExcept (t, t', none)
   noFrontDeskChange (t, t')
   }
```

FIG. 6.7 Hotel locking model, part 1.

```
pred checkout (t, t': Time, g: Guest) {
  let occ = FrontDesk.occupant {
    some occ.t.g
    occ.t' = occ.t - Room->g
    }
  FrontDesk.lastKey.t = FrontDesk.lastKey.t'
  noRoomChangeExcept (t, t', none)
  noGuestChangeExcept (t, t', none)
  }

pred checkin (t, t': Time, g: Guest, r: Room, k: Key) {
  g.keys.t' = g.keys.t + k
  let occ = FrontDesk.occupant {
    no occ.t [r]
    occ.t' = occ.t + r->g
    }
  let lk = FrontDesk.lastKey {
    lk.t' = lk.t ++ r->k
    k = nextKey (lk.t [r], r.keys)
    }
  noRoomChangeExcept (t, t', none)
  noGuestChangeExcept (t, t', g)
  }

pred noFrontDeskChange (t, t': Time) {
  FrontDesk.lastKey.t = FrontDesk.lastKey.t'
  FrontDesk.occupant.t = FrontDesk.occupant.t'
  }

pred noRoomChangeExcept (t, t': Time, rs: set Room) {
  all r: Room - rs | r.currentKey.t = r.currentKey.t'
  }

pred noGuestChangeExcept (t, t': Time, gs: set Guest) {
  all g: Guest - gs | g.keys.t = g.keys.t'
  }
```

FIG. 6.8 Hotel locking model, part 2.

```
fact Traces {
    init (TO/first ())
    all t: Time - TO/last() | let t' = TO/next (t) |
        some g: Guest, r: Room, k: Key |
            entry (t, t', g, r, k)
            or checkin (t, t', g, r, k)
            or checkout (t, t', g)
}

assert NoBadEntry {
    all t: Time, r: Room, g: Guest, k: Key | let t' = TO/next(t) |
        let o = FrontDesk.occupant.t [r] |
            entry (t, t', g, r, k) and some o => g in o
}

fact NoIntervening {
    all t: Time - TO/last() | let t' = TO/next (t), t" = TO/next(t') |
        all g: Guest, r: Room, k: Key |
            checkin (t, t', g, r, k) => (entry (t', t", g, r, k) or no t")
}

check NoBadEntry for 5 but 3 Room, 3 Guest, 9 Time
```

FIG. 6.9 Hotel locking model, part 3.

traditional treatment of requirements as just like specifications, but at a "higher level." Michael Jackson has developed a systematic theory of requirements called "problem frames" that explains how to structure and reason about software development problems that involve interaction between a system and its environment. His theory also explains the distinction between simply observable events (such as entering the room) and events that are better characterized by definition (such as acquiring occupancy). The ideas that are most relevant to this example can be found in several of the short pieces in his essay collection [38] (in particular "Definitions," "Designations," "Domains," "Machines," and "Requirements"), and are elaborated more fully in his book on problem frames [39].

What does this analysis say about hotel rooms in practice?

When you enter the room for the first time, you should use your own key. If a bellhop lets you in with a master key, the lock will not be recoded, and any valuables you leave in the room will be vulnerable until the next time you reenter the room.

6.2.4 An Event-Based Variation

We've seen how Alloy doesn't have a fixed idiom for modeling state machines, so you're free to use whatever idiom works best for the model at hand. To illustrate this freedom, figs. 6.10–6.12 show a variation of the hotel locking model of figs. 6.7–6.9. The state space and the transitions are exactly the same, but this model uses events rather than operations.

Instead of writing a predicate for each operation, a signature is declared whose atoms represent a set of events. For example, the *Checkin* signature represents the set of all events in which a guest checks in. The constraints that were in the predicate now appear instead as signature facts.

Arguments to operation predicates now become fields of the event signatures. The signature hierarchy can be used to factor out common arguments; thus *RoomKeyEvent* is the set of events that involve a room and a key, in addition to pre- and poststates and a guest.

The *Traces* fact takes a rather different form in this model:

```
1  fact Traces {
2      init (TO/first ())
3      all t: Time - TO/last() | let t' = TO/next (t) |
4          some e: Event {
5              e.pre = t and e.post = t'
6              currentKey.t != currentKey.t' => e in Entry
7              occupant.t != occupant.t' => e in Checkin + Checkout
8              (lastKey.t != lastKey.t' or keys.t != keys.t')
9                  => e in Checkin
10          }
11  }
```

As before, the first constraint (line 2) says that the initial condition holds at the first time instant. The quantified constraint says that, for any pair of consecutive time instants, there is an event from one to the other (5), and that, if certain state changes occur, an event in a particular set must happen. For example, if the *occupant* relation changes, then either a *Checkin* or a *Checkout* event must have occurred (7).

```
module examples/hotelEvents
open util/ordering[Time] as TO
open util/ordering[Key] as KO

sig Key, Time {}

sig Room {
   keys: set Key,
   currentKey: keys one -> Time
   }
fact DisjointKeySets {
   Room <: keys : Room lone -> Key
   }

one sig FrontDesk {
   lastKey: (Room -> lone Key) -> Time,
   occupant: (Room -> Guest) -> Time
   }

sig Guest {
   keys: Key -> Time
   }

fun nextKey (k: Key, ks: set Key): set Key {
   KO/min (KO/nexts (k) & ks)
   }

pred init (t: Time) {
   no Guest.keys.t
   no FrontDesk.occupant.t
   all r: Room | FrontDesk.lastKey.t [r] = r.currentKey.t
   }

abstract sig Event {
   pre, post: Time,
   guest: Guest
   }

abstract sig RoomKeyEvent extends Event {
   room: Room,
   key: Key
   }
```

FIG. 6.10 An event-based variation of the hotel locking model, part 1.

```
sig Entry extends RoomKeyEvent {} {
    key in guest.keys.pre
    let ck = room.currentKey |
        (key = ck.pre and ck.post = ck.pre) or
        (key = nextKey(ck.pre, room.keys) and ck.post = key)
    }

sig Checkin extends RoomKeyEvent {} {
    keys.post = keys.pre + guest -> key
    let occ = FrontDesk.occupant {
        no occ.pre [room]
        occ.post = occ.pre + room -> guest
        }
    let lk = FrontDesk.lastKey {
        lk.post = lk.pre ++ room -> key
        key = nextKey (lk.pre [room], room.keys)
        }
    }

sig Checkout extends Event {} {
    let occ = FrontDesk.occupant {
        some occ.pre.guest
        occ.post = occ.pre - Room -> guest
        }
    }

fact Traces {
    init (TO/first ())
    all t: Time - TO/last() | let t' = TO/next (t) |
        some e: Event {
            e.pre = t and e.post = t'
            currentKey.t != currentKey.t' => e in Entry
            occupant.t != occupant.t' => e in Checkin + Checkout
            (lastKey.t != lastKey.t' or keys.t != keys.t')
                => e in Checkin
            }
        }
    }
```

FIG. 6.11 An event-based variation of the hotel locking model, part 2.

```
assert NoBadEntry {
    all e: Entry | let o = FrontDesk.occupant.(e.pre) [e.room] |
        some o => e.guest in o
    }
check NoBadEntry for 5 but 3 Room, 3 Guest, 9 Time, 8 Event

fact NoIntervening {
    all c: Checkin |
        c.post = TO/last ()
        or some e: Entry {
            e.pre = c.post
            e.room = c.room
            e.guest = c.guest
            }
    }
```

FIG. 6.12 An event-based variation of the hotel locking model, part 3.

The *NoIntervening* fact becomes easier to express in this style:

```
1   fact NoIntervening {
2       all c: Checkin |
3           c.post = TO/last ()
4           or some e: Entry {
5               e.pre = c.post
6               e.room = c.room
7               e.guest = c.guest
8               }
9       }
```

It says that every *Checkin* event is either the last event to occur (3), or is followed immediately by some *Entry* event with the same room and guest (4).

One major advantage of this idiom is that, because events are atoms, it's easier to tell which events are occurring in traces output by the analyzer. Fig. 6.13 shows a counterexample corresponding to that of fig. 6.6, which is produced when the *NoIntervening* fact is omitted. I've chosen a visualizer setting that shows events in their prestates, so the event in each snapshot is the one that is about to occur.

Discussion

What are the attractions of this style of modeling?

Making events concrete produces nicer visualizations, and allows some properties to be written more succinctly and directly. Another advantage is that signature extension can be used to factor out common properties of events. Here, we used this only to share the declarations of event arguments, but it could be used in other ways—for example, to declare more traditional frame conditions and share them between event classes. This kind of sharing is easier to express between signatures than between predicates, because predicates are explicitly parameterized, but signature extension (like inheritance in an object-oriented language, and like schema inclusion in Z) works with free variables.

Could you have written the frame conditions more traditionally?

Yes, the frame conditions from the previous version could have been incorporated verbatim. I used the more unusual style of frame condition to emphasize the flexibility that an idiomless language like Alloy gives you.

Who invented this style of frame condition?

The basic idea is due to Ray Reiter [57], and was elaborated in the context of software modeling in collaboration with Alex Borgida and John Mylopoulos [7].

When is this style of frame condition suitable?

It works well exactly when conventional frame conditions are most cumbersome. Suppose we have m state components, and k operations, each of which modifies just one state component. Then in the conventional style, each operation would require a frame condition for each of the $m - 1$ state components that remains unchanged, so there would be $k \times (m - 1)$ equalities in total. Reiter's scheme, on the other hand, requires just one implication for each operation, m in total, saying that if a particular state component changed, then its associated operation must have occurred.

In contrast, if every operation modifies every state component but one, traditional frame conditions will require only one equality per operation, giving a total of k, whereas Reiter's scheme would require m implications each listing $k - 1$ operation names in the consequent.

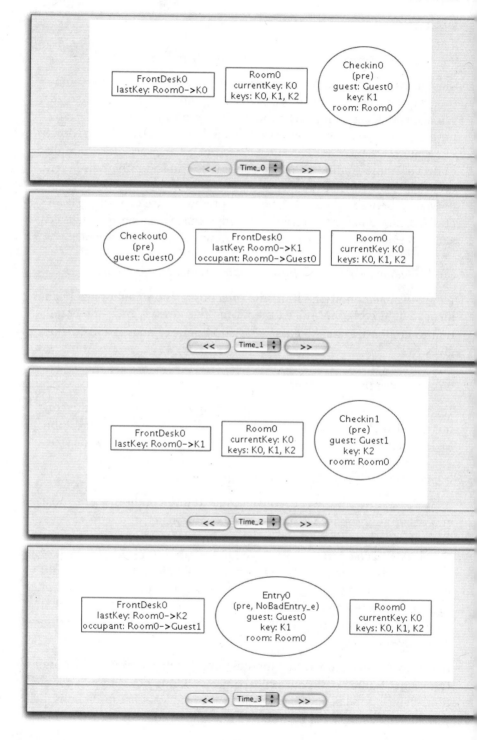

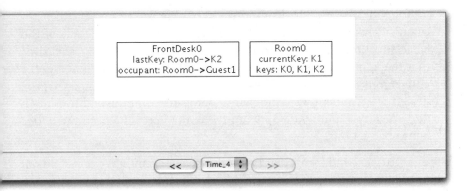

FrontDesk0
lastKey: Room0->K2
occupant: Room0->Guest1

Room0
currentKey: K1
keys: K0, K1, K2

<< | Time_4 | >>

FIG. 6.13 (Left and above) A sample trace showing unauthorized entry for the event-based variation.

With respect to this simple comparison, Reiter's scheme is equivalent to the use of "modifies" clauses that indicate, for each operation, which state components may change. The advantage of Reiter's scheme, however, is that it requires no extra-logical notions, and can accommodate more complex forms, such as frame conditions that are dependent on the state in which an operation is invoked.

6.3 Media Asset Management

For organizing a large collection of media files, such as photos, movies, or soundtracks, the built-in facilities of a file system are usually not good enough. Applications for "media asset management" allow you to view large collections in thumbnail form; to move, rename, copy and backup files; to attach labels and captions; to generate webpages; and so on. The main advantages over the standard file system's interface is that you can form catalogs that crosscut the directory structure, and apply batch operations to collections of files at once.

This example is a model of a few of the essential functions of one of the popular applications, iView Media Pro. I developed it to illustrate how modeling can give you insight into very basic functions: the kind that seem obvious at first glance, but are subtler when examined carefully. This kind of modeling is ideally performed in the early stages of developing a program such as Media Pro, but is also useful later, when new functionality threatens to compromise the clarity of the key abstractions.

Although I'd used (and been impressed by) Media Pro for several years,
when I constructed this model, I hadn't understood the details of the
basic functions. I was motivated by occasional unpleasant surprises
that made me wonder whether they might have been designed differently. From the modeling experience, I came to the conclusion that the
design was eminently sensible, and that aside from the addition of an
undo facility, I found no opportunity for an improvement in the underlying abstractions.

Constructing and analyzing the model gave me a number of insights. It
would belabor them to show the model in its intermediate forms, and to
attempt to explain how they arose. Instead, I'll present the final version
of the model, with a separate summary of the insights gained.

6.3.1 Catalog and Application State

The state of the entire application consists of a set of open catalogs (each
with its own state, which we'll come to shortly), a current catalog, and a
cut buffer holding a set of assets:

```
module examples/assets
sig ApplicationState {
   catalogs: set Catalog,
   catalogState: catalogs -> one CatalogState,
   currentCatalog: catalogs,
   buffer: set Asset
   }
sig Catalog, Asset {}
```

The role of a catalog in Media Pro is like the role of a document in a
word processor, and the cut buffer is primarily for moving assets between catalogs. The presence of an asset in a catalog is a purely organizational notion; the location of the asset's file on disk is not affected by
its movement among catalogs.

An individual catalog's state (shown as a model diagram in fig. 6.14)
consists of its assets, which are partitioned into assets that are shown
and assets that are hidden, and a selection, which is either undefined or
is a set of assets:

```
sig CatalogState {
   assets: set Asset,
   part hidden, showing: set assets,
   selection: set assets + Undefined
   }
one sig Undefined {}
```

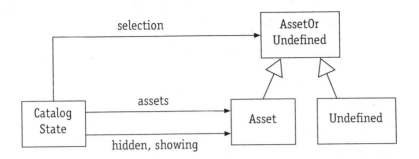

FIG. 6.14 Model diagram for the catalog state declarations.

The hiding and showing of assets is a mechanism that allows the user to focus on a particular subset. Some of the batch actions (such as cut/ copy, rename, rebuild thumbnail) are applied only to selected assets; others (such as webpage generation) are applied to all the assets that are showing. Typical usage often involves selecting a set of assets, hiding them (or the others), and then selecting a subset again, or performing some action.

Because it would be undesirable for actions to be applied to assets that are hidden, the selected assets must always be showing. So we record an invariant saying that the selection is either undefined, or is a nonempty set of assets that are showing:

```
pred catalogInv (cs: CatalogState) {
    cs.selection = Undefined
        or (some cs.selection and cs.selection in cs.showing)
    }
```

The invariant on the whole state simply applies this invariant to the state of each catalog:

```
pred appInv (xs: ApplicationState) {
    all cs: xs.catalogs | catalogInv (xs.catalogState[cs])
    }
```

6.3.2 Operations

We'll model the operations associated with hiding and showing assets, and the operations of the cut buffer.

To show the assets that are selected, and hide the rest, the user executes the "show selected" command:

```
pred showSelected (cs, cs': CatalogState) {
    cs.selection != Undefined
    cs'.showing = cs.selection
    cs'.selection = cs.selection
    cs'.assets = cs.assets
    }
```

Note the precondition that the selection be defined. If no asset is selected, the command's menu entry is grayed out.

To hide the selected assets and show the rest, the user executes the "hide selected" command:

```
pred hideSelected (cs, cs': CatalogState) {
    cs.selection != Undefined
    cs'.hidden = cs.hidden + cs.selection
    cs'.selection = Undefined
    cs'.assets = cs.assets
    }
```

The asymmetry between these operations is a bit surprising at first. The show command *replaces* the set of shown assets, and leaves the selection unchanged. The hide command, in contrast, *augments* the set of hidden assets, and clears the selection.

The cut command is described by this operation:

```
1   pred cut (xs, xs': ApplicationState) {
2       let cs = xs.currentCatalog.(xs.catalogState), sel = cs.selection {
3           sel != Undefined
4           xs'.buffer = sel
5           some cs': CatalogState {
6               cs'.assets = cs.assets - sel
7               cs'.showing = cs.showing - sel
8               cs'.selection = Undefined
9               xs'.catalogState =
10                  xs.catalogState ++ xs.currentCatalog -> cs'
11              }
12          }
13      xs'.catalogs = xs.catalogs
14      xs'.currentCatalog = xs.currentCatalog
15      }
```

Its precondition is that the selection is defined (3). Its effect is to replace the contents of the buffer with the selection (4), to remove the selected assets from the catalog (6) and from the set of shown assets (7), and to clear the selection (8). All these actions are performed in the context of the current catalog; to make this clear, a variable is introduced for the current catalog's state (2). Only the current catalog has a change of state (10). Finally, two frame conditions (13, 14) say that neither the set of open catalogs nor the choice of current catalog is changed.

The paste operation is similar:

```
16  pred paste (xs, xs': ApplicationState) {
17      let cs = xs.currentCatalog.(xs.catalogState), buf = xs.buffer {
18          xs'.buffer = buf
19          some cs': CatalogState {
20              cs'.assets = cs.assets + buf
21              cs'.showing = cs.showing + (buf - cs.assets)
22              cs'.selection = buf - cs.assets
23              xs'.catalogState =
24                  xs.catalogState ++ xs.currentCatalog -> cs'
25          }
26      }
27      xs'.catalogs = xs.catalogs
28      xs'.currentCatalog = xs.currentCatalog
29  }
```

It has no precondition (since the buffer, unlike the selection, can be empty but cannot be undefined). Its effect is to add the assets in the buffer to the assets of the current catalog (20); and to augment the set of shown assets with the new assets that have been added (21), which also become selected (22).

6.3.3 Analyses

In our previous examples, the assertions we checked captured essential properties: that one leader is elected, that no unauthorized entry occurs, and so on. This example is more typical of what happens in practice. No single property seems to capture the essence of the design, but there are a number of simple sanity checks that can be formulated, and which can be very effective in exposing errors and confusions.

One simple and common class of sanity checks is that operations preserve invariants. For example, we can check that if the invariant on catalog state holds before the hide command is issued, then it will also hold after:

```
assert HidePreservesInv {
    all cs, cs': CatalogState |
        catalogInv (cs) and hideSelected (cs, cs') => catalogInv (cs')
    }
check HidePreservesInv
```

This check is sufficient to expose the error of not clearing the selection. Suppose that the operation were to read

```
pred hideSelected (cs, cs': CatalogState) {
    cs.selection != Undefined
    cs'.hidden = cs.hidden + cs.selection
    cs'.selection = cs.selection
    cs'.assets = cs.assets
    }
```

instead of

```
pred hideSelected (cs, cs': CatalogState) {
    cs.selection != Undefined
    cs'.hidden = cs.hidden + cs.selection
    cs'.selection = Undefined
    cs'.assets = cs.assets
    }
```

The analyzer would then produce a counterexample in which the operation results in a hidden asset being selected.

Another class of useful sanity checks involves algebraic properties. Here, for example, we might expect the cut and paste actions to be inverses of one another, so that each acts as an undo for the other. We can assert that a cut followed by a paste results in a final state equivalent to the initial state:

```
assert CutPaste {
    all xs, xs', xs": ApplicationState |
        appInv (xs) and cut (xs, xs') and paste (xs', xs")
            => sameApplicationState (xs, xs")
    }
check CutPaste
```

where equivalence is defined as follows:

```
pred sameApplicationState (xs, xs': ApplicationState) {
    xs'.catalogs = xs.catalogs
    all c: xs.catalogs |
        sameCatalogState (c.(xs.catalogState), c.(xs'.catalogState))
    xs'.currentCatalog = xs.currentCatalog
    xs'.buffer = xs.buffer
    }

pred sameCatalogState (cs, cs': CatalogState) {
    cs'.assets = cs.assets
    cs'.showing = cs.showing
    cs'.selection = cs.selection
    }
```

The assertion is invalid, for a rather inconsequential reason: the cut replaces the contents of the buffer, and the paste doesn't retrieve the old contents (which it would if the cut buffer were a stack, as in the emacs text editor). To confirm that this is the only reason, we can comment out the line

```
xs'.buffer = xs.buffer
```

in *sameApplicationState*, rerun the analysis, and note that a counterexample is no longer found.

Similarly, we can check a paste followed by a cut:

```
assert PasteCut {
    all xs, xs', xs": ApplicationState |
        (appInv (xs) and paste (xs, xs') and cut (xs', xs"))
            => sameApplicationState (xs, xs")
    }
check PasteCut
```

This also fails, because of the change to the selection. Commenting out the line

```
cs'.selection = cs.selection
```

in *sameCatalogState* confirms that there are no additional problems (but see subsection 6.3.4 below).

Sometimes, when writing an operation, a property to check comes to mind. For example, noting that the paste operation adds to the set of shown assets, we might assert that it has no effect on the hidden set of the current catalog:

```
module examples/assets
sig Catalog, Asset {}
sig ApplicationState {
    catalogs: set Catalog,
    catalogState: catalogs -> one CatalogState,
    currentCatalog: catalogs,
    buffer: set Asset
    }
sig CatalogState {
    assets: set Asset,
    part hidden, showing: set assets,
    selection: set assets + Undefined
    }
one sig Undefined {}

pred catalogInv (cs: CatalogState) {
    cs.selection = Undefined
        or (some cs.selection and cs.selection in cs.showing)
    }
pred appInv (xs: ApplicationState) {
    all cs: xs.catalogs | catalogInv (xs.catalogState[cs])
    }
```

FIG. 6.15 Media asset model, state and invariants.

```
assert PasteNotAffectHidden {
    all xs, xs': ApplicationState |
        (appInv (xs) and paste (xs, xs')) =>
            let c = xs.currentCatalog |
                xs'.catalogState[c].hidden = xs.catalogState[c].hidden
    }
check PasteNotAffectHidden
```

This assertion is valid.

Figs. 6.15–6.17 bring together the parts of the model that have been discussed.

```
pred showSelected (cs, cs': CatalogState) {
    cs.selection != Undefined
    cs'.showing = cs.selection
    cs'.selection = cs.selection
    cs'.assets = cs.assets
    }
pred hideSelected (cs, cs': CatalogState) {
    cs.selection != Undefined
    cs'.hidden = cs.hidden + cs.selection
    cs'.selection = Undefined
    cs'.assets = cs.assets
    }
pred cut (xs, xs': ApplicationState) {
let cs = xs.currentCatalog.(xs.catalogState), sel = cs.selection {
    sel != Undefined
    xs'.buffer = sel
    some cs': CatalogState {
        cs'.assets = cs.assets - sel
        cs'.showing = cs.showing - sel
        cs'.selection = Undefined
        xs'.catalogState =
            xs.catalogState ++ xs.currentCatalog -> cs'
        }
    }
xs'.catalogs = xs.catalogs
xs'.currentCatalog = xs.currentCatalog
}
pred paste (xs, xs': ApplicationState) {
    let cs = xs.currentCatalog.(xs.catalogState), buf = xs.buffer {
        xs'.buffer = buf
        some cs': CatalogState {
            cs'.assets = cs.assets + buf
            cs'.showing = cs.showing + (buf - cs.assets)
            cs'.selection = buf - cs.assets
            xs'.catalogState =
                xs.catalogState ++ xs.currentCatalog -> cs'
            }
        }
    xs'.catalogs = xs.catalogs
    xs'.currentCatalog = xs.currentCatalog
    }
```

FIG. 6.16 Media asset model, operations.

assert HidePreservesInv {
  all cs, cs': CatalogState |
    catalogInv (cs) **and** hideSelected (cs, cs') => catalogInv (cs')
  }
check HidePreservesInv

assert CutPaste {
  all xs, xs', xs": ApplicationState |
    appInv (xs) **and** cut (xs, xs') **and** paste (xs', xs")
      => sameApplicationState (xs, xs")
  }
check CutPaste

pred sameApplicationState (xs, xs': ApplicationState) {
  xs'.catalogs = xs.catalogs
  all c: xs.catalogs |
    sameCatalogState (c.(xs.catalogState), c.(xs'.catalogState))
  xs'.currentCatalog = xs.currentCatalog
  xs'.buffer = xs.buffer
  }

pred sameCatalogState (cs, cs': CatalogState) {
  cs'.assets = cs.assets
  cs'.showing = cs.showing
  cs'.selection = cs.selection
  }

assert PasteNotAffectHidden {
  all xs, xs': ApplicationState |
    (appInv (xs) **and** paste (xs, xs')) =>
      let c = xs.currentCatalog |
        xs'.catalogState[c].hidden = xs.catalogState[c].hidden
  }
check PasteNotAffectHidden

FIG. 6.17 Media asset model, assertions.

6.3.4 Insights

The construction and analysis of this little model gave me some insights into the mechanisms of selecting, showing, and hiding:

· The selection is not just a set; it's either undefined, or a set containing one or more assets. This prevents you from selecting zero assets (for which there seems to be no purpose), and from issuing the command to show the selected assets when none are selected, which would cause all assets to be hidden.

· The show and hide commands, as noted, are asymmetric. The show command *replaces* the set of shown assets, and leaves the selection unchanged. The hide command, in contrast, *augments* the set of hidden assets, and clears the selection. This reflects another asymmetry: that the selection is always of assets that are showing. If the show command were to augment rather than replace, it would have no effect! Or, put another way, both commands are really about hiding: the hide command hides the assets selected, and the show command hides the assets that are shown but not selected.

· Executing the paste command leaves the pasted assets selected. This allows some degree of undo by a subsequent cut, although the undo isn't complete because the original selection is lost.

· The case in which a paste is executed and the cut buffer shares assets with the catalog is surprisingly subtle. Initially, I got it wrong, and wrote

```
pred paste (xs, xs': ApplicationState) {
    xs'.catalogs = xs.catalogs
    xs'.currentCatalog = xs.currentCatalog
    let cs = xs.currentCatalog.(xs.catalogState), buf = xs.buffer {
        xs'.buffer = buf
        some cs': CatalogState {
            cs'.assets = cs.assets + buf
            cs'.showing = cs.showing + buf
            cs'.selection = buf
            xs'.catalogState =
                xs.catalogState ++ xs.currentCatalog -> cs'
        }
    }
}
```

so that the set of shown assets is augmented by, and the selection is replaced by, the entire contents of the buffer, rather than the buffer restricted to those assets not already in the catalog. Both assertions *PasteNotAffectHidden* and *PasteCut* failed for unexpected reasons. The former failed because pasting an asset that was already hidden caused it to be shown (and thus removed from the hidden set); the latter failed additionally because the resulting selection included the originally present assets, so a subsequent cut leaves the catalog with fewer assets than it started with before the paste-cut sequence. An experiment with Media Pro revealed the more complicated design of paste, which seems wise, because it preserves the algebraic property *PasteCut* (at least ignoring the selection) which most users probably expect to hold.

Discussion

Is the existential quantifier in the cut and paste operations needed to allocate fresh catalog state?

No. No notion of allocation is necessary in a declarative specification. Instead of writing

```
pred cut (xs, xs': ApplicationState) {
    some cs': CatalogState {
    cs'.assets = expression
    xs'.catalogState = xs.catalogState ++ xs.currentCatalog -> cs'
    }
    ...
    }
```

we could equally well have written

```
pred cut (xs, xs': ApplicationState) {
    let cs' = xs'.catalogState [xs.currentCatalog] |
    cs'.assets = expression
    all c: Catalog - xs.currentCatalog |
    xs'.catalogState [c] = xs.catalogState [c]
    ...
    }
```

but the existential quantifier is convenient because it allows the relational override operator to be used.

Aren't your insights rather trivial?

Perhaps some readers will think I'm making a mountain out of a mole-hill; after all, none of the issues I discuss are "showstoppers," which if confused in the design could not be fixed later. The point, rather, is that to make a dependable and usable application you need to get all these things right *eventually*.

Can usability issues really be addressed in the abstract?

Of course some design issues, especially those involving usability, cannot be resolved in the abstract. But that's no reason to ignore them during design. Focusing on them early will catch many problems, even if not all, and will save you a lot of reworking later. Moreover, a usability study is most effective when viewed as an experiment in which a hypothesis is being tested. If you don't have a coherent design with clean abstractions, you don't have a hypothesis. You can't tweak an incoherent user interface design into a usable and elegant one any more than you can test a pile of spaghetti code into a robust code base.

6.4   Memory Abstractions

Memory systems have long been a favorite subject for modeling and analysis. This example is included to show the application of Alloy to a well-understood problem. As a pedagogical example, it illustrates the use of nondeterminism (in the descriptions of flushing and loading), of abstraction functions for relating models at different levels of abstraction, and of Alloy's module system to separate the models from one another and from the checks that relate them.

6.4.1   Abstract Memory

A model of a simple abstract memory is shown in fig. 6.18. The module is parameterized by *Addr*, the set of addresses, and *Data*, the set of data values that can be stored. The *Memory* signature represents the possible states of the memory. The *Canonicalize* fact ensures that memories with the same contents are represented by the same atom.

The contents of the memory are modeled by the field *data* mapping addresses to data values. The mapping is a partial function; each address maps to at most one data value. The initialization of the memory is described by the predicate *init*: the memory is initially empty, with no mappings at all. Later, in subsection 6.4.3, we'll relate this model to a less abstract model in which there is always a data value for every address, set arbitrarily at the start.

Writes to the memory are described by the *write* predicate. The data mapping of the new memory (*m'*) is the data mapping of the old memory (*m*) overridden by the mapping from the address *a* to the data value *d*.

Reads, described by the *read* predicate, are more interesting. If there is a data value associated with the address being looked up, that value is returned. Otherwise, the value is unconstrained, and any value may be returned.

Two examples of simple checks that can be applied to this model are, first, that a read of an address returns the value just written:

```
assert WriteRead {
    all m, m': Memory, a: Addr, d1, d2: Data |
        write (m, m', a, d1) and read (m', a, d2) => d1 = d2
    }
check WriteRead
```

and, second, that performing a second identical write has no effect:

```
module examples/abstractMemory [Addr, Data]

sig Memory {
   data: Addr -> lone Data
   }

fact Canonicalize {
   no disj m, m': Memory | m.data = m'.data
   }

pred init (m: Memory) {
   no m.data
   }

pred write (m, m': Memory, a: Addr, d: Data) {
   m'.data = m.data ++ a -> d
   }

pred read (m: Memory, a: Addr, d: Data) {
   let d' = m.data [a] | some d' implies d = d'
   }
```

FIG. 6.18 Simple abstract memory.

```
assert WriteIdempotent {
   all m, m', m": Memory, a: Addr, d: Data |
      write (m, m', a, d) and write (m', m", a, d) => m' = m"
   }
check WriteIdempotent
```

Discussion

Why canonicalize the memory values?

The alternative would be to introduce a predicate, *sameMemory* say, that evaluates to true when applied to two memories with identical data mappings. This predicate would then be used in place of equality tests. Either approach works fine, but canonicalization is slightly more convenient, because it avoids the error of forgetting to use the equivalence predicate rather than equality, and because instances generated by the analyzer are easier to understand, since memories with different names are always structurally different.

Why doesn't read *take a second memory argument?*

Since *read* does not change the state of the memory, there is no need to have a second argument, *m′* say, to represent the poststate. Sometimes, however, this is preferable. In a less abstract model in which the read operation might load data to a cache from main memory, the second argument would be required. To check that model against this abstract model, it would be convenient to have the second argument in the abstract model too, to avoid a separate check that the loading read does not affect the abstract state.

6.4.2 Cache Memory

A model of a simple cache memory is shown in fig. 6.19. This time, the signature representing the system states (*cacheMemory*) has two fields mapping addresses to data values, one for the main memory and one for the cache.

Both reading and writing involve only the cache. The *write* operation alters the cache and leaves the main memory unchanged. The *read* operation returns the data value from the cache, and has a precondition that such a value exist. The idea is that prior to executing a read, the system may execute a load if necessary to bring the requested address into the cache. Prior to a write, it may execute a flush to make room in the cache for the new entry.

The *load* and *flush* operations are nondeterministic. Rather than specifying a particular caching policy, they cover all policies by leaving open the question of which entries are loaded and flushed.

The *WriteRead* and *WriteIdempotent* checks could be applied to this model too (with the references to the signature *Memory* replaced by references to *CacheSystem*). More interesting checks involve loading and flushing. For example, we can check that a load interposed between a read and a write has no observable effect:

```
assert LoadNotObservable {
    all c, c', c": CacheSystem, a1, a2: Addr, d1, d2, d3: Data |
        {
        read (c, a2, d2)
        write (c, c', a1, d1)
        load (c', c")
        read (c", a2, d3)
        } implies d3 = (if a1 = a2 then d1 else d2)
    }
check LoadNotObservable
```

```
module examples/cacheMemory [Addr, Data]

sig CacheSystem {
    main, cache: Addr -> lone Data
    }

pred init (c: CacheSystem) {
    no c.main + c.cache
    }

pred write (c, c': CacheSystem, a: Addr, d: Data) {
    c'.main = c.main
    c'.cache = c.cache ++ a -> d
    }

pred read (c: CacheSystem, a: Addr, d: Data) {
    some d
    d = c.cache [a]
    }

pred load (c, c': CacheSystem) {
    some addrs: set c.main.Data - c.cache.Data |
        c'.cache = c.cache ++ addrs <: c.main
    c'.main = c.main
    }

pred flush  (c, c': CacheSystem) {
    some addrs: some c.cache.Data {
        c'.main = c.main ++ addrs <: c.cache
        c'.cache = c.cache - addrs -> Data
        }
    }
```

FIG. 6.19 Cache memory.

This assertion says that if a read, write, load, and read are performed in that order, then the data value returned from the second read will either match the value written (if the second read address matches the write address), or the value read initially (if it does not).

No counterexample is found; the assertion is valid. On the other hand, suppose we'd made a mistake in specifying the load operation, allowing any entries to be copied to the cache from main memory, irrespective of whether their addresses match addresses of entries in the cache:

```
pred load (c, c': CacheSystem) {
  some addrs: set Addr |
    c'.cache = c.cache ++ addrs <: c.main
  c'.main = c.main
  }
```

The analyzer now finds a counterexample showing fresh values in the cache (which have yet to be flushed) being overwritten.

Discussion

Why no canonicalization of memory values for the caching version?

This model, unlike the previous one of the abstract memory, does not include a canonicalization fact. Our example involves no comparisons of cache memories, but it will involve comparisons of abstract memories (when we check that loading and flushing have no abstract effect).

6.4.3 Fixed-Size Memory

In the abstract memory model of subsection 6.4.1, the memory grows dynamically as writes to new addresses are made, even though the set of possible addresses is fixed. For a memory implemented in hardware, a more realistic model, shown in fig. 6.20, assigns a value to every address in every state.

The initialization predicate is now empty: any initial assignment of data values is allowed, so long as the multiplicity of the declaration of the field *data* is obeyed, so that each address has a defined data value associated with it. The read operation no longer distinguishes the case of whether the address is present, and simply returns the data value for the given address.

This model could be subjected to the same kind of internal analyses as the abstract memory model—nothing new here.

6.4.4 A Quick Introduction to Abstraction Functions

We've now seen three variants of the memory model: an abstract memory model, and two more concrete models, one accommodating arbitrary initialization, and one describing caching. If we observed the behaviors of these two, we would expect them to conform to the abstract model. That is, if all you could see was which operations occurred, the addresses passed to them, and the data values passed into the write operation and out of the read, every execution of one of the concrete sys-

```
module examples/fixedSizeMemory [Addr, Data]
sig Memory {
  data: Addr -> one Data
  }

pred init (m: Memory) {
  }

pred write (m, m': Memory, a: Addr, d: Data) {
  m'.data = m.data ++ a -> d
  }

pred read (m: Memory, a: Addr, d: Data) {
  d = m.data [a]
  }
```

FIG. 6.20 Fixed-size memory.

tems would be indistinguishable from some execution of the abstract system.

To determine whether a concrete operation

```
pred concreteOp (s, s': State) {...}
```

produces behaviors acceptable to an abstract operation

```
pred abstractOp (s, s': State) {...}
```

we can assert that every transition of the concrete operation is a transition of the abstract one:

```
assert Refinement {
  all s, s': State | concreteOp (s, s') => abstractOp (s, s')
  }
```

For example, we could check that the write operation from our abstract model

```
pred write (m, m': Memory, a: Addr, d: Data) {
  m'.data = m.data ++ a -> d
  }
```

meets the more abstract description

```
pred writeWeak (m, m': Memory, a: Addr, d: Data) {
  m'.data [a] = d
  }
```

which (unhelpfully) allows corruption on every address except the one written, with the assertion

```
assert WriteRefinement {
    all m, m': Memory, a: Addr, d: Data |
        write (m, m', a, d) => writeWeak (m, m', a, d)
}
```

To compare across memory models, however, this simple approach won't work: the operations compared apply to different state spaces. A classic paper by Tony Hoare [28] introduced a solution to this problem that is now well-known and widely used. An *abstraction function* is defined that maps concrete states to corresponding abstract states.

Suppose our operations are

```
pred concreteOp (s, s': ConcreteState) {...}
pred abstractOp (s, s': AbstractState) {...}
```

Then we try to find an abstraction function

```
fun alpha (s: ConcreteState): AbstractState {...}
```

that makes this assertion valid:

```
assert AbstractionRefinement {
    all s, s': ConcreteState |
        concreteOp (s, s') => abstractOp (alpha(s), alpha(s'))
}
```

If such an abstraction function can be found, the observable behaviors of the concrete model—in which everything is visible except the state itself—will conform to the abstract model.

Discussion

What exactly is the notion of conformance here?

We're using *trace inclusion* as the yardstick. A trace is an execution history: a sequence of events, each representing a single step in which an operation fires. An event can be described in full by the name of the operation and the values taken by the inputs and outputs in that step. Note that the pre- and poststates are not part of the event, because they are regarded as invisible from outside. Each machine, abstract and concrete, has a trace set that summarizes its behavior. The concrete machine conforms to the abstract machine if its trace set is a subset of the trace set of the abstract model.

If the concrete machine conforms in this way, it never does anything *bad*. On the other hand, conformance doesn't guarantee that it does anything *good*. In particular, the concrete machine that has no traces at all conforms to any abstract machine! To ensure that good things happen, the notion of conformance needs to be extended. If each operation represents a request for service and its fulfillment, we might require that the concrete operations be just as *applicable*: that is, whenever a trace can be extended with an event in the abstract machine, there is a corresponding event in the concrete machine (or, more generally, an appropriate sequence of events). This would ensure that the concrete machine never refuse to respond to a request that the abstract machine would have responded to.

This kind of extension is not easily formulated or checked in Alloy, because it requires an unbounded universal quantification over states. The assertion we'd need would say something like this: for every concrete prestate, the concrete operation is applicable (that is, there exists a concrete poststate satisfying the operation constraint) whenever the correspond abstract operation is applicable. This existential quantifier over the concrete poststate becomes an unbounded universal quantifier when it's negated to find counterexamples, so it can't be handled by Alloy. See section 5.3 for a detailed discussion of this problem.

Does the abstraction function method always work?

The method is *sound*, which means that if you can find an abstraction function that satisfies the refinement condition, then it follows that the concrete machine conforms to the abstract machine. It's not *complete*, however: just because the concrete machine conforms does not imply that an abstraction function exists. The problem with the standard method arises only rarely, when the abstract and concrete machines exhibit nondeterminism at different points but with the same observable effect.

The method can be made complete in one of two ways. You can generalize to an abstraction *relation*, but this isn't desirable for Alloy, because it requires an unbounded universal quantification. Alternatively, you can augment the concrete model with additional state variables in a way that doesn't alter the observable behavior, but makes it possible to find an abstraction function. Two kinds of variables are added, history and prophecy variables, depending on whether the troublesome nondeterminism is resolved earlier or later in the concrete machine. Use of a history variable is illustrated below, in subsection 6.4.6.

What if you pick the wrong abstraction function?

It doesn't matter what function you pick, so long as it satisfies the refinement condition, and one additional condition. It must be *total*, so that it gives an interpretation for every concrete state. This condition is not easily checked in Alloy, because it requires an unbounded universal (see section 5.3), but you can often write the abstraction function in such a way that it's easy to see that it's total, and you can simulate it (just by running the function in the Alloy Analyzer) to check that it's consistent.

Must the abstraction function really map every concrete state?

Not necessarily. You can introduce an invariant. So long as every concrete operation preserves the invariant—easily checked in Alloy (see section 6.3.1)—the refinement condition can be restricted to those prestates that satisfy it, and then the abstraction function need only map them.

6.4.5 Abstraction Function for Cache Memory

To check the cache model against the abstract model, we create a new Alloy module:

```
module examples/checkCache [Addr, Data]
open cacheMemory [Addr, Data] as cache
open abstractMemory [Addr, Data] as amemory
```

We then declare an abstraction function, saying that the abstract memory associated with a cache system is obtained by taking the contents of the main memory, and overriding them with the contents of the cache:

```
fun alpha (c: CacheSystem): Memory {
{m: Memory | m.data = c.main ++ c.cache}
}
```

Now we can write the assertions to check the operations. For read and write, we have:

```
assert ReadOK {
all c: CacheSystem, a: Addr, d: Data, m: Memory |
    cache/read (c, a, d) and m = alpha (c)
        => amemory/read (m, a, d)
}
check ReadOK
```

```
assert WriteOK {
    all c, c': CacheSystem, a: Addr, d: Data, m, m': Memory |
        cache/write (c, c', a, d)
        and m = alpha (c) and m' = alpha (c')
            => amemory/write (m, m', a, d)
}
check WriteOK
```

The load and flush operations don't have counterparts in the abstract model; their effect should not even be detectable from an abstract perspective. So we check them against the abstract operation that does nothing:

```
assert LoadOK {
    all c, c': CacheSystem, m, m': Memory |
        cache/load (c, c')
        and m = alpha (c) and m' = alpha (c')
            => m = m'
}
check LoadOK

assert FlushOK {
    all c, c': CacheSystem, m, m': Memory |
        cache/flush (c, c')
        and m = alpha (c) and m' = alpha (c')
            => m = m'
}
check FlushOK
```

6.4.6 History Variables

Showing that fixed-size memory conforms to the abstract model is impossible with an abstraction function alone. But the fixed-size memory does indeed conform: the arbitrary initial values correspond to the addresses in the abstract memory that have no data values associated with them, and when a read operation returns one of these arbitrary values, the abstract model would allow it, because, in the abstract setting, the address would have been missing from the mapping—a case in which the abstract read operation does not constrain the value returned.

Unfortunately, however, after the initial state, you can no longer tell by looking at the fixed-size memory's address/data mapping which addresses have been written to, and which still hold their initial junk values. A solution to this dilemma is to extend the model with an extra state component that maintains this distinction, as shown in fig. 6.21.

This state component, *unwritten*, is called a *history variable*, because it holds additional history about the behavior—in this case the set of addresses that have not yet been written to.

Now, using the augmented state, we can formulate an abstraction function, and check the operations as before, but using the augmented concrete model rather than the original one. The new abstraction function and the refinement assertions are shown in fig. 6.22.

Discussion

Why is an abstraction function needed at all for the fixed-size memory? Doesn't its state match the state of the abstract memory?

The state of the cache model clearly differs from the state of the abstract model, because it separates the memory into two mappings. But you may wonder whether the fixed-size memory state is different: like the abstract memory, the state comprises a single field called *data* mapping addresses to data values.

First, distinct signatures represent distinct sets of atoms, even if their fields have the same name. The ability to use fields of the same name is a convenience—a form of overloading that Alloy resolves automatically. Alloy doesn't permit two distinct signatures with the same name; even though both of these are called *Memory*, they are declared in different modules, so their full names are unique.

Second, even if we rewrote the models so that the fixed-size and abstract memories shared the same state signature, an abstraction function would still be needed. Consider checking the initialization predicates. The abstract memory requires the address/data mapping to be empty initially, whereas the fixed-size memory requires it to be full!

The issue here is that, even if the *names* of the two state spaces match, and they are represented by the same set of atoms, a single state can have different *interpretations* in the two models. In fact, to interpret a state of the fixed-size memory in terms of the abstract memory, we need to distinguish addresses that have been written, and addresses that still hold their arbitrary values from initialization. This is what led us to introduce the history variable. Even in the absence of the history variable, an abstraction function is needed to bridge two state spaces when their interpretations differ. As another example, think of testing one

```
module examples/fixedSizeMemory_H [Addr, Data]
open fixedSizeMemory [Addr, Data] as memory

sig Memory_H extends memory/Memory {
    unwritten: set Addr
    }

pred init (m: Memory_H) {
    memory/init (m)
    m.unwritten = Addr
    }

pred read (m: Memory_H, a: Addr, d: Data) {
    memory/read (m, a, d)
    }

pred write (m, m': Memory_H, a: Addr, d: Data) {
    memory/write (m, m', a, d)
    m'.unwritten = m.unwritten - a
    }
```

FIG. 6.21 Extension of fixed-size memory model with a history variable.

arithmetic implementation against another in which the byte ordering differs: the testing framework will need to apply conversions, even though both implementations represent an integer as a byte.

Why did you write the abstraction function as a predicate rather than as a function?

Simply to illustrate a different style; it's still a function, even though it's defined implicitly. The predicate form is perhaps preferable because it doesn't use the set comprehension. You might think that defining the abstraction function as an Alloy function (as in subsection 6.4.5) ensures that it is truly a function from concrete to abstract states. Unfortunately, this isn't true: if the comprehension property is badly written, a single concrete state might map to a set of more than one abstract state. You'd still have a function in the sense of the Alloy keyword (because the result is a single set of abstract states) but you wouldn't have an abstraction function, because the mapping from states to states would not be one-to-one.

module examples/checkFixedSize [Addr, Data]
open fixedSizeMemory_H [Addr, Data] **as** fmemory
open abstractMemory [Addr, Data] **as** amemory

pred alpha (fm: fmemory/Memory, am: amemory/Memory) {
    am.data = fm.data - (fm.unwritten -> Data)
    }

assert initOK {
    all fm: fmemory/Memory, am: amemory/Memory |
      fmemory/init (bm) **and** alpha (bm, am)
        => amemory/init (am)
    }
check initOK

assert readOK {
    all fm: fmemory/Memory, a: Addr, d: Data,
    am: amemory/Memory |
      fmemory/read (fm, a, d) **and** alpha (fm, am))
        => amemory/read (am, a, d)
    }
check readOK

assert writeOK {
    all fm, fm': fmemory/Memory, a: Addr, d: Data,
    am: amemory/Memory |
      fmemory/write (fm, fm', a, d)
      and alpha (fm, am) **and** alpha (fm', am')
        => amemory/write (am, am', a, d)
    }
check writeOK

FIG. 6.22 Abstraction function and refinement assertions
for history-extended machine.

Appendix A: Exercises

These exercises are divided into sections. The exercises in the early sections are designed to help develop skills in using relational logic and the basic linguistic constructs of Alloy, so they tend to be more mathematical in flavor. The exercises in the later sections are more open-ended, and more characteristic of what modeling involves in practice.

The exercises of section A.1 assume only chapter 3 as background, and do not require any familiarity with the language constructs of 4. Nevertheless, most readers will enjoy the exercises more, and learn more from them, if they experiment with the Alloy Analyzer as they go along. I've therefore provided templates that show how to use the analyzer in each exercise without requiring knowledge of the full language.

The exercises of the remaining sections can all be attempted after reading only chapters 3 and 4, except for A.5.3 which refers to an example in chapter 6.

Exercises that are easy and should not require any deep thinking are marked with a small heart (♥). Exercises that are particularly challenging are marked with a small clubs symbol (♣).

A.1   Logic Exercises

The exercises in this section give practice in writing expressions and constraints in the relational logic. They don't require any knowledge of the full Alloy language, but many of them show how to embed the expressions and constraints within an Alloy model, so that you can use the analyzer to generate instances and give you concrete feedback.

♥A.1.1   Properties of Binary Relations

The following Alloy model constrains a binary relation to have a collection of standard properties:

```
module exercises/properties

pred show () {
    some r: univ -> univ {
        some r              -- nonempty
        r.r in r            -- transitive
        no iden & r         -- irreflexive
        ~r in r             -- symmetric
        ~r.r in iden        -- functional
        r.~r in iden        -- injective
        univ in r.univ      -- total
        univ in univ.r      -- onto
    }
}
run show for 4
```

A finite binary relation cannot have all these properties at once. Which individual properties, if eliminated, allow the remaining properties to be satisfied? For each such property eliminated, give an example of a relation that satisfies the rest.

You can use the Alloy Analyzer to help you. The *run* command instructs the analyzer to search for an instance satisfying the constraints in a universe of at most 4 atoms. To eliminate a property, just comment it out (with two hyphens in a row at the start of the line).

♥A.1.2   Relational and Predicate Calculus Styles

The properties in problem A.1.1 were written in a relational calculus style. Rewrite each in a predicate calculus style instead. For example, the non-emptiness property can be reformulated as

some x, y: **univ** | x -> y **in** r

Each of your reformulations can be cast as an Alloy assertion, so you can use the analyzer to check it. For example, to check the reformulation of non-emptiness, you would write

assert ReformulateNonEmptinessOK {
  all r: **univ** -> **univ** |
    some r **iff** (**some** x, y: **univ** | x -> y)
  }
check ReformulateNonEmptinessOK

and then execute the check to see if there are counterexamples—values of the relation r that satisfy one formulation but not the other.

♥A.1.3 Relational Properties in Modeling

Suppose you are modeling each of the following relationships as a binary relation. What properties (drawn from the list in problem A.1.1) would you expect each to have?

(a) the *sibling* relationship, between children with the same parents;

(b) the *links* relationship, between a host on a network and the hosts it is linked to;

(c) the *contains* relationship, between a directory in a file system and its contents;

(d) the *group* relationship, between graphical elements in a drawing program and groups (collections of elements that are selected and deselected together);

(e) the *sameGroup* relationship, between graphical elements in the same group;

(f) the *supersedes* relationship, between a file in one file system and a file in another file system, which holds when the first file is a newer version of the second file.

(g) the *substitutableFor* relationship, between two components, when the first can be substituted for the second in any system in some class; for example, one power supply may be substituted for another if it provides the same voltage and at least as much power.

♥*A.1.4 Refactoring Navigation Expressions*

When writing "navigation expressions," you may notice repeated subexpressions that can be factored out, making the overall expression more succinct. For example, the expression *p.mother.brother + p.father.brother*, denoting *p*'s uncle, can be written instead as *p.(mother + father).brother*. Simplifications like this rely on the assumption that certain algebraic identities hold, such as

(a) distributivity of join over union: $s.(p + q) = s.p + s.q$;

(b) distributivity of join over difference: $s.(p - q) = s.p - s.q$; and

(c) distributivity of join over intersection: $s.(p \& q) = s.p \& s.q$

for a given set *s* and binary relations *p* and *q*.

For each putative identity, say whether it holds, and if not, give a counterexample.

Here is an example of how you might check the first using the Alloy Analyzer:

```
module exercises/distribution
assert union {
   all s: set univ, p, q: univ->univ | s.(p + q) = s.p + s.q
   }
check union for 4
```

The command tells the analyzer to find a counterexample within a universe of 4 elements. When you find that a property does not hold, try and obtain the smallest counterexample you can, by reducing the scope (for example, replacing *for 4* by *for 2*).

A.1.5 Characterizing Trees

A *tree* is a relation that satisfies some properties. What exactly are these properties? Express them in relational logic, and illustrate with a few examples.

Here is a template to help you:

```
module exercises/tree
pred isTree (r: univ->univ) { ... }
run isTree for 4
```

Just replace the ellipsis with some constraints on the relation *r*, and execute the command to visualize some sample instances. You may need to add some constraints to make the instances nontrivial.

A.1.6   Spanning Trees

A *spanning tree* of a graph is a tree-like subgraph that covers all the nodes. Make this definition precise, and give an example of a graph with two distinct spanning trees.

Here is a template to help you:

```
module exercises/spanning
pred isTree (r: univ -> univ) { ... }
pred spans (r1, r2: univ -> univ) { ... }
pred show (r, t1, t2: univ -> univ) {
    spans (t1, r) and isTree (t1)
    spans (t2, r) and isTree (t2)
    t1 not = t2
    }
run show for 3
```

Hint: It's up to you whether you consider the graph and trees to be directed or undirected. The undirected case is a bit trickier, and more interesting.

Spanning trees have many uses. In networks, they're often used to set up connections. In the Firewire protocol, for example, a spanning tree is automatically discovered, and the root of the tree becomes a leader that coordinates communication.

A.1.7   Characterizing Rings

Some communication protocols organize nodes in a network into a *ring*, with links from node to node forming a circle. Characterize, as simply and concisely as you can, the constraints on *next*, the relation from node to node, that ensures that it forms a ring.

Here is a sample Alloy model into which you can insert the constraints, and then execute the command to see if the instances you obtain are indeed rings:

```
module exercises/ring
sig Node {next: set Node}
pred isRing () {
    ... your constraints here
    }
run isRing for exactly 4 Node
```

♣A.1.8 Defining Acyclicity for an Undirected Graph

An undirected graph can be represented as a binary relation, constrained to be symmetric. Write constraints on such a relation that rule out cycles. Here is a suitable template:

```
module exercises/undirected
sig Node {adjs: set Node}
pred acyclic () {
   adjs = ~adjs
   ... your constraints here
   }
run acyclic for 4
```

A.1.9 Axiomatizing Transitive Closure

Transitive closure is not axiomatizable in first-order logic. In short, that means that if you want to express it, you need a special operator, because it can't be defined in terms of other operators. Here's a bogus attempt to do just that; your challenge is to use the Alloy Analyzer to find the flaw.

Recall that the transitive closure of a binary relation r is the smallest transitive relation R that includes r. Let's say R is a transitive cover of r if R is transitive and includes r. To ensure that R is the smallest transitive cover, we can say that removing any tuple a->b from R gives a relation that is *not* a transitive cover of r. Formalize this by completing the following template:

```
module exercises/closure

pred transCover (R, r: univ->univ) {
   ... your constraints here
   }
pred transClosure (R, r: univ->univ) {
   transCover (R, r)
   ... your constraint here
   }

assert Equivalence {
   all R, r: univ->univ | transClosure (R, r) iff R = ^r
   }
check Equivalence for 3
```

Now execute the command, examine the counterexample, and explain what the bug is. The official definition of UML 1.0 had this problem.

A.1.10   Address Book Constraints and Expressions

In this exercise, you'll get some practice writing expressions and constraints for a simple multilevel address book. Consider a set *Addr* of addresses, and a set *Name* consisting of two disjoint subsets *Alias* and *Group*. The mapping from names to addresses is represented by a relation *address*, but a name can map not only to an address but also to a name.

First, write the following *invariants*—constraints which you'd expect an address book to satisfy:

(a) There are no cycles; if you resolve a name repeatedly, you never reach the same name again.

(b) All names eventually map to an address.

Second, write the following *simulation constraints*, which you might add during the exploration of a model in order to see more interesting instances:

(c) The address book has at least two levels.

(d) Some groups are non-empty.

Finally, write expressions for each of the following, without using comprehension syntax:

(e) the set of names that are members of groups;

(f) the set of groups that are empty;

(g) the mapping from aliases to the addresses they refer to, directly or indirectly;

(h) the mapping from names to addresses which, when a name maps to some addresses directly, and some other addresses indirectly, includes only the direct addresses.

Here's how to use the analyzer to help you with this problem. Take the following template, which declares the various sets and the *address* relation, and fill in the invariants and simulation constraints:

```
module exercises/addressBook1

abstract sig Name {
    address: set Addr + Name
    }
sig Alias, Group extends Name {}
sig Addr {}
```

fact {
    ... *invariants*
    }
pred show () {
    ... *simulation constraints*
    }
run show **for** 3

As you fill them in, execute the *run* command; the tool will generate sample instances. Then, when you have an interesting instance, enter a candidate expression into the evaluator, and the tool will show you its value for that particular instance. You may find that you need to add more simulation constraints to obtain an instance that nicely illustrates the meaning of an expression.

A.1.11 Modeling The Tube

In this exercise, you'll write some generic constraints about railway lines, and then apply them to the London Underground.

The diagram of fig. A.1 shows a simplified portion of the London Underground. (You can find the real thing at *http://tube.tfl.gov.uk/.*) There are three lines shown: the Jubilee line running north to south from Stanmore to Waterloo; the Central Line running west to east from West Ruislip and Ealing Broadway to Epping; and the Circle line running clockwise through Baker Street. The snapshot of fig. A.2 shows an instance of an Alloy model that corresponds to it.

Let's model all the stations in a railway as the set *Station*. A particular line *Line* will be represented as a set of stations *Line* served by that line, with the same name as the line, and a binary relation *line* over those stations, with the same name but starting with a lower case letter.

Formalize each of these statements in the Alloy logic:

(a) Station S is served by line $L1$ but not by line $L2$.

(b) Line L forms a circle.

(c) Line L forms a straight line.

(d) Line L is a straight line, until it branches into two straight lines at station S.

(e) The ends of line L are stations $S1$ (at the start) and $S2$ (at the end).

(f) It is possible to travel from station $S1$ to station $S2$ on line L.

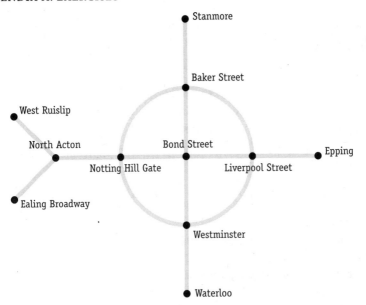

FIG. A.1 A simplified portion of the London Underground.

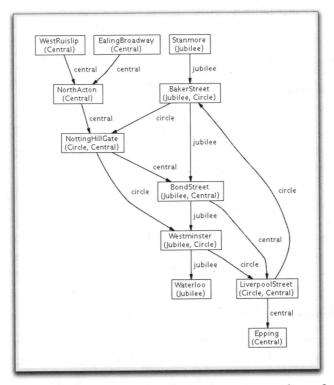

FIG. A.2 An instance generated by the Alloy Analyzer corresponding to fig. A.1.

(g) At station S, two branches of L merge into one.

(h) [Hard!] If you get on an L line train at station $S1$, you will eventually reach station $S2$.

(i) Now construct a model of the portion of the Underground shown in fig. A.1, and run the Alloy Analyzer to see if you can obtain a snapshot similar to that shown in fig. A.2.

Here is a template to show you how to use the analyzer for this problem:

```
module exercises/tube

abstract sig Station {
    jubilee, central, circle: set Station
    }
sig Jubilee, Central, Circle in Station {}
one sig
    Stanmore, BakerStreet, BondStreet, Westminster, Waterloo,
    WestRuislip, EalingBroadway, NorthActon, NottingHillGate,
        LiverpoolStreet, Epping
    extends Station {}

fact {
    ... your constraints here
    }
pred show () {}
run show
```

Just write the constraints in the body of the fact, and execute the command to generate sample instances. The constraints you need are instantiations of the generic constraints. For example, the generic constraint S in L says that station S is served by line L; you might write here

```
BakerStreet in Jubilee
```

to say that Baker Street is served by the Jubilee line. If you have read chapter 4, you could write the model more elegantly by defining functions and predicates for the generic constraints. Don't cheat by just entering the instance directly, for example by writing

```
jubilee = Stanmore -> BakerStreet + BakerStreet -> BondStreet ...
```

If you do this you won't have a model that is true of the Underground as a whole, because it won't accommodate additional, intermediate stations. Worse, you'll miss the opportunity to use the analyzer to find errors in your generic constraints.

A.2 Extending Simple Models

The problems in this section exercise the full Alloy language, but give you the initial structure of the model.

A.2.1 Telephone Switch Connections

Consider the following model of connections in a telephone network:

```
module exercises/phones

sig Phone {
    requests: set Phone,
    connects: lone Phone
    }
```

The signature *Phone* represents a set of telephones. For a phone *p*, *p.requests* is a set of phones that *p* is requesting connections to, some of which may have been granted, and *p.connects* is the phone that *p* is currently connected to (or none).

(a) Simulate the model by adding a predicate and running it. Add some constraints to the predicate to ensure that you don't get boring cases; for example, you might say that there should be some requests and some connections.

(b) Add two invariants: that every connection has a matching request (on the assumption that requests don't disappear until the connections they spawned are torn down), and that there are no conference calls (in which a phone is involved in more than one connection).

(c) Now incorporate call forwarding, by extending the state with a new relation *forward* from phones to phones, where *p.forward*, if nonempty, is the phone that an incoming call to *p* should be forwarded to. Change the constraint relating *requests* and *connects* to account for forwarding. Simulate some interesting examples of call forwarding, adding some extra simulation constraints if necessary.

A.2.2   *Invariant Preservation in an Address Book*

In this problem, you are given a model of a simple address book program, with operations to add, delete, viol and look up a name, and an invariant characterizing the address book's well-formedness properties. Your task is to show that the add and delete operations break the invariant, and to fix them by strengthening their preconditions.

Here is the basic model:

```
module exercises/addressBook2

sig Addr, Name {}
sig Book {
    addr: Name -> (Name + Addr)
    }

pred inv (b: Book) {
    let addr = b.addr |
        all n: Name {
            n not in n.^addr
            some addr.n => some n.^addr & Addr
            }
    }

pred add (b, b': Book, n: Name, t: Name + Addr) {
    b'.addr = b.addr + n -> t
    }
pred del (b, b': Book, n: Name, t: Name + Addr) {
    b'.addr = b.addr - n -> t
    }
fun lookup (b: Book, n: Name): set Addr {
    n.^(b.addr) & Addr
    }
```

Note that names are mapped both to addresses and to other names, resulting in a multilevel lookup.

The invariant says that no name should map to itself, directly or indirectly, and that if a name is itself mapped to, then the name is mapped, directly or indirectly, to at least one address. An operation is said to *preserve* an invariant if, when invoked in any state satisfying the invariant, it always results in another state satisfying the invariant.

(a) The invariant is defined formally in the predicate *inv*. Explain in words, informally, what the invariant says.

(b) Generate some examples of address books that satisfy the invariant, and some examples that violate it in different ways. To do this, you'll need to add predicates and commands to run them.

(c) Generate some examples of executions of the operations, again by adding and running appropriate predicates.

(d) Find counterexamples showing that neither *add* nor *delete* preserves the invariant. To do this, you'll need to define assertions that invoke the operations and the invariant, and commands to check them. Reduce the scope if necessary to obtain the smallest counterexample possible.

(e) Elaborate the two operations with additional preconditions—constraints on the prestates—that ensure the invariant is preserved, and rerun the preservation check to show that you have succeeded. Increase the scope to give you more confidence, and briefly justify your choice of scope.

(f) Rerun your simulations from (c) to check that you haven't inadvertently overconstrained the operations.

A.2.3   Inmate Assignments

A program is needed to assign inmates to cells in a prison. The assignment must avoid placing two inmates in the same cell if they are members of different gangs.

Here is a suitable template:

```
module exercises/prison

sig Gang {members: set Inmate}
sig Inmate {room: Cell}
sig Cell {}

pred safe () {
    ... your constraints here
    }

pred show () {
    ... your constraints here
    }
run show
```

(a) Complete the predicate *safe* characterizing a safe assignment, and generate examples of both safe and unsafe assignments by running the simulation predicate *show*, with appropriate invocations of *safe* as its constraint.

(b) Write a new predicate called *happy*, saying that gang members only share cells with members of the same gang. A safe assignment is not necessarily a happy assignment. By writing an assertion and a command to check it, find a counterexample, and explain why not.

(c) Add a constraint as a fact that ensures that safety will indeed imply happiness. Run your simulation predicate again to make sure that you haven't introduced an inconsistency, and check the assertion again to make sure it now has no counterexample.

A.3 Classic Puzzles

The exercises in this section give practice in writing Alloy and structuring small models.

♥A.3.1 A Surprising Syllogism

A song by Doris Day goes

"Everybody loves my baby
but my baby don't love nobody but me."

David Gries has pointed out that, from a strictly logical point of view, this implies "I am my baby." Check this, by formalizing the song as some constraints, and Gries's inference as an assertion. Then modify the constraints to express what Doris Day probably meant, and show that the assertion now has a counterexample.

♥A.3.2 Ceilings and Floors

A song by Paul Simon goes

"One man's ceiling is another man's floor."

Does this imply that one man's floor is another man's ceiling? Formalize the two constraints in Alloy, and check an assertion that the first implies the second. If you get counterexamples that don't make sense because of implicit assumptions, add them as new constraints, and check again.

A.3.3   Barber Paradox

Consider the set of all sets that do not contain themselves as members. Does it contain itself? This paradox was discovered by Bertrand Russell in 1901, and revealed an inconsistency in Frege's naive set theory. A variant of the paradox, also attributed to Bertrand Russell, asks: in a village in which the barber shaves every man who doesn't shave himself, who shaves the barber?

Here's a statement of the paradox in Alloy:

```
module exercises/barbers
sig Man {shaves: set Man}
one sig Barber extends Man {}
fact {
    Barber.shaves = {m: Man | m not in m.shaves}
    }
```

(a) Use the analyzer to show that the model is indeed inconsistent, at least for a village of small size.

(b) Feminists have noted that the paradox disappears if the existence of women is acknowledged. Make a new version of the model that classifies villagers into men (who need to be shaved) and women (who don't), and show that there is now a simple solution.

(c) A more drastic solution, noted by Edsger Dijkstra [12], is to allow the possibility of there being no barber. Modify the original model accordingly, and show that there is now a solution.

(d) Finally, try a variant of the original model that allows multiple barbers, and show there is again a solution.

♥A.3.4 Halmos's Handshaking Problem

This is a famous problem invented by the mathematician Paul Halmos [24]. Solving the problem by constructing a logical argument is quite challenging, but finding a solution with Alloy is easy.

> Alice and Bob invited four other couples over for a party. Some of them knew each other and some didn't; some were polite and some were not. So there was some handshaking, although not every pair of guests shook hands (and of course nobody shook her own hand or her partner's hand). Being curious, Alice went round and asked at the end of the party how many hands each person had shaken. She got nine different answers from the nine people. How many hands did Bob shake?

(a) Solve the problem by modeling it in Alloy, and using the analyzer to find a solution.

(b) Solving for 10 people will take longer than solving for 4 or 6, so use a smaller number until your confident that your model makes sense.

(c) Might there be another solution, in which Bob shook a different number of hands? Extend your model to allow this to be checked. You might want to refactor it a bit so that the two candidate solutions don't lead to two sets of almost identical constraints.

A.3.5   Goat, Cabbage, Wolf

A farmer wants to ferry across a river a goat, a cabbage, and a wolf, but his boat only has room for him to take one at a time. If he leaves the goat with the cabbage, the goat will eat it; if he leaves the goat with the wolf, the goat will be eaten. How does he do it? Solve the problem by modeling it in Alloy, and using the analyzer to find a solution.

Hint: the standard distribution of Alloy includes a module util/ordering that defines a total ordering. You may find it useful in ordering the steps the farmer takes.

♣A.3.6   Surgeon's Gloves

Another famous problem by Paul Halmos. A surgeon must operate on three patients, but has only two pairs of gloves. There must be no cross-contamination: the surgeon must not come into contact with the blood of any patient, and no patient must come into contact with the blood of another patient. The surgeon needs two hands to work. How does she do it?

Express this problem in Alloy, and use the analyzer to find a solution.

Hint: There are 4 things that need covering (3 patients and one surgeon). The gloves offer 4 resources. The formalization of this problem is much trickier than for the handshake problem. You'll need to express the constraints that the surgeon has to be able to handle the patients (via gloves); to express how contamination is passed on; and the no-contamination condition itself. You might want to associate with each operation a pre and poststate, each of which carries a contamination relation that says what has contaminated what.

A.4 Metamodels

The exercises in this section give practice in constructing metamodels. A metamodel is a model of a collection of models. It need not share the qualities of the models it captures. For example, a metamodel of state machines doesn't have to be dynamic itself: a state machine is just a structure that can be given a dynamic interpretation.

A.4.1 State Machine Definition

A *state machine* has one or more initial states, and a transition relation connecting each state to its successors. Construct an Alloy model of a state machine, and, by adding constraints and having the analyzer solve them, generate a variety of examples of machines:

(a) a *deterministic* machine, in which each state has at most one successor;

(b) a *nondeterministic* machine, in which some states have more than one successor;

(c) a machine with *unreachable* states;

(d) a machine without *unreachable* states;

(e) a *connected* machine in which every state is reachable from every other state;

(f) a machine with a *deadlock*: a reachable state that has no successors;

(g) a machine with a *livelock*: the possibility of an infinite execution in which a state that is always reachable is never reached.

✦A.4.2 State Machine Simulation

Consider two state machines *M1* and *M2* with labeled transitions. A relation *r* from the states of *M1* to the states of *M2* is a *simulation* of *M1* in *M2* if and only if

· whenever *r* relates a state *s1* in *M1* to a state *s2* in *M2*, and *M1* has a transition labeled *a* from *s1* to *s1'*, *M2* also has a transition labeled *a* from *s2* to *s2'* for some *s2'* related by *r* to *s1'*, and

· whenever *s1* is an initial state of *M1*, there is an initial state *s2* of *M2* where *s1* and *s2* are related by *r*.

The relation r is a *bisimulation* if, in addition, $\sim r$ is a simulation of $M2$ in $M1$.

A *trace* of a state machine is a finite sequence of transition labels formed by starting in an initial state and following a path along transitions. The behaviour of a machine can be described by the set of traces it exhibits.

(h) Construct an Alloy model of a state machine with traces, and simulation relations, and generate some examples of machines with their associated trace sets.

(i) Add the notion of simulation, and generate some examples of machines related by simulations.

(j) If there is simulation between two machines, must they have the same trace set? Use Alloy to check this hypothesis. How about a bisimulation?

A.4.3   Metamodel of Alloy

Write an Alloy model of Alloy models. Limit your model to signatures and fields and the relationships between them. To show that your model is sufficiently rich to describe itself, add simulation constraints to get the tool to generate an instance that corresponds to it.

A.4.4   Metamodel of Java

Construct and explore a metamodel of Java, as follows. First, model the class/interface hierarchy, treating classes and interfaces as atoms that are related to one another by relations such as *extends* and *implements*. Then model the declarations of instance variables by associating a source and target class or interface with each. Now model the heap itself as a collection of objects, each of which has an assigned runtime type, and write the constraints that ensure that the heap is well-typed. Use the analyzer to generate some interesting examples.

A.5 Small Case Studies

The exercises in this section involve the construction of small models in well-defined settings.

♣A.5.1 Unix File System

In this exercise, you'll model how pathnames are resolved in the Unix file system, and you'll check some simple properties.

In the Unix file system, each file is represented by an *inode*. The inode includes some basic properties of the file (permission bits, file type, and so on), and has a sequence of ten addresses that point to disk blocks containing the file's data.

In addition, there are three further *indirect* addresses. The first involves one extra level of indirection: it points to a block containing addresses, rather than data, of blocks which hold the data. The second involves two levels of indirection: it points to an address block that points to address blocks that point to data blocks. The third involves three levels.

All the inodes are stored in an array called the *inode table*. The index of a given inode in this array is its *inumber*. A directory is represented as a file whose data consists of a list of inumber/filename pairs. The root directory is associated with some fixed inumber.

Files and directories have *pathnames*. The empty pathname / corresponds to the root directory. In general, given a pathname *p* denoting a directory *d*, the pathname *p/n* denotes the file or directory named *n* in directory *d*. To resolve a pathname, the file system starts at the root directory, and looks up the prefix of the file's pathname. This gives an inumber, which it then looks up in the inode table. The inode obtained is either the file or directory required (if no more of the pathname remains), or another directory, for which the process is repeated (on the rest of the pathname).

This description intentionally includes details that are not relevant to how pathnames are resolved. For example, you will need to consider whether the order of addresses in an inode matters, and if not, what simpler structure than a sequence would suffice.

(a) Start by building a model of the basic structure of inodes, inumbers and blocks. Ignore indirect addressing. Explore some sample structures by writing simulation constraints, adding any invariants that you discover you omitted.

(b) Build a model of pathnames, treating a pathname as a list, consisting of a name (the first element) and a pathname (the rest). Explore some sample pathnames by writing simulation constraints, adding any invariants that you discover you omitted.

(c) Now you're going to combine the two parts of your model, and define a function that models lookup: given a pathname, it will return a set of inodes. You'll want to define lookup recursively, but Alloy functions cannot be recursive. Instead, you can declare a relation corresponding to the lookup, which is defined by a constraint in which the relation name appears on both sides.

(d) Formulate and check two assertions: that each pathname resolves to at most one inode, and that no two distinct pathnames resolve to the same inode. Which of these did you expect to hold? If your analysis reveals flaws in your model, correct them.

(e) Finally, add the notion of indirect addressing. Try to do it in a modular fashion, with as little disruption as possible to your model of name lookup.

♣A.5.2 Railway Switching

In this exercise, you'll construct a simple model of a railway switching system, and you'll check that a switching policy ensures no collisions. You'll make some simplifying assumptions, for example, that a train occupies one track segment at a time, but you'll learn techniques that apply in general, especially how to model a physical environment that allows many arbitrary behaviors (in this case the train movements), and how to separate the requirement (that no collisions occur) from assumptions (that drivers obey signals).

(a) Model the track layout as a collection *Segment* of track segments, with a relation *next* from *Segment* to *Segment*. Segments are physically disjoint, touching each other only at their endpoints, and are directional, with trains assumed to travel from one endpoint to the other. The endpoints are not represented explicitly, though. Instead, we are representing the connection of the exit end of *s1* to the entrance end of *s2* by *next* mapping *s1* to *s2*. Generate some sample layouts, and obtain some nice visualizations using the Alloy Analyzer.

(b) To model the possibility of collision, we might just say that two trains can collide only when they are on the same segment. For a more general notion, which allows for the possibility of a collision between trains on segments that are, for example, parallel to each other, we can declare a relation *overlaps* that represents, very abstractly, the physical layout of the track, mapping a segment *s1* to a segment *s2* when it would be dangerous for one train to be on *s1* and another to be on *s2* at the same time. What properties would you expect this relation to have: is it reflexive, symmetric, transitive? Add the relation to your model, along with a fact recording whichever of these properties you think should hold.

(c) Now you're going to introduce time-varying state. Declare a signature *Train* to represent a set of trains, and a signature *TrainState*, with a relation *on* from *Train* to *Segment* to represent their positions. (Remember that each train can occupy only a single segment.) Define an additional field *occupied* in *TrainState* that holds the set of segments occupied by trains. Generate and visualize some sample states; you'll probably want to use coloring to indicate the occupied the segments.

(d) To describe all physically possible train movements, introduce an operation on *TrainState* that takes as arguments two train states (representing the pre- and poststates), and a set of trains that move, and constrains the train states so that, in this step, each train that moves passes from a segment to one of its successors under the *next* relation. Generate and visualize some sample executions of this operation.

(e) To model the signaling system, introduce a signature *GateState* with a field *closed* whose value is a set of segments, representing those segments beyond which a train is not supposed to travel. Note that there's no need to introduce gates or lights as explicit atoms. Write a predicate that captures legal movements whose arguments are a *GateState*, a *TrainState* and a set of *Trains* that move.

(f) Write a safety condition on *TrainState* saying that trains never occupy overlapping segments, and generate some sample states that satisfy and violate the condition.

(g) The hardest part is designing the mechanism—the policy that determines when gates should be closed. Rather than prescribing exactly when and which gates should be closed, we want to write a condition that imposes some minimal conditions. In this way, we'll actually be checking a whole family of possible mechanisms. Write the policy as a predicate that takes as arguments a *GateState* and a

TrainState. It may say, for example, that if several occupied segments share a successor, then at most one can have an open gate.

(h) Finally, put all the parts together: write an assertion that says that when the trains move, if the mechanism obeys the gate policy, and the train movements are legal, then a collision does not occur (that is, the system does not transition from a safe state to an unsafe state). Check this assertion, and if you find counterexamples, study them carefully, and adjust your model. Most likely, your gate policy will be at fault.

(i) When you are satisfied that the gate policy works as expected (preventing collisions), make sure that you have not overconstrained the model, by generating and visualizing some interesting train movements.

A.5.3 Hotel Locking

In this exercise, you'll build a model of a hotel locking scheme similar to the one described in section 6.2.

In this scheme, described in US Patent 4511946, each keycard holds two separate numbers acting as keys. Each lock likewise has two keys. When the first key on the card matches the first key in the lock, and the second key on the card matches the second key in the lock, the lock opens. When the first key on the card matches the second key in the lock, the door also opens, but the lock is rekeyed with its first and second keys matching the first and second keys of the card respectively. The front desk holds a record of the last key issued for each room, and in addition a set of keys that have been issued. A new card is formed by using the last key issued as the first key, and a fresh key for the second.

(a) Construct a model of this scheme, with operations for checking in, checking out, and entering a room, and use the Alloy Analyzer to generate some scenarios.

(b) Formulate a safety condition that captures the purpose of the scheme—denying access to intruders—and check the model against this condition, reporting any counterexample you find.

(c) This analysis is likely to reveal errors in your model or safety condition. Correct them, check that the safety condition is satisfied, and—to ensure that you have not inadvertently overconstrained the model—regenerate your initial scenarios (at least those that are still valid).

(d) Suppose the hotel guest can make new cards, using the keys from cards obtained legitimately. Alter the entry operation accordingly, and check that the safety condition still holds.

(e) Suppose the scheme is changed so that the door unlocks when the first key on the card matches the first key in the lock (and in this case ignores the second key). Show that in this case, the scheme is susceptible to attack by a dishonest guest who makes new cards.

A.6 Open-Ended Case Studies

Here are some ideas for small case studies in modeling and analysis. They are ordered roughly according to difficulty, easiest first, and might each take between a couple of hours and a few days of work, depending on the depth of the study and the complexity of features considered.

(a) *Organizational Structure.* Model the structure of the organization in which you work, and generate sample instances of the structure. Consider how there might be different, cross-cutting structures for different kinds of function, and explore how these are related to one another.

(b) *Folders in an email client.* Model the folder structure of an email client, with mailboxes containing messages, and folders containing mailboxes, along with operations for moving messages around and altering the folder hierarchy. Consider carefully how to handle special mailboxes, such as an inbox for incoming messages, boxes for messages to be sent and already sent, a box for draft messages, and a box of deleted messages. What properties do these special boxes share with regular boxes and with each other? Do they typically have additional properties?

(c) *Conference Calling.* View a phone system as a collection of endpoints and a centralized database that maintains information about which endpoints are connected to each other. Model the structure of this database, along with the operations that modify it when a conference call is established, when endpoints are added and dropped, etc. Simulate some interesting scenarios, and formulate and check some assertions.

(d) *Do/undo/redo.* Model a standard mechanism for undoing and redoing actions in an application, and analyze it against some fundamental properties formulated as assertions.

(e) *Trash.* Model an operating system's "trash" or "deleted items" folder to which deleted items are moved and from which they can be reinstated. You might want to compare the design in different systems. In Mac OSX, the notion is quite simple: items can be moved out of the trash, but there is no function to reinstate a file or folder in its old location. Windows, in contrast, offers much more elaborate functionality. Can you characterize the essence of trashing as a collection of assertions that relate the basic operations (eg., of creation, deletion, undeletion, etc.) algebraically?

(f) *Domain Name System.* Model and analyze the structure of host names in the standard domain name system, the structure of DNS databases, and the mechanism for resolving names. What kinds of guarantee does DNS offer?

(g) *Elevator control.* Consider a bank of elevators that serves some number of floors. Can you construct a model that describes how elevators behave in response to requests purely in terms of declarative rules? For example, a rule might be: an elevator cannot pass a floor without stopping if there is a request to stop a that floor that came from the pressing of a button within the elevator itself.

(h) *Version control.* Model the abstract view underlying a version control system (such as CVS or Subversion), and the mechanisms it uses. Formulate some critical properties and check them.

(i) *Layers in Photoshop.* Construct an abstract model of Adobe Photoshop's layer functionality, in which an image can be constructed from a stack of layers, each consisting either of a matrix of pixels, or of a transformation function applied to the result of the layers beneath.

Appendix B:
Alloy Language Reference

B.1 Lexical Issues

The permitted characters are the printing characters of the ASCII character set, with the exception of

· backslash \
· backquote `

and, of the ASCII nonprinting characters, only space, horizontal tab, carriage return, and linefeed. Since the encoding of linebreaks varies across platforms, the Alloy Analyzer accepts any of the standard combinations of carriage and linefeed.

The nonalphanumeric symbols are used as operators or for punctuation, with the exception of

· dollar sign $;
· percent sign %;
· question mark ?;
· underscore _;
· single and double quote marks (' and ").

Dollar, percent and question mark are reserved for use in future versions of the language. Underscore and quotes may be used in identifiers. Single and double quote marks (numbered 39 and 34 in ASCII) should not be confused with typographic quote marks and the prime mark, which are not acceptable characters. If text is prepared in a word processor, ensure that a 'smart quotes' feature is not active, since it might generate typographic quote marks from simple ones.

Characters between -- or // and the end of the line, and from /* to */, are treated as comments. Multiple-line comments may not be nested.

Noncomment text is broken into tokens by the following separators:

· whitespace (space, tab, linebreak);
· nonalphanumeric characters (except for underscore and quote marks).

The meaning of the text is independent of its format; in particular, line-breaks are treated as whitespace just like spaces and tabs.

Keywords and identifiers are case sensitive.

Identifiers may include any of the alphabetic characters, and, except as the first character, numbers, underscores, question mark and exclamation point, and quote marks. A hyphen may not appear in an identifier, since it is treated as an operator.

A numeric constant consists of a sequence of digits between 0 and 9, whose first digit is not zero.

The following sequences of characters are recognized as single tokens:

- the double colon :: used for receiver syntax;
- the implication operator =>;
- the integer comparison operators >= and =<;
- the product arrow ->;
- the restriction operators <: and :>;
- the relational override operator ++;
- conjunction && and disjunction ||;
- the comment markings --, //, /* and */.

The negated operators (such as !=) are not treated as single tokens, so they may be written with whitespace between the negation and comparison operators.

The following are reserved as keywords and may not be used for identifiers:

abstract	all	and	as	assert
but	check	disj	else	exactly
extends	fact	for	fun	iden
if	iff	implies	in	Int
int	let	lone	module	no
none	not	one	open	or
part	pred	run	set	sig
some	sum	then	univ	

B.2 Namespaces

Each identifier belongs to a single namespace. There are three namespaces:

- module names and module aliases;

- signatures, fields, paragraphs (facts, functions, predicates and assertions), and bound variables (arguments to functions and predicates, and variables bound by let and quantifiers);
- command names.

Identifiers in different namespaces may share names without risk of name conflict. Within a namespace, the same name may not be used for different identifiers with one exception: bound variables may shadow each other, and may shadow field names. Conventional lexical scoping applies; the innermost binding applies.

B.3 Grammar

The grammar uses the standard BNF operators:

- x^* for zero or more repetitions of x;
- x^+ for one or more repetitions of x;
- $x \mid y$ for a choice of x or y;
- [x] for an optional x.

In addition,

- $x,^*$ means zero or more comma-separated occurrences of x;
- $x,^+$ means one or more comma-separated occurrences of x.

To avoid confusion with grammar symbols, square brackets, star, plus and the vertical bar are set in bold type when they are to be interpreted as terminals.

Every name ending *Id* is an identifier, and is to be treated as a terminal. The terminal *number* represents a numeric constant.

```
module ::= header import* paragraph*
header ::= module [path] moduleId [[ sigId,+ ]]
path ::= directoryId / [path]
import ::= open [path] moduleId [[ sigRef,* ]] [as aliasId]

paragraph ::=
    sigDecl | factDecl | funDecl | predDecl | assertDecl | runCmd | check-
Cmd

sigDecl ::=
    [abstract] [mult] sig sigID,+ [extends sigRef] sigBody
    | [mult] sig sigID,+ in sigRef sigBody
sigBody ::= { decl,* } [constraintSeq]
```

factDecl ::= **fact** *[*factId*]* constraintSeq
assertDecl ::= **assert** *[*assertId*]* constraintSeq
funDecl ::= **fun** *[*sigRef **::***]* funId (decl,*) : declExpr { expr }
predDecl ::= **pred** *[*sigRef **::***]* predId (decl,*) constraintSeq

runCmd ::=
   *[*commandId **:***]* **run** funRef *[*scope*]*
   *[*commandId **:***]* **run** predRef *[*scope*]*
checkCmd ::= *[*commandId **:***]* **check** assertRef *[*scope*]*

scope ::= **for** number
   | **for** *[*number **but***]* typescope,⁺
typescope ::= *[***exactly***]* number scopeable
scopeable ::= sigRef | **int**

decl ::= *[***part** | **disj***]* varId,⁺ : declExpr
letDecl ::= varId = expr
declExpr ::= declSetExpr | declRelExpr
declSetExpr ::= *[*mult*]* expr
declRelExpr ::= declRelExpr′ *[*mult*]* -> *[*mult*]* declRelExpr′
declRelExpr′ ::= declRelExpr | expr
mult ::= **lone** | **one** | **some**

expr ::= *[*@*]* varId | sigRef | **this** |
   | **none** | **univ** | **iden**
   | unOp expr | expr binOp expr | expr[expr]
   | { decl,⁺ | *[*constraint*]* }
   | **let** letDecl,⁺ | expr
   | **if** constraint **then** expr **else** expr
   | **Int** intExpr
   | *[*expr **::***]* funRef (expr,*)
   | (expr)

intExpr ::= number | **#** expr | **sum** expr | **int** expr
   | **if** constraint **then** intExpr **else** intExpr
   | intExpr intOp intExpr
   | **let** letDecl,... | intExpr
   | **sum** decl,⁺ | intExpr
   | (intExpr)
intOp ::= **+** | **-**

constraintBody ::= constraintSeq | | | constraint
constraintSeq ::= { constraint* }
constraint ::= expr [neg] compOp expr
    | quantifier expr
    | intExpr [neg] intCompOp intExpr
    | neg constraint | constraint logicOp constraint
    | constraint thenOp constraint [elseOp constraint]
    | quantifier decl,⁺ constraintBody
    | **let** letDecl,⁺ constraintBody
    | [expr ::] predRef (expr,*)
    | expr : declExpr
    | constraintSeq
    | (constraint)

thenOp ::= **implies** | =>
elseOp ::= **else** | ,

neg ::= **not** | !
logicOp ::= && | || | **iff** | <=> | **and** | **or**
quantifier ::= **all** | **no** | mult
binOp ::= + | - | & | . | -> | <: | :> | ++
unOp ::= ~ | * | ^
compOp ::= **in** | =

intCompOp ::= < | > | = | =< | >=

funRef ::= [moduleRef] funId
predRef ::= [moduleRef] predId
assertRef ::= [moduleRef] assertId
sigRef ::= [moduleRef] sigId | **Int** | **univ**
moduleRef ::= [path] moduleId [[sigRef,*]] / | aliasId /

B.4   Precedence and Associativity

The precedence order for logical operators, tightest first, is

- negation operators: *!* and *not*;
- conjunction: *&&* and *and*;
- implication: *=>*, *<=>*, *implies* and *iff*;
- disjunction: *||* and *or*.

The precedence order for expression operators, tightest first, is

- unary operators: ~, ^ and *;
- dot join: . ;
- restriction operators: <: and :>;
- brackets join: [];
- arrow product: ->;
- intersection: &;
- override: ++;
- union and difference: + and -.

Note that in particular dot binds more tightly than brackets, so *a.b[c]* is parsed as *(a.b)[c]*.

All binary operators associate to the left, with the exception of implication, which associates to the right. So, for example, $p \Rightarrow q \Rightarrow r$ is parsed as $p \Rightarrow (q \Rightarrow r)$, and *a.b.c* is parsed as *(a.b).c*.

In an implication, an else-clause is associated with its closest then-clause. So the constraint

$$p \Rightarrow q \Rightarrow r, s$$

for example, is parsed as

$$p \Rightarrow (q \Rightarrow r, s)$$

B.5   Semantic Basis

B.5.1 Instances and Meaning

A model's meaning is several collections of *instances*. An instance is a binding of values to variables. Typically, a single instance represents a state, or a pair of states (corresponding to execution of an operation), or an execution trace. The language has no built-in notion of state machines, however, so an instance need not represent any of these things.

The collections of instances assigned to a model are:

- A set of *core instances* associated with the facts of the model, and the constraints implicit in the signature declarations. These instances have as their variables the signatures and their fields, and they bind values to them that make the facts and declaration constraints true.
- For each function or predicate, a set of those instances for which the facts and declaration constraints of the model as a whole are true,

and additionally the constraint of the function or predicate is true. The variables of these instances are those of the core instances, extended with the arguments of the function or predicate.

- For each assertion, a set of those instances for which the facts and declaration constraints of the model as a whole are true, but for which the constraint of the assertion is false.

A model without any core instances is *inconsistent,* and almost certainly erroneous. A function or predicate without instances is likewise inconsistent, and is unlikely to be useful. An assertion is expected not to have any instances: the instances are *counterexamples,* which indicate that the assertion does not follow from the facts.

The Alloy Analyzer finds instances of a model automatically by search within finite bounds (specified by the user as a *scope*; see subsection B.7.5 below). Because the search is bounded, failure to find an instance does not necessarily mean that one does not exist. But instances that are found are guaranteed to be valid.

B.5.2 Relational Logic

Alloy is a first-order relational logic. The values assigned to variables, and the values of expressions evaluated in the context of a given instance, are *relations.* These relations are first order: that is, they consist of tuples whose elements are atoms (and not themselves relations).

Alloy has no explicit notion of sets, scalars, or tuples. A set is simply a unary relation; a scalar is a singleton, unary relation; and a tuple is a singleton relation. The type system distinguishes sets from relations because they have different arity, but does not distinguish tuples and scalars from more general relations.

There is no function application operator. Relational join is used in its place, and is syntactically cleaner that it would be in a language that distinguished sets and scalars. For example, given a relation f that is functional, and x and y constrained to be scalars, the constraint

$$x.f = y$$

constrains the image of x under the relation f to be the set y. So long as x is in the domain of f, this constraint will have the same meaning as it would if the dot were interpreted as function application, f as a function, and x and y as scalar-typed variables. But if x is out of the domain of f, the expression $x.f$ will evaluate to the empty set, and since y is constrained to be a scalar (that is, a singleton set), the constraint as a whole will be false. In a language with function application, various meanings are possible, depending on how partial functions are handled. An advantage of the Alloy approach is that it sidesteps this issue.

The declaration syntax of Alloy has been designed so that familiar forms have their expected meaning. Thus, when X is a set, the quantified constraint

> **all** x: X | F

has x range over scalar values. That is, the constraint F is evaluated for bindings of x to singleton subsets of X.

The syntax of Alloy does in fact admit higher-order quantifications. For example, the assertion that join is associative over binary relations may be written

> **assert** {**all** p, q, r: **univ** -> **univ** | (p.q).r = p.(q.r)}

Many such constraints become first order when presented for analysis, since (as here) the quantified variables can be skolemized away. If a constraint remains truly higher order, the Alloy Analyzer will warn the user that analysis is likely to be infeasible.

Alloy provides rudimentary support for integers. There is a class of expressions whose values are integers. Integer values may not be bound to variables in instances, but there is a special class of integer atoms that are associated with primitive integer values, and which may appear in relations that are bound to variables like any other atoms. See subsection B.7.7 for more details.

B.6   Types and Overloading

Alloy's type system was designed with a different aim from that of a programming language. There is no notion in a modeling language of a "runtime error," so type soundness is not an issue. Instead, the type system is designed to allow as many reasonable models as possible, without generating false alarms, while still catching prior to analysis those errors that can be explained in terms of the types of declared fields and variables alone.

We expect most users to be able to ignore the subtleties of the type system. Error messages reporting that an expression is ill-typed are never spurious, and always correspond to a real error. Messages reporting failure to resolve an overloaded field reference can always be handled by a small and systematic modification, explained below.

B.6.1 Type Errors

Three kinds of type error are reported:

- An *arity error* indicates an attempt to apply an operator to an expression of the wrong arity, or to combine expressions of incompatible arity. Examples include taking the closure of a nonbinary relation; restricting a relation to a non-set; taking the union, intersection, or difference, or comparing with equality or subset, two relations of different arity.

- A *disjointness error* indicates an expression in which two relations are combined in such a way that the result will always be the empty relation, irrespective of their value. Examples include taking the intersection of two relations that do not intersect; joining two relations that have no matching elements; and restricting a relation with a set disjoint from it. Applying the overriding operator to disjoint relations also generates a disjointess error, even though the result may not be the empty relation, since the relations are expected to overlap (a union sufficing otherwise).

- A *redundancy error* indicates that an expression (usually appearing in a union expression) is redundant, and could be dropped without affecting the value of the enclosing constraint. Examples include expressions such as *(a+b)&c* and constraints such as *c in a+b*, where one of *a* or *b* is disjoint from *c*.

Note that unions of disjoint types *are* permitted, because they might not be erroneous. Thus the expression *(a+b).c*, for example, will be type correct even if *a* and *b* have disjoint types, so long as the type of the leftmost column of *c* overlaps with the types of the right-hand columns of both *a* and *b*.

B.6.2 Field Overloading

Fields of signatures may be overloaded. That is, two distinct signatures may have fields of the same name, so long as the signatures do not represent sets that overlap. Field references are resolved automatically.

Resolution of overloading exploits the full context of an expression, and uses the same information used by the type checker. Each possible resolving of an overloaded reference is considered. If there is exactly one that would not generate a type error, it is chosen. If there is more than one, an error message is generated reporting an ambiguous reference.

Resolution takes advantage of all that is known about the types of the possible resolvents, including arity, and the types of all columns (not only the first). Thus, in contrast to the kind of resolution used for field dereferencing in object-oriented languages (such as Java), the reference to f in an expression such as $x.f$ can be resolved not only by using the type of x but by using in addition the context in which the entire expression appears. For example, if the enclosing expression were $a+x.f$, the reference f could be resolved by the arity of a.

If a field reference cannot be resolved, it is easy to modify the expression so that it can be. If a field reference f is intended to refer to the field f declared in signature S, one can replace a reference to f by the expression $S <: f$. This new expression has the same meaning, but is guaranteed to resolve the reference, since only the f declared in S will produce a non-empty result. Note that this is *not* a special casting syntax. It relies only on the standard semantics of the domain restriction operator.

B.6.3 Subtypes

The type system includes a notion of subtypes. This allows more errors to be caught, and permits a finer-grained namespace for fields.

The type of any expression is a *union type* consisting of the union of some relation types. A *relation type* is a product of basic types. A basic type is either a signature type, the predefined universal type *univ*, or the predefined empty type *none*. The basic types form a lattice, with *univ* as its maximal, and *none* as its minimal, element. The lattice is obtained from the forest of trees of declared signature types, augmented with the subtype relationship between top-level types and *univ*, and between *none* and all signature types.

The union consisting of no relation types is used in type checking to represent ill-typed expressions, and is distinct from the union consisting of a relation type that is a product of *none*'s (which is used for expressions constructed with the constant *none*, representing an intentionally empty relation).

The semantics of subtyping is very simple. If one signature is a subtype of another, it represents a subset. The immediate subtypes of a signature are disjoint. Two subtypes therefore overlap only if one is, directly or indirectly, a subtype of the other. The type system computes a type for an expression that is an approximation to its value. Consider, for example, the join

    e1 . e2

where the subexpressions have types

    e1 : A->B
    e2 : C->D

If the basic types B and C do not overlap, the join gives rise to a disjointness error. Otherwise, one of B or C must be a subtype of the other. The type of the expression as a whole will be A->D.

No casts are needed, either upward or downward. If a field f is declared in a signature S, and sup and sub are respectively variables whose types are a supertype and subtype of S, both $sup.f$ and $sub.f$ will be well-typed. In neither case is the expression necessarily empty. In both cases it may be empty: if sup is not in S or f is declared to be partial and sub is outside its domain. On the other hand, if d is a variable whose type D is disjoint from the type of S—for example, because both S and D are immediate subtypes of some other signature—the expression $d.f$ will be ill-typed, since it must always evaluate to the empty relation.

B.6.4 Functions and Predicates

Invocations of functions and predicates are type-checked by ensuring that the actual argument expressions are not disjoint from the formal arguments. The types of formals are *not* used to resolve overloading of field names in actual expressions.

The constraints implicit in the declarations of arguments of functions and predicates are conjoined to the body constraint when a function or predicate is run. When a function or predicate is invoked, however, these implicit constraints are ignored. You should therefore not rely on such declaration constraints to have a semantic effect; they are intended as redundant documentation. A future version of Alloy may include a checking scheme that determines whether actual expressions have values compatible with the declaration constraints of formals.

B.6.5 Integers and Type Checking

Only integer expressions take on primitive integer values. The parser distinguishes between relational expressions and integer expressions, so type information is not needed to resolve the overloading of the plus and minus operators (which act as addition and subtraction for integer expressions, and union and difference for relational expressions). In a constraint such as

    # S + S =1

the plus symbol will be parsed as a relational operator (and the # operator will be applied to the entire left-hand side), since otherwise the constraint as a whole would not be syntactically valid.

The *Int* type, which represents the predefined signature for integer-carrying objects, is treated by the type system like any other basic type. It is disjoint from all other basic types except for the universal type *univ*.

B.6.6 Multiplicity Keywords

Alloy uses the following *multiplicity keywords* shown with their interpretations:

- *lone*: zero or one;
- *one*: exactly one;
- *some*: one or more.

To remember that *lone* means zero or one, it may help to think of the word as short for "less than or equal to one."

These keywords are used in several contexts:

- as quantifiers in quantified constraints: the constraint *one x: S | F*, for example, says that there is exactly one *x* that satisfies the constraint *F*;

- as quantifiers in quantified expressions: the constraint *lone e*, for example, says that the expression *e* denotes a relation with containing at most one tuple;

- in set declarations: the declaration *x: some S*, for example, where *S* has unary type, declares *x* to be a set of elements drawn from *S* that is nonempty;

- in relation declarations: the declaration *r: A one->one B*, for example, declares *r* to be a one-to-one relation from *A* to *B*.

- in signature declarations: the declaration *one sig S {...}*, for example, declares *S* to be a signature whose set contains exactly one element.

When declaring a set variable, the default is *one*, so in a declaration *x: X* in which *X* has unary type, *x* will be constrained to be a scalar. In this case, the *set* keyword overrides the default.

B.7 Language Features

B.7.1 Module Structure

The productions discussed in this section are

> **module** ::= header import* paragraph*
> header ::= **module** *[path]* moduleId *[* **[** sigId,⁺ **]** *]*
> import ::= **open** *[path]* moduleId *[* **[** sigRef,* **]** *]* *[* **as** aliasId *]*
> paragraph ::= sigDecl | factDecl | funDecl | predDecl | assertDecl
> | runCmd | checkCmd
> path ::= id / *[path]*
> sigRef ::= *[moduleRef]* sigId | **Int** | **univ**
> moduleRef ::= *[path]* moduleId *[* **[** sigRef,* **]** *]* | aliasId
> funRef ::= *[moduleRef]* funId
> predRef ::= *[moduleRef]* predId
> assertRef ::= *[moduleRef]* assertId

An Alloy model consists of one or more *files*, each containing a single *module*. One "main" module is presented for analysis; it *imports* other modules directly (through its own imports) or indirectly (through imports of imported modules).

A module consists of a header identifying the module, some imports, and some paragraphs:

> **module** ::= header import* paragraph*

A model can be contained entirely within one module, in which case no imports are necessary. A module without paragraphs is syntactically valid but useless.

The paragraphs of a module are signatures, facts, functions, predicates, assertions, run commands, and check commands:

> paragraph ::= sigDecl | factDecl | funDecl | predDecl | assertDecl
> | runCmd | checkCmd

Signatures represent sets and are assigned values in analysis; they therefore play a role similar to static variables in a programming language. Facts, functions, and predicates are packagings of constraints. Commands are used to instruct the Alloy Analyzer to perform various analyses. A module exports as components all paragraphs except for commands; only the commands of the main module are relevant in an analysis.

A module is named by a *path* and a *module identifier*, and may be *parameterized* by one or more signature parameters:

> header ::= **module** *[path]* moduleId *[[* sigId,⁺ *]]*
> path ::= id / *[path]*

The path must correspond to the directory location of the module's file with respect to a default root directory. A set of root directories may be specified in the Alloy Analyzer, so that libraries and domain-specific models, for example, may be kept in different locations. A module with the module identifier *m* must be stored in the file named *m.als*.

A separate import is needed for each imported module. It gives the path and name of the imported module, instantiations of its parameters (if any), and optionally an alias:

> import ::= **open** *[path]* moduleId *[[* sigRef,* *]]* *[as* aliasId*]*
> sigRef ::= *[moduleRef]* sigId | **Int** | **univ**

There must be an instantiating signature parameter for each parameter of the imported module. An instantiating signature may be a type, subtype, or subset, or one of the predefined types *Int* and *univ*. If the imported module declares a signature that is an extension of a signature parameter, instantiating that parameter with a subset or with *Int* will be an error.

A single module may be imported more than once. The result is *not* to create multiple copies of the same module, but rather to make a single module available under different names.

A component of an imported module is referred to by its *qualified name*, consisting of the module reference and the component name:

> sigRef ::= *[moduleRef]* sigId | **Int** | **univ**
> funRef ::= *[moduleRef]* funId
> predRef ::= *[moduleRef]* predId
> assertRef ::= *[moduleRef]* assertId

When a component reference would be ambiguous, it *must* be qualified. Components declared in the same module in which they are referenced need not be qualified. A module may also be given an *alias* when imported to allow more succinct qualified names. If an alias is declared, the regular module name may not be used.

The module reference may be either the path and module identifier of the imported module along with any instantiating parameters (exactly as it appears in the import statement), or an alias if one was declared in the import:

> moduleRef ::= *[path]* moduleId *[[* sigRef,* *]]* / | aliasId /

Paragraphs may appear in a module in any order. There is no requirement of definition before use. The order of import statements is also immaterial, even if one provides instantiating parameters to another.

The signature *Int* is a special predefined signature representing integers, and can be used without an explicit import.

A module may not contain references to components of another module that it does not import, even if that module is imported along with it in another module.

Module names occupy their own namespace, and may thus coincide with the names of signatures, paragraphs, arguments, or variables without conflict.

B.7.2 Signature Declarations

The productions discussed in this section are

> sigDecl ::=
>   *[abstract]* *[mult]* **sig** sigID,⁺ *[extends* sigRef*]* sigBody
> | *[mult]* **sig** sigID,⁺ **in** sigRef sigBody
> sigRef ::= *[moduleRef]* sigId | **Int**
> sigBody ::= **{** decl,* **}** *[constraintSeq]*
> constraintSeq ::= **{** constraint* **}**
> moduleRef ::= *[path]* moduleId *[[* sigRef,* *]]* | aliasId
> mult ::= **lone** | **one** | **some**

A *signature* represents a set of atoms. There are two kinds of signature. A signature declared using the *in* keyword is a *subset signature*:

> sigDecl ::= *[mult]* **sig** sigID,⁺ **in** sigRef sigBody

All other signatures are *type signatures*:

> sigDecl ::= *[abstract]* *[mult]* **sig** sigID,⁺ *[extends* sigRef*]* sigBody

A type signature plays the role of a type or subtype in the type system. A type signature that does not extend another signature is a *top-level* signature, and its type is a *top-level type*. A signature that extends another signature is said to be a *subsignature* of the signature it extends, and its type is taken to be a subtype of the type of the signature extended. A signature may not extend itself, directly or indirectly. The type signatures therefore form a type hierarchy whose structure is a forest: a collection of trees rooted in the top-level types.

Top-level signatures represent mutually disjoint sets, and subsignatures of a signature are mutually disjoint. Any two distinct type signatures are thus *disjoint* unless one extends the other, directly or indirectly, in which case they *overlap*.

A subset signature represents a set of elements that is a subset of the union of its *parents*: the signatures listed in its declaration. These may be subset or type signatures. A subset signature may not be extended, and subsets of a signature are not necessarily mutually disjoint. A subset signature may not be its own parent, directly or indirectly. The subset signatures and their parents therefore form a directed acyclic graph, rooted in type signatures. The type of a subset signature is in general a union of top-level types or subtypes, consisting of the parents of the subset that are types, and the types of the parents that are subsets.

An *abstract signature*, marked *abstract*, is constrained to hold only those elements that belong to one of the signatures that extends it. If there are no extensions, the marking has no effect. The intent is that an abstract signature represents a classification of elements that is refined further by more 'concrete' signatures. If it has no extensions, the *abstract* keyword is likely an indication that the model is incomplete.

Any multiplicity keyword (with the exception of *set*, since it has no effect) may be associated with a signature, and constrains the signature's set to have the number of elements specified by the multiplicity.

The body of a signature declaration consists of declarations of *fields* and an optional *signature fact* constraining the elements of the signature:

> sigBody ::= { decl,* } *[*constraintSeq*]*

A subtype signature *inherits* the fields of the signature it extends, along with any fields that signature inherits. A subset signature inherits the fields of its parent signatures, along with their inherited fields.

A signature may not declare a field whose name conflicts with the name of an inherited field. Moreover, two subset signatures may not declare a field of the same name if their types overlap. This ensures that two fields of the same name can only be declared in disjoint signatures, and there is always a context in which two fields of the same name can be distinguished. If this were not the case, some overloadings would never be resolvable.

Like any other fact, the signature fact is a constraint that always holds. Unlike other facts, however, a signature fact is implicitly quantified over the signature set. Given the signature declaration

sig S {...} { *F* }

the signature fact *F* is interpreted as if one had written an explicit fact

fact { **all this:** S | *F′* }

where *F′* is like *F*, but has each reference to a field *f* of S (whether declared or inherited) replaced by *this.f*. Prefixing a field name with the special symbol @ suppresses this implicit expansion.

Declaring multiple signatures at once in a single signature declaration is equivalent to declaring each individually. Thus the declaration

sig A, B **extends** C {f: D}

for example, introduces two subsignatures, *A* and *B*, of *C*, and for each declares a field *f*.

B.7.3 Declarations

The productions discussed in this section are

```
decl ::= [part | disj] varId,⁺ : declExpr
declExpr ::= declSetExpr | declRelExpr
declSetExpr ::= [mult] expr
declRelExpr ::= declRelExpr′ [mult] -> [mult] declRelExpr′
declRelExpr′ ::= declRelExpr | expr
mult ::= lone | one | some
```

The same declaration syntax is used for fields of signatures, arguments to functions and predicates, and quantified variables, all of which we shall here refer to as *variables*. The interpretation for fields, which is slightly different, is explained second.

A declaration introduces one or more variables, and constrains their values and type:

```
decl ::= [part | disj] varId,⁺ : declExpr
```

A declaration has two effects:

- Semantically, it constrains the *value* a variable can take. The relation denoted by the variable (on the left) is constrained to be a subset of the relation denoted by the declaration expression (on the right). When more than one variable is declared at once, the keywords *disj* and *part* may be used. The keyword *disj* constrains the declared variables to be mutually disjoint. The keyword *part* constrains them additionally to form a partition of the relation denoted by the declaration expression. Multiplicity constraints, explained below, constrain the value of a variable further.

- For the purpose of type checking, a declaration gives the variable a *type*. A type is determined for the declaration expression, and that type is assigned to the variable. Any variable that appears in the declaration expression must have been declared already, either earlier in the sequence of declarations in which this declaration appears, or earlier elsewhere. For a quantified variable, this means within an enclosing quantifier; for a field of a signature, this means that the field is inherited; for a function or predicate argument, this means in the argument declarations of the enclosing function or predicate.

Note that the declaration expression of a field declaration in a signature may not refer to fields declared in other signatures, unless they are inherited.

The declaration expression is an arbitrary expression. If the expression denotes a set (that is, a unary relation), it may be prefixed by a multiplicity keyword:

declExpr ::= [mult | **set**] expr
mult ::= **lone** | **one** | **some**

If the keyword is omitted, the declared variable is constrained by default to be a *scalar* (that is, to be a singleton set). The keyword *set* eliminates this constraint; *lone* weakens it to allow the variable to denote an "option": either a singleton set or the empty set; *some* constrains the variable to denote a nonempty set; and *one* has no effect, being equivalent to omission.

If the expression does not denote a set (that is, its arity is two or more), multiplicity keywords may not be used as a prefix. If the expression is formed with the arrow operator, the arrow itself may be elaborated with multiplicity keywords:

declRelExpr ::= declRelExpr' [mult] -> [mult] declRelExpr'
declRelExpr' ::= declRelExpr | expr
mult ::= **lone** | **one** | **some**

If the declaration expression has the form *e1 m->n e2*, where *m* and *n* are multiplicity keywords, the declaration imposes a *multiplicity constraint* on the declared variable. An arrow expression of this form denotes the relation whose tuples are concatenations of the tuples in *e1* and the tuples in *e2*. If the marking *n* is present, the relation denoted by the declared variable is required to contain, for each tuple *t1* in *e1*, *n* tuples that begin with *t1*. If the marking *m* is present, the relation denoted by the declared variable is required to contain, for each tuple *t2* in *e2*, *m* tuples that end with *t2*. The markings are interpreted as follows:

- *lone* means zero or one;
- *one* means exactly one;
- *some* means one or more.

When the expressions *e1* and *e2* are unary, these reduce to familiar notions. For example, a declaration expression of the form X->*one* Y makes the variable a total function from X to Y; the expression X->*lone* Y makes it an partial function; and X *one*->*one* Y makes it a bijection.

Multiplicity markings can be used in nested arrow expressions. For example, a declaration of the form

r: *e1* *m* -> *n* (*e2* *m'* -> *n'* (*e3*)

produces the constraints described above (due to the multiplicity keywords *m* and *n*), but it produces additional constraints (due to *m'* and *n'*). The constraints for the nested expression are the same multiplicity constraints as for a top-level arrow expression, but applied to each image of a tuple under the declared relation that produces a value for the nested expression. For example, if *e1* denotes a set, the constraint is equivalent to the constraint of the declaration

all x: e1 | x.r : *e2* *m'* -> *n'* (*e3*

If *e1* is not a set, the quantification must range over the appropriate tuples. For example, if *e1* is binary, the constraint would be equivalent to the constraint of the declaration

all x, y: **univ** | x->y **in** e1 => x.(y.r) : *e2* *m'* -> *n'* (*e3*

Declarations within a signature have essentially the same interpretation. But for a field *f*, the declaration constraints apply not to *f* itself but to *this.f*: that is, to the value obtained by dereferencing an element of the signature with *f*. Thus, for example, the declaration

sig S {f: e}

does not constrain *f* to be a subset of *e* (as it would if *f* were a regular variable), but rather implies

all this: S | this.f **in** e

Moreover, any field appearing in *e* is expanded according to the rules of signature facts (see section B.7.2). A similar treatment applies to multiplicity constraints and *disj/part*. In this case, for example, if *e* denotes a unary relation, the implicit multiplicity constraint will make *this.f* a scalar, so that *f* itself will denote a total function on *S*.

Type checking of fields has the same flavor. The field *f* is not assigned the type *e*, but rather the type of the expression *S->e*. That is, the domain of the relation *f* has the type *S*, and *this.f* has the same type as *e*.

B.7.4 Constraint Paragraphs

The productions discussed in this section are

```
factDecl ::= fact [factId] constraintSeq
predDecl ::= pred [sigRef ::] predId ( decl,* ) constraintSeq
funDecl ::= fun [sigRef ::] funId ( decl,*) : declExpr { expr }
assertDecl ::= assert [assertId] constraintSeq
constraintSeq ::= { constraint* }
constraint ::= ... | [expr ::] predRef ( expr,* )
expr ::= ... | [expr ::] funRef ( expr,* )
```

A *fact* is a constraint that always holds. A *predicate* is a template for a constraint that can be instantiated in different contexts. A *function* is a template for an expression. An *assertion* is a constraint that is intended to follow from the facts of a model; it is thus an intentional redundancy. Assertions can be checked by the Alloy Analyzer; functions and predicates can be simulated.

A fact can be named for documentation purposes. An assertion can be named or anonymous, but since a command to check an assertion must name it, an anonymous assertion cannot be checked. Functions and predicates must always be named.

A fact consists of an optional name and a constraint, given as a sequence of constraints, which are implicitly conjoined:

```
factDecl ::= fact [factId] constraintSeq
```

A predicate declaration consists of the name of the predicate, some argument declarations, and a constraint, given as a sequence of constraints, which are implicitly conjoined:

```
predDecl ::= pred [sigRef ::] predId ( decl,* ) constraintSeq
```

The argument declarations may include a first argument declared anonymously. When a predicate is declared in the form

pred S::f (...) {...}

the first argument is taken to be a scalar of signature *S*, which is referred to within the body of the predicate using the keyword *this*, as if the declaration had been written

pred f (**this**: S, ...) {...}

A function declaration consists of the name of the function, some argument declarations, and an expression:

funDecl ::= **fun** *[sigRef ::]* funId (decl,*) : declExpr **{ expr }**

The argument declarations include a declaration expression for the result of the function, corresponding to the value of the expression. The first argument may be declared anonymously, exactly as for predicates.

A predicate may be invoked as a constraint by providing an expression for each argument:

constraint ::= *[expr ::]* predRef (expr,*)

A function likewise may be invoked as an expression by providing an expression for each argument:

expr ::= *[expr ::]* funRef (expr,*)

Invocation can be viewed as textual inlining. An invocation of a predicate gives a constraint which is obtained by taking the constraint of the predicate's body, and replacing the formal arguments by the corresponding expressions of the invocation. Likewise, invocation of a function gives an expression obtained by taking the expression of the function's body, and replacing the formal arguments of the function by the corresponding expressions of the invocation. Recursive invocations are not currently supported.

A function or predicate invocation may present its first argument in receiver position. So instead of writing

p (a, b, c)

for example, one can write

a::p (b, c)

The form of invocation is not constrained by the form of declaration. Although often a function or predicate will be both declared with an anonymous receiver argument and used with receiver syntax, this is not necessary. The first argument may be presented as a receiver irrespective of the format of declaration, and the first argument may be declared anonymously irrespective of the format of use. In particular, it can be convenient to invoke a function or predicate in receiver form when the first argument is not a scalar, even though it cannot be declared with receiver syntax in that case.

Within a module, no two constraint paragraphs may be declared with the same name, nor may a constraint paragraph have the same name as a signature.

B.7.5 Commands

The productions discussed in this section are

> runCmd ::=
>   [commandId :] **run** funRef [scope]
>   [commandId :] **run** predRef [scope]
> checkCmd ::= [commandId :] **check** assertRef [scope]
> scope ::= **for** number
> | **for** [number **but**] typescope,+
> typescope ::= [**exactly**] number scopeable
> scopeable ::= sigRef | **int**
> sigRef ::= [moduleRef] sigId | **Int** | **univ**

A command is an instruction to the Alloy Analyzer to perform an analysis. Analysis involves constraint solving: finding an *instance* that satisfies a constraint. A *run* command causes the analyzer to search for an *example* that witnesses the consistency of a function or a predicate. A *check* command causes it to search for a *counterexample* showing that an assertion does not hold.

A command to run a function or predicate consists of an optional command name, the keyword *run*, a reference to the function or predicate, and, optionally, a scope specification:

> runCmd ::=
>   [commandId :] **run** funRef [scope]
>   [commandId :] **run** predRef [scope]

Similarly, a command to check an assertion consists of an optional command name, the keyword *check*, a reference to the assertion, and, optionally, a scope specification:

> checkCmd ::= [commandId :] **check** assertRef [scope]

The command name is used in the user interface of the Alloy Analyzer (or at the command line) to select the command to be executed. In the graphical user interface, the command is selected from a pop-up menu; the only reason for the command name is to allow commands to be more easily recognized when there are many commands for the same assertion, function, or predicate. No two commands in a module may have the same command names.

As explained in section B.5, analysis always involves solving a constraint. For a predicate with body constraint P, the constraint solved is

P and F and D

where F is the conjunction of all facts, and D is the conjunction of all declaration constraints, including the declarations of the predicate's arguments. Note that when the predicate's body is empty, the constraint is simply the facts and declaration constraints of the model. An empty predicate is often a useful starting point in analysis to determine whether the model is consistent, and, if so, to examine some of its instances.

For a function named f whose body expression is E, the constraint solved is

f = E and F and D

where F is the conjunction of all facts, and D is the conjunction of all declaration constraints, including the declarations of the function arguments. The variable f stands for the value of the expression.

Note that the declaration constraints of a predicate or function are used when that function or predicate is run, but are ignored when the predicate or function is invoked.

For an assertion whose body constraint is A, the constraint solved is

F and D and not A

namely the negation of

F and D implies A

where F is the conjunction of all facts, and D is the conjunction of all declaration constraints.

An instance found by the analyzer will assign values to the following variables:

· the signatures and fields of the model;

· for an instance of a predicate or function, the arguments of the function or predicate, one of which will be named *this* if the first argument is declared anonymously;

· for an instance of function, a variable denoting the value of the expression, with the same name as the function itself.

The analyzer may also give values to skolem constants as witnesses for existential quantifications. Whether it does so, and whether existentials inside universals are skolemized, depends on preferences set by the user.

The search for an instance is conducted within a *scope*, which is specified as follows:

scope ::= **for** number
    | **for** *[*number **but***]* typescope,⁺
typescope ::= *[***exactly***]* number scopeable
scopeable ::= sigRef | **int**
sigRef ::= *[*moduleRef*]* sigId | **Int** | **univ**

The *scope specification* of a command places bounds on the sizes of the sets assigned to type signatures, thus making the search finite. Only type signatures are involved; subset signatures may not be bounded in a scope specification. For the rest of this section, "signature" should be read as synonymous with "type signature."

The bounds are determined as follows:

· If no scope specification is given, a default scope of 3 elements is used: each top-level signature is constrained to represent a set of at most 3 elements.

· If the scope specification takes the form *for N*, a default of *N* is used instead.

· If the scope specification takes the form *for N but ...*, every signature listed following *but* is constrained by its given bound, and any top-level signature whose bound is not given implicitly is bounded by the default *N*.

· Otherwise, for an explicit list without a default, each signature listed is constrained by the given bound.

Implicit bounds are determined as follows:

· If an abstract signature has no explicit bound, but its subsignatures have bounds, implicit or explicit, its bound is the sum of those of its subsignatures.

· If an abstract signature has a bound, explicit or by default, and all but one of its subsignatures have bounds, implicit or explicit, the bound of the remaining subsignature is the difference between the abstract signature's bound and the sum of the bounds of the other subsignatures.

· A signature declared with the multiplicity keyword *one* has a bound of 1.

· If an implicit bound cannot be determined for a signature by these rules, the signature has no implicit bound.

If a scope specification uses the keyword *exactly*, the bound is taken to be both an upper and lower bound on the cardinality of the signature. The rules for implicit bounds are adjusted accordingly. For example, an abstract signature whose subsignatures are constrained exactly will likewise be constrained exactly.

The scope specification must be

· *consistent*: at most one bound must be associated with any signature, implicitly, explicitly, or by default;

· *complete*: every top-level signature must have a bound;

· *uniform*: a signature without a bound may not have a subsignature that has a bound.

By default, the predefined signature *Int* is limited to 3 elements, so that there may be at most 3 integer objects appearing in an instance or counterexample. The bound on the integer values represented by these integer objects, and on the values of integer expressions, may be altered by assigning a bound to *int*. A bound of k for *int* limits integer values to be between 0 and $2^k -$. Its default is 5, so integers by default range from 0 to 31.

B.7.6 Expressions

The productions discussed in this section are

```
expr ::= [@] varId | sigRef | this |
    | none | univ | iden
    | unOp expr | expr binOp expr | expr[ expr ]
    | { decl,⁺ | [constraint] }
    | let letDecl,⁺ | expr
    | if constraint then expr else expr
    | ( expr )
letDecl ::= varId = expr
binOp ::= + | - | & | . | -> | <: | :> | ++
unOp ::= ~ | * | ^
```

There are two kinds of expression in Alloy: relational expressions and integer expressions. When mentioned without qualification, the term "expression" refers to a relational expression.

Every relational expression denotes a relation. A set is represented as a relation of arity one, and a scalar is represented as a singleton set. A tuple is a singleton relation.

Alloy's analysis involves finding solutions to constraints. For any candidate instance that may be a solution to the constraint, each expression of the constraint has a value given by the instance's bindings of values to variables.

An expression may consist simply of a variable name, signature reference, or the special argument *this*:

    expr ::= *[@]* varId | sigRef | **this** |

If the variable denotes a field name, its value is the value bound to that field in the instance being evaluated. In contexts in which field names are implicitly dereferenced—that is, in signature declaration expressions and signature facts—the prefix @ preempts dereferencing (see subsection B.7.2). If there is more than one field of the given name, the reference is resolved, or rejected if ambiguous (see section B.6).

If a variable denotes a quantified or let-bound variable, its value is determined by the binding. If the variable is an argument of a function or predicate, the analysis at hand must be a *run* of that function or predicate (since if the function or predicate is invoked, its meaning is obtained by inlining and the argument has been replaced) and the variable's value is bound speculatively to each possible value during search.

An expression may be a relational constant:

    expr ::= **none | univ | iden**

The three constants *none*, *univ*, and *iden* denote respectively the empty unary relation (that is, the set containing no elements), the universal unary relation (the set containing every element), and the identity relation (the binary relation that relates every element to itself).

Note that *univ* and *iden* are interpreted over the universe of all atoms. So a constraint such as

    iden in r

will be unsatisfiable unless the relation *r* has type *univ->univ*. To say that *r* is a reflexive relation, you might write instead t <: **iden in** r

for example, where *r* has type *t->t*.

An expression may be a compound expression:

    expr ::= unOp expr | expr binOp expr | expr[expr]
    binOp ::= + | - | & | . | ->
    unOp ::= ~ | * | ^

The value of a compound expression is obtained from the values of its constituents by applying the operator given. The meanings of the operators are as follows:

- ~*e*: transpose of *e*;
- ^*e*: transitive closure of *e*;
- *e*: reflexive-transitive closure of *e*;
- *e1* + *e2*: union of *e1* and *e2*;
- *e1* - *e2*: difference of *e1* and *e2*;
- *e1* & *e2*: intersection of *e1* and *e2*;
- *e1* . *e2*: join of *e1* and *e2*;
- *e2* [*e1*]: join of *e1* and *e2*;
- *e1*->*e2*: product of *e1* and *e2*;
- *e2* <: *e1*: domain restriction of *e1* to *e2*;
- *e1* :> *e2*: range restriction of *e1* to *e2*;
- *e1* ++ *e2*: relational override of *e1* by *e2*.

For the first three (the unary operators), *e* is required to be binary. For the set theoretic operations (union, difference, and intersection) and for relational override, the arguments are required to have the same arity. For the restriction operators, the argument *e2* is required to be a set.

Note that *e1[e2]* is equivalent to *e2.e1*, but the dot and brackets operators have different precedence.

The *transpose* of a relation is its mirror image: the relation obtained by reversing each tuple. The *transitive closure* of a relation is the smallest enclosing relation that is transitive (that is, relates *a* to *c* whenever there is a *b* such that it relates *a* to *b* and *b* to *c*). The *reflexive-transitive closure* of a relation is the smallest enclosing relation that is transitive and reflexive (that is, includes the identity relation).

The union, difference, and intersection operators are the standard set theoretic operators, applied to relations viewed as sets of tuples. The *union* of *e1* and *e2* contains every tuple in *e1* or in *e2*; the *intersection* of *e1* and *e2* contains every tuple in both *e1* and in *e2*; the *difference* of *e1* and *e2* contains every tuple in *e1* but not in *e2*.

The *join* of two relations is the relation obtained by taking each combination of a tuple from the first relation and a tuple from the second relation, and if the last element of the first tuple matches the first element of the second tuple, including the concatenation of the two tuples, omitting the matching elements.

The *product* of two relations is the relation obtained by taking each combination of a tuple from the first relation and a tuple from the second relation, and including their concatenation.

The *domain restriction* of e1 to e2 contains all tuples in e1 that start with an element in the set e2. The *range restriction* of e1 to e2 contains all tuples in e1 that end with an element in the set e2. These operators are especially handy in resolving overloading (see section B.6).

The *relational override* of e1 by e2 contains all tuples in e2, and additionally, any tuples of e1 whose first element is not the first element of a tuple in e2.

An expression may be a *comprehension expression*:

> expr ::= { decl,⁺ | [constraint] }

The expression

> {x1: e1, x2: e2, ... | F}

denotes the relation obtained by taking all tuples $x1 \rightarrow x2 \rightarrow \ldots$ in which x1 is drawn from the set e1, x2 is drawn from the set e2, and so on, and the constraint F holds. The expressions e1, e2, and so on, must be unary, and may not be prefixed by multiplicity keywords. More general declaration forms are not permitted, except for the use of the *disj* and *part* keywords.

An expression may be a *let expression*:

> expr ::= **let** letDecl,⁺ | expr
> letDecl ::= varId = expr

The expression

> **let** v1 = e1, v2 = e2, ... | e

is equivalent to the expression e, but with each bound variable v1, v2, etc. replaced by its assigned expression e1, e2, etc. Variables appearing in let declaration expressions must have been previously declared. Recursive bindings are not permitted.

An expression may be an *if expression*:

> expr ::= **if** constraint **then** expr **else** expr

The expression

> **if** F **then** e1 **else** e2

has the value of expression *e1* when the constraint *F* is true, and the value of expression *e2* otherwise.

The meaning of an *invocation expression*

> expr ::= *[*expr **::***]* funRef **(** expr,* **)**

is explained in section B.7.4.

The meaning of the *Integer expression*

> expr ::= **Int** intExpr

is explained in section B.7.7.

An expression may be parenthesized to force a particular ordering of application of operators:

> expr ::= **(** expr **)**

B.7.7 Integers

The productions discussed in this section are

> constraint ::= intExpr *[neg]* intCompOp intExpr
> expr ::= **Int** intExpr
> intExpr ::= number | **#** expr | **sum** expr | **int** expr
> | **if** constraint **then** intExpr **else** intExpr
> | intExpr intOp intExpr
> | **let** letDecl,... | intExpr
> | **sum** decl,⁺ | intExpr
> | **(** intExpr **)**
> intOp ::= **+** | **-**
> intCompOp ::= **<** | **>** | **=** | **=<** | **>=**

There are two kinds of integers in Alloy. The predefined signature *Int* denotes a set of *integer-carrying objects* that may appear as atoms in relations. Integer operators may not be applied to these objects directly. Integer expressions are distinguished syntactically from relational expressions, and have *primitive integer values* which may be combined and compared using arithmetic operators. Primitive integer values may not appear as atoms in relations, and cannot be quantified over.

Distinct integer objects never carry the same primitive integer value. So the following assertion always holds:

> **assert** IntegersCanonical {**no disj** i, j: **Int** | **int** i = **int** j}

A primitive integer value may be obtained from a relational expression whose value is a set of integer objects:

> intExpr ::= **sum** expr | **int** expr

Both integer expressions **int** e and **sum** e have an integer value that is the sum of the integer values associated with integer objects in the set denoted by the relational expression e. There is no semantic difference between the two. The intent is that *sum* be used to indicate explicitly that the expression is expected not to be a singleton. Usually, the *int* operator will be applied to an expression denoting a single Integer object, but it is defined over a set of Integer objects so that it always has a value.

A primitive integer value may be obtained from a relational expression of any type using a *cardinality expression*:

> intExpr ::= # expr

The integer expression #e has an integer value corresponding to the cardinality of e—that is, the number of tuples in the relation denoted by the relational expression e.

A *numeric constant* may be used as an integer expression:

> intExpr ::= number

A numeric constant is a sequence of one or more digits, of which the first is not zero.

Integers may be combined using standard arithmetic operators for addition and subtraction:

> intExpr ::= intExpr intOp intExpr
> intOp ::= + | -

The integer expression $i+j$ evaluates to the sum of the values of the integer expressions i and j; the integer expression $i-j$ evaluates to the value of the integer expression i minus the value of the integer expression j. Note that the plus and minus symbols are overloaded: they are treated as arithmetic operators within integer expressions, and as relational operators within relational expressions.

A *sum expression* computes the sum of the values of an integer expression over a range of bindings:

> intExpr ::= **sum** decl,⁺ | intExpr

The integer expression

> **sum** x: X, y: Y, ... | ie

evaluates to the sum of the values that the integer expression *ie* can take for all distinct bindings of the variables *x*, *y*, and so on. The most general declaration forms are permitted, although analysis may not be feasible when the bindings are not first order.

If-then-else and let can be applied to integer expressions:

> intExpr ::=
>   **if** constraint **then** intExpr **else** intExpr
> | **let** letDecl,... | intExpr

with the same meaning as for relational expressions, but with integer values instead.

Integer valued expressions can be compared:

> constraint ::= intExpr *[neg]* intCompOp intExpr
> intCompOp ::= < | > | = | =< | >=

The meaning of the comparison operators is as follows:

- The constraint $i = j$ is true when the integer expressions i and j have the same value.
- The constraint $i < j$ is true when i is less than j.
- The constraint $i > j$ is true when i is greater than j.
- The constraint $i =< j$ is true when i is less than or equal to j.
- The constraint $i >= j$ is true when i is greater than or equal to j.

The "less than or equal to" operator is written unconventionally with the equals symbol first so that it does not have the appearance of an arrow, which might be confused with a logical implication.

A constraint in which the comparison operator is negated,

> e1 **not** *op* e2

is equivalent to the constraint obtained by moving the negation outside:

> **not** e1 *op* e2

The negation operators *!* and *not* have the same meaning.

Integer objects are obtained from integer values with the *Int* operator:

> expr ::= **Int** intExpr

The expression **Int** *ie* denotes the Integer object associated with the value of the integer expression *ie*; it is equivalent to

> {i: **Int** | **int** i = ie}

It is possible that, in a particular analysis, the scope is too small to provide such an integer. In that case, *Int ie* denotes the empty set. Note that because no two integer-carrying objects hold the same integer value, it will never denote a set of more than one object.

B.7.8 Constraints

The productions discussed in this section are

> constraint ::=
>   quantifier expr
> | expr *[neg]* compOp expr
> | neg constraint | constraint logicOp constraint
> | constraint thenOp constraint *[elseOp constraint]*
> | quantifier decl,⁺ constraintBody
> | **let** letDecl,⁺ constraintBody
> | expr : declExpr
> | constraintSeq
> | **(** constraint **)**
> constraintBody ::= constraintSeq | **|** constraint
> constraintSeq ::= **{** constraint* **}**
> letDecl ::= varId = expr
> thenOp ::= **implies** | =>
> elseOp ::= **else** | **,**
> neg ::= **not** | **!**
> logicOp ::= **&&** | **||** | **iff** | <=> | **and** | **or**
> quantifier ::= **all** | **no** | mult
> mult ::= **lone** | **one** | **some**
> compOp ::= **in** | **:** | =
> declExpr ::=
>   *[mult | **set***] expr
> | expr *[mult]* -> *[mult]* expr

Elementary constraints are formed by applying quantifiers to relational expressions, or by comparing relational or integer expressions.

A *quantified expression* takes the form

    constraint ::= quantifier expr
    quantifier ::= **all** | **no** | mult
    mult ::= **lone** | **one** | **some**

Its meaning depends on the quantifier chosen:

- The constraint **no** *e* is true when *e* evaluates to a relation containing no tuple.
- The constraint **some** *e* is true when *e* evaluates to a relation containing one or more tuple.
- The constraint **lone** *e* is true when *e* evaluates to a relation containing at most one tuple.
- The constraint **one** *e* is true when *e* evaluates to a relation containing exactly one tuple.

The constraint **all** *e* is rejected by a static semantic check: it has no meaning.

A *comparison constraint* takes the form

    constraint ::= expr [neg] compOp expr
    compOp ::= **in** | **=**

Its meaning depends on the comparison operator:

- The constraint *e1* **in** *e2* is true when the relation that *e1* evaluates to is a subset of the relation that *e2* evaluates to.
- The constraint *e1* **=** *e2* is true when the relation that *e1* evaluates to the same relation as *e2*.Equality:operator defined:

Note that relational equality is extensional: two relations are equal when they contain the same tuples.

A constraint in which the comparison operator is negated,

    e1 **not** *op* e2

is equivalent to the constraint obtained by moving the negation outside:

    not e1 *op* e2

The negation operators **!** and **not** have the same meaning.

Comparisons on integer expressions are covered in subsection B.7.7.

A *negated constraint* takes the form

    constraint ::= neg constraint
    neg ::= **not** | **!**

The constraint **not** F is true when the constraint F is false, and vice versa. The negation operators **not** and **!** are interchangeable.

A *compound constraint* combines smaller constraints with logical operators:

    constraint ::=
        constraint logicOp constraint
        | constraint thenOp constraint [elseOp constraint]
    logicOp ::= **&&** | **||** | **iff** | **<=>** | **and** | **or**
    thenOp ::= **implies** | **=>**
    elseOp ::= **else** | **,**

The meaning of the logical operators is as follows:

- The constraint F **and** G is true when F is true and G is true.
- The constraint F **or** G is true when one or both of F and G are true.
- The constraint F **iff** G is true when F and G are both false or both true.
- The constraint F **implies** G is true when F is false or G is true.
- The constraint F **implies** G **else** H is true when both F and G are true, or when F is false and H is true.

The logical operators may be written interchangeably as symbols: **&&** for **and**, **||** for **or**, **=>** for **implies**, **<=>** for **iff**, and a comma (**,**) for **else**.

A *constraint sequence* is a sequence of constraints enclosed in braces:

    constraint ::= constraintSeq
    constraintSeq ::= **{** constraint* **}**

The constraint

    { F G H ... }

is equivalent to the conjunction

    F **and** G **and** H **and** ...

If the sequence contains no constraints, the constraint is true.

A *quantified constraint* consists of one or more declarations and a body:

    constraint ::= quantifier decl,⁺ constraintBody

```
constraintBody ::= constraintSeq | | constraint
constraintSeq ::= { constraint* }
quantifier ::= all | no | mult
mult ::= lone | one | some
```

It makes no difference whether the constraint body is a single constraint preceded by a vertical bar, or a constraint sequence. The two forms are provided so that the vertical bar can be omitted when the body is a sequence of constraints. Some users prefer to use the bar in all cases, writing, for example,

> all x: X | { F }

Others prefer never to use the bar, and use the braces even when the constraint sequence consists of only a single constraint:

> all x: X { F }

These forms are all acceptable and are interchangeable.

The meaning of the constraint depends on the quantifier:

- The constraint **all** $x: e \mid F$ is true when the constraint F is true for all bindings of the variable x.
- The constraint **no** $x: e \mid F$ is true when the constraint F is true for no bindings of the variable x.
- The constraint **some** $x: e \mid F$ is true when the constraint F is true for one or more bindings of the variable x.
- The constraint **lone** $x: e \mid F$ is true when the constraint F is true for at most one binding of the variable x.
- The constraint **one** $x: e \mid F$ is true when the constraint F is true for exactly one binding of the variable x.

The range and type of the bound variable is determined by its declaration (see subsection B.7.3). In a sequence of declarations, each declared variable may be bound by the declarations or previously declared variables. For example, in the constraint

> all x: e, y: S - x | F

the variable x varies over the values of the expression e (assumed to represent a set), and the variable y varies over all elements of the set S except for x. When more than one variable is declared, the quantifier is interpreted over bindings of all variables. For example,

> one x: X, y: Y | F

is true when there is exactly one binding that assigns values to x and y that makes F true. So although a quantified constraint with multiple declarations may be regarded, for some quantifiers, as a shorthand for nested constraints, each with one declaration, this is not in general true. Thus

> **all** x: X, y: Y | F

is short for

> **all** x: X | **all** y: Y | F

but

> **one** x: X, y: Y | F

is not short for

> **one** x: X | **one** y: Y | F

A quantified constraint may be higher-order: that is, it may bind non-scalar values to variables. Whether the constraint is analyzable will depend on whether it can be skolemized by the analyzer, and if not, how large the scope is.

A *let constraint* allows a variable to be introduced, to highlight an import subexpression or make the constraint shorter by factoring out a repeated subexpression:

> constraint ::= **let** letDecl,⁺ constraintBody
> letDecl ::= varId = expr

The constraint

> **let** x1 = e1, x2 = e2, ... | F

is equivalent to the constraint F with each occurrence of the bound variable *x1* replaced by the expression *e1*, *x2* by *e2*, and so on. Like all declarations, let declarations are interpreted in order, and may not be recursive.

Predicate invocation is discussed in subsection B.7.4.

A *declaration constraint* allows a multiplicity constraint to be placed on an expression:

> constraint ::= declConstraint
> declConstraint ::= expr : declExpr
> declExpr ::=
>   *[mult |* **set***]* expr
>   *|* expr *[mult]* -> *[mult]* expr

Declaration constraints are useful for two reasons. First, they allow multiplicity constraints to be placed on arbitrary expressions, where declarations themselves only allow them to be placed on variables. Thus,

> p.q : t **one**->**one** t

for example, says that the join of p and q is a bijection. Second, they allow additional multiplicity constraints to be expressed that cannot be expressed in declarations. For example, the relation r of type A->B can be declared as a field of A:

> **sig** A {r: **set** B}

Since the declaration constraints apply to the relations *this.r*, they cannot constrain the multiplicity of the relation from B's perspective. To say that r maps at most one A to each B, one could add as a fact the declaration constraint

> r: A **lone**->B

Another deficiency of declarations that can be overcome is that they only allow multiplicities around one arrow to be given. For a relation p of type A->B->C, a declaration of the form

> **all** r: A->**some** (B->C) | ...

makes r total on A. The constraint that R maps a pair from A->B to each element of C cannot be expressed in this declaration because it requires a different parsing of the expression, associating the arrows to the left rather than the right. To express this constraint, one could use a declaration constraint like this:

> **all** r: A->**some** (B->C) | r: (A->B) **some**->C => ...

A constraint may be parenthesized to force a particular ordering of application of operators:

> constraint ::= (constraint)

Appendix C:
Kernel Semantics

This appendix gives a succinct definition of the underlying logic in terms of the operators of conventional set theory.

An Alloy model comprises, in essence, a collection of declarations of relations (the signatures and their fields), and a collection of named formulas. The meaning of the model is a set of instances, for each named formula, each instance assigning a relational value to each of the declared relations. Here, we'll consider a simplified language consisting only of simple formulas, and we'll define the meaning of a formula as a function from instances to boolean values; the set of instances described is then, implicitly, those instances on which the function evaluates to true. Although this language is much smaller than the full Alloy language, it captures its semantic essence, and it is relatively straightforward to translate the constructs of the full language into it.

C.1 Semantics of the Alloy Kernel

The syntax of formulas is given by these productions:

```
formula ::= elemFormula | compFormula | quantFormula
elemFormula ::= expr in expr | expr = expr
compFormula ::= not formula | formula and formula
quantFormula ::= all var : expr | formula
```

and the syntax of expressions by:

```
expr ::= rel | var | none | expr binop expr | unop expr
binop ::= + | & | - | . | ->
unop ::= ~ | ^
```

The syntactic category *rel* represents free relation variables (the signatures and fields), whereas *var* represents variables bound by quantifiers. The constants *iden* and *univ* are not defined here, since they depend on the context of the model's declarations (*univ* denoting the union of the top-level signatures, and *iden* the identity relation over that union).

In standard denotational style, we'll define a function M that interprets formulas, mapping a formula in the context of an instance to a boolean value, and a function M that interprets expressions, mapping an expression in the context of an instance to a relation value:

M: Formula, Instance → Boolean
E: Expression, Instance → RelationValue

An instance is a function from relation variables to relation values. A relation value is a set of tuples of atoms, and all the tuples in a particular relation value can be assumed to contain the same number of elements (although in fact this constraint is unnecessary [14]).

Here are the definitions of the formula operators:

$M[\textbf{not } f]i = \neg\, M[f]i$
$M[f \textbf{ and } g]i = M[f]i \wedge M[g]i$
$M[\textbf{all } x: e \,|\, f]i = \wedge\{M[f]\, (i \oplus x \mapsto v) \mid v \subseteq E[e]i \wedge \#v = 1\}$
$M[p \textbf{ in } q]i = E[p]i \subseteq E[q]i$
$M[p = q]i = (E[p]i = E[q]i)$

The universally quantified formula is true for an instance i when its body is true for every instance in which i is extended by an assignment of some singleton subset of the value of the bounding expression to the quantified variable. We are assuming here that bounding expressions are unary, so that these subsets represent scalars.

The *in* operator is just conventional subset; it is given the ambiguous name "*in*" so that it can serve naturally as both a membership operator, relating an element to a set or a tuple to a relation, and as a subset operator, relating one set or relation to another. Equality is simply subset in both directions; it is included here just to make it clear that equality is the simple conventional notion of equality of sets or relations, with none of the distinctions between identity and contents often made in object-oriented languages.

Here are the definitions of the expression operators:

$E[\textbf{none}]i = \varnothing$
$E[p + q]i = E[p]i \cup E[q]i$
$E[p \& q]i = E[p]i \cap E[q]i$
$E[p - q]i = E[p]i \setminus E[q]i$
$E[p \cdot q]i =$
    $\{(p_1,...,p_{n-1},\, q_2,...,q_m) \mid (p_1,...,p_n) \in E[p]i \wedge (q_1,...,q_m) \in E[q]i \wedge p_n = q_1\}$
$E[p \rightarrow q]i = \{(p_1,...,p_n,\, q_1,...,q_m) \mid (p_1,...,p_n) \in E[p]i \wedge (q_1,...,q_m) \in E[q]i\}$
$E[\sim p]i = \{(p_2,\, p_1) \mid (p_1,\, p_2) \in E[p]i\}$
$E[\wedge p]i = \{(x, y) \mid \exists p_1,...p_n \mid (x, p_1),\, (p_1, p_2),\, ...\,(p_n, y) \in E[p]i\}$

The +, & and - operators are the standard set operators – union, intersection and difference. The ~ and ^ are the standard relational operators for transpose and transitive closure, defined over binary relations. Dot is a generalized relational composition (or join), and arrow is a cartesian product. Note that all these operators are total, so there are no undefined expressions in Alloy.

Finally, the value of an expression containing just a relation name is the value assigned to that relation by the instance:

$$E[r]i = i(r)$$

If the relation name is ambiguous (because fields of different signatures have the same name), the meaning is simply the union of the values assigned by the instance to each of the relations that the name might refer to.

C.2   Semantics of Integer Expressions and Formulas

Alloy supports integers to a limited degree. The elements of the language extension can be summarized by these productions:

intExpr ::= number | # expr | **sum** expr | **int** expr | intExpr intOp intExpr

intFormula ::= intExpr intCompOp intExpr

intCompOp ::= < | > | = | =< | >=

intOp ::= + | -

number = 0 | 1 | ..

expr ::= .. | **Int** intExpr

An *intExpr* is an expression whose value is an integer; the semantics of formulas involving such expressions is completely standard. Such an expression is obtained either from an integer literal, by combining other such expressions, or by applying one of the three operators *#*, *sum* and *int* to an Alloy relational expression. The operator *#* is the cardinality operator; the meaning of *#e* is simply the number of tuples in *e*.

For the expressions *int e* and *sum e*, type checking ensures that the relational expression *e* denotes a unary relation (that is, a set) of atoms of a special predefined type *Int*. Each atom in the set *Int* is associated with an integer value by a relation *I2i*; this relation is considered a free variable like an explicitly declared relation, and is likewise given a value by an instance. Both expressions *int e* and *sum e* actually have the same meaning: their value is the sum of the integer values associated by *I2i* with the atoms in the set *e*. But when *int* is used, the relational expression is assumed to denote a scalar, and when *sum* is used, the relational expression is assumed to denote a set that may contain more than one *Int* atom. Currently, the Alloy Analyzer does not check this, however.

A relational value can be obtained from an integer value by applying the operator *Int*. The meaning of *Int ie* is the set of atoms in *Int* whose value is mapped to the integer value of *ie* by the relation *I2i*. Since *I2i* is constrained to be an injective function, this set contains at most one element. In Alloy terminology, therefore, *Int ie* is an option, denoting either a scalar (when there is an *Int* atom associated with the integer *ie*), or an empty set (otherwise).

In an analysis, the scope setting bounds separately the size of the set *Int* and the bit width of the largest positive and negative integer. This allows cases to be handled in which the number of integers stored in relations is much smaller than the size of the largest integer value. Limiting the range of integers makes exhaustive analysis possible, at a cost: the standard semantics for integers cannot be preserved. In particular, generation axioms (for example, that every integer has a successor) do not apply: the formula

all i: **Int** | **some** j: **Int** | **int** j = **int** i + 1

is not valid. Consequently, analyses involving integers may produce spurious instances. The same problem arises whenever a signature is intended to represent a set for which a generator axiom would be desirable but cannot be expressed without eliminating all finite instances (see [44] and section 5.3).

Appendix D:
Diagrammatic Notation

Multiplicity symbols
* any number (default)
? zero or one
! exactly one
+ one or more

S	*S* is a set

S is an abstract set:
all its elements are contained
by subsets that extend it

S m

S is a set with multiplicity *m*

S m

S is a set with multiplicity *m* ;
if present, m must be ? or !
and defaults to ! if missing

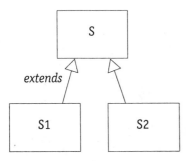

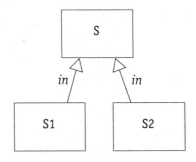

S1 and *S2* are subsets of *S*,
and are disjoint;
no label means extends

S1 and *S2* are subsets of *S*
and are not necessarily disjoint
from each other (or from other sets
that extend *S*)

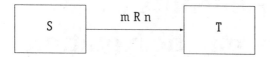

R is a relation from S to T with multiplicities m and n,
corresponding to the textual constraint $R: S\ m \to n\ T$;
R may be any relational expression

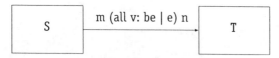

For any value of variable v drawn from bounding expression be,
expression e denotes a relation from S to T with multiplicities m
and n, corresponding to the constraint $all\ v: be \mid e: S\ m \to n\ T$

When e is an expression in which the special form $<C>$ occurs,
for an expression C denoting a set, the occurrence of e in the
label is short for $all\ v: C \mid e'$ where e' is e with $<C>$ replaced by v

Appendix E:
Alternative Approaches

The models in this appendix were contributed by Michael Butler, John Fitzgerald, Martin Gogolla, Peter Gorm Larsen, and Jim Woodcock, and are included here with their permission.

Alloy is only one of several approaches to the modeling and analysis of software abstractions. This appendix briefly describes four of these alternatives: B, OCL, VDM, and Z. Its purpose is both to help those in search of an approach that matches their needs, and—for readers already familiar with other approaches—to highlight the respects in which they differ from Alloy.

I chose these four approaches because of their ability to capture complex structure succinctly and abstractly. They are all well known, and each has an active and enthusiastic community of users and researchers. Other modeling and analysis approaches can be used effectively for software design in specialized domains: there are many model checkers, for example, that can check protocols and concurrent algorithms, but they are not considered here since (with the exception of FDR) they tend to have only rudimentary support for structuring of data.

Some features are common to all the approaches, including Alloy. They all offer a notation that can capture software abstractions more succinctly and directly than a programming language can; all of them, despite differences in syntax and semantics, view the state in terms of classical mathematical structures, such as sets and relations, and describe behaviors declaratively, using constraints. Lightweight tools are available for all of them, in which constraints are evaluated against concrete cases, and new tool projects are underway for all these approaches that are likely to extend their power and applicability greatly.

At the same time, there are important differences. B is more operational in flavor; its notation is more like an abstract programming language than a specification language. OCL has a very different syntax from the others, reminiscent of Smalltalk. In B and VDM, and to some extent Z and OCL, a particular notion of state machine is hardwired, in contrast to Alloy, which is designed to support a variety of idioms, each as easy (or difficult!) to express as the others. B, VDM and Z were designed more with proof in mind than lightweight analysis, and so, unlike Alloy and OCL, are supported by specialized theorem provers.

All these languages predate Alloy, which has benefited greatly from their experience. Alloy was designed for similar applications, but with more emphasis on automatic analysis. In pursuit of this goal, the language was stripped down to the bare essentials of structural modeling, and was developed hand-in-hand with its analysis. Any feature that would thwart analysis was excluded. Consequently, Alloy's analysis is more powerful than the lightweight analyses offered by the other approaches, which (with the exception of ProB) are mostly "animators" that execute a model on given test cases. Unlike an animator, the Alloy Analyzer does not require the user to provide initial conditions and inputs; it does not restrict the language to an executable subset; and, because it covers the entire space within the scope, it is more effective at uncovering subtle bugs. The idea of analysis is built in to the language itself: assertions can be recorded as part of a specification, and the scopes (which bound the analysis) are confined to commands. The other approaches use tool-specific extensions instead.

Another goal in the design of Alloy was to be unusually small and simple; it has fewer concepts than the other languages, and is in some respects more flexible. For example, Alloy unifies all data structuring within the notion of a relation; it uses the same relational join for indexing, dereferencing structures and applying functions; its signatures can simulate the schemas of Z and the classes of OCL; and its assertions can express invariant preservations, refinements and temporal properties over traces.

These benefits are not, of course, without some cost. Alloy is less expressive than the other languages. Whereas Alloy's structures are strictly first order, B, VDM and Z all support higher-order structures and quantifications. Carroll Morgan's well known telephone switching specification [54] in Z, for example, represents the connections as a set of sets of endpoints. Such a structure is not directly representable in Alloy; you'd need to model the connections as a relation between endpoints, or as a set of connection atoms, each mapped to its endpoints. Morgan's ingenious characterization of the behavior of the switch, with a higher-order formula constraining the connection structure to be maximal, would not be expressible at all in Alloy. A more significant (but less fundamental) deficiency of Alloy in this regard is its relatively poor support for sequences and integers.

Aside from occupying a different point in the spectrum of expressiveness versus analyzability, the other languages naturally have their own particular merits. B offers a more direct path to implementation; OCL is integrated with UML, the modeling language of choice for many companies; VDM supports both explicit and implicit forms of modeling; and Z has higher-order features that have been found very useful in the structuring of large specifications.

A single problem is used to illustrate all the approaches. For each alternative approach, a model was constructed by an expert. Michael Butler developed the B version, using the ProB tool; Martin Gogolla developed the OCL version using the USE tool; Peter Gorm Larsen and John Fitzgerald developed the VDM version using VDMTools; and Jim Woodcock developed the Z version using the Z/Eves theorem prover and the Jaza animator. Unfortunately, there was not sufficient space to include all their work in full. In particular, Martin Gogolla wrote a second model showing that OCL could accommodate the "time-instant" idiom used in the Alloy specification as easily as the standard pre/post idiom, and constructed an ASSL procedure for generating test cases automatically; and Jim Woodcock proved precondition theorems for all operations, and the *NoIntruder* assertion with the help of Z/Eves.

E.1 An Example

To illustrate the different approaches, we'll use an example of a scheme for recodable hotel-door locks, similar to (but simpler than) the one that appears in chapter 6. The purpose of the modeling and analysis is to determine whether the scheme is effective in preventing unauthorized access. An Alloy model is shown in figs. E.1 and E.2.

Fig. E.1 shows the declarations of the components of the state space, and the initialization. Each key card is marked with two keys (line 5); these markings are fixed, and do not change over time. The remaining components are time-varying, as can be seen by the presence of the *Time* column in their declarations: the current key for each room (8); the front desk record of keys issued so far (11), and of which keys were issued for which rooms in the immediately previous checkin (12); and the set of cards held by each guest (15).

At initialization, the record at the front desk associating keys with rooms matches the current keys of the room locks themselves (18), no keys have been issued, and no guests hold cards (19).

```
1   module hotel
2   open util/ordering [Time]

3   sig Key, Time {}
4   sig Card {
5       fst, snd: Key
6       }
7   sig Room {
8       key: Key one -> Time
9       }
10  one sig Desk {
11      issued: Key -> Time,
12      prev: (Room -> lone Key) -> Time
13      }
14  sig Guest {
15      cards: Card -> Time
16      }

17  pred init (t: Time) {
18      Desk.prev.t = key.t
19      no issued.t and no cards.t
20      }
```

FIG. E.1 Hotel locking example, in Alloy: part 1.

Fig. E.2 shows the operations corresponding to checking in and entering a room, the definition of execution traces, and an assertion expressing the intended effect of the scheme in terms of denied access.

When a guest *g* checks in at the front desk to a room *g*, the guest is given a card (5) whose first key is the last key that was issued for that room (3), and whose second key is fresh (4). The desk's records are updated accordingly (6, 7). There is no change to the keys in the locks (9).

A guest can enter a room so long as he or she is holding a card (12) whose first or second key matches the current key of the room's lock. If the second key matches, the lock's key remains the same (14); if the first key matches, the lock is recoded with the second key (15). No changes are made to the front desk's records (17) or to the sets of keys that guests hold (18).

To shorten the example, no operation is given for checking out. The use of a key by a new guest should invalidate previously issued keys, so

```
1   pred checkin (t, t': Time, r: Room, g: Guest) {
2     some c: Card {
3       c.fst = r.(Desk.prev.t)
4       c.snd not in Desk.issued.t
5       cards.t' = cards.t + g -> c
6       Desk.issued.t' = Desk.issued.t + c.snd
7       Desk.prev.t' = Desk.prev.t ++ r -> c.snd
8       }
9     key.t = key.t'
10    }

11  pred enter (t, t': Time, r: Room, g: Guest) {
12    some c: g.cards.t |
13      let k = r.key.t {
14        c.snd = k and key.t' = key.t
15        or c.fst = k and key.t' = key.t ++ r -> c.snd
16        }
17    issued.t = issued.t' and prev.t = prev.t'
18    cards.t = cards.t'
19    }

20  fact Traces {
21    init (first())
22    all t: Time - last () |
23      some g: Guest, r: Room |
24        checkin (t, next(t), r, g) or enter (t, next(t), r, g)
25    }

26  assert NoIntruder {{
27    no t1: Time, disj g, g': Guest, r: Room |
28      let t2 = next(t1), t3 = next(t2), t4 = next (t3) {
29        enter (t1, t2, r, g)
30        enter (t2, t3, r, g')
31        enter (t3, t4, r, g)
32        }
33    }
34  check NoIntruder for 3 but 6 Time, 1 Room, 2 Guest
```

FIG. E.2 Hotel locking example, in Alloy: part 2.

whenever a guest checks in, the previous occupant is implicitly checked out.

If you're reading this appendix before you've read the rest of the book, a few comments about Alloy might be helpful:

- A signature introduces a set, and some relations that have that set as their first column. For example, the declaration for *sig Card* introduces the set *Card* of key cards, and two relations, *fst* and *snd*, from *Card* to *Key*.

- Multiplicities of relations are sometimes implicit, as in the declaration of *fst* and *snd*, each of which maps a *Card* to one *Key*, and sometimes explicit using keywords, as in the declaration of *key* in *Room*, which for a given room, maps one element of *Key* to each element of *Time*. The keyword *lone* means at most one (and can be read "less than or equal to one"), so the declaration of *prev* says that, for a given *Desk*, and at a given *Time*, each *Room* is associated with at most one *Key*.

- The dot operator is relational join. Scalars are treated semantically as singleton sets, and sets are treated as unary relations. Thus *cards.t* is the relation that associates elements of *Guest* with elements of *Card* at time *t*, *c.fst* is the first key of card *c*, and *r.key.t* is the current key of room *r* at time *t*.

- The arrow operator -> is a cartesian product, and is used in the operations to form tuples; + is union; - is difference; and ++ is relational override.

Importing the built-in ordering module (fig. E.1, line 2) introduces a total ordering on time steps, the elements of the signature *Time*. The *Traces* fact (fig. E.2, line 20) constrains the ordering so that the initialization condition holds in the first state, and so that any state (except the last) and its successor are related by either the *checkin* or the *enter* operation.

The assertion (26) claims that three *enter* events cannot occur in sequence for the same room, with the intervening one performed by one guest, and the first and third by another. In other words, two guests can't use the same room at the same time.

The check command for this assertion instructs the analyzer to consider all traces involving 3 cards, 3 keys, 6 time instants, one room and two guests. Executing it produces a counterexample trace in 2 seconds (on a PowerMac G5), consisting of the following steps (shown graphically in the visualizer's output of fig. E.3):

· Initially, the room *Room0* holds key *Key0* in its lock, and the desk associates the room with the key, but holds no record of previously issued keys. Note that the room has been marked with the label *NoIntruder_r*: it will be the witness to the violation of the assertion *NoIntruder*, corresponding to the quantified variable *r*.

· In the second state, following a *checkin*, *Guest0* has acquired a card whose first and second keys are *Key0* and *Key1* respectively, and the desk has recorded *Key0* as issued. Note that the guest has been labeled *NoIntruder_g*, indicating that this guest will be the witness playing the role of the variable *g* in the assertion.

· In the third state, following another *checkin*, a second guest, *Guest1*, has acquired a card whose first and second keys are *Key1* and *Key0* respectively—the same keys as *Guest0*, but in a different order—and the desk has recorded *Key1* as issued. This new guest has been marked with the label *NoIntruder_g'*, indicating that it will be the witness playing the role of the variable *g'* in the assertion—the intruder.

· In the fourth state, the first entry has occurred—of *Guest0*—and the room key has been changed to *Key1*.

· In the fifth state, the second, illegal, entry has occurred—of *Guest1*— and the room key has been changed back to *Key0*.

· In the sixth and final state, the third entry has occurred—of *Guest0* again—and the room key has been changed back to *Key1*.

The fault lies in the initial condition. Because *Key0*, the initial key of *Room0*, was not recorded as having been issued, it was possible to issue it twice, thus setting up the cycle. The keys already in the locks should have been recorded as issued initially:

```
pred init (t: Time) {
  Desk.prev.t = key.t
  Desk.issued.t = Room.key.t and no cards.t
}
```

With this change, the analysis exhausts the entire space without finding a counterexample. For greater confidence, we can increase the scope. Extending the scope to 4 keys and cards, 7 time instants, two guests and one room

check NoIntruder **for** 4 **but** 7 Time, 2 Guest, 1 Room

reveals another counterexample, in which a guest checks in twice, with another guest checking in between the two. These two guests can then

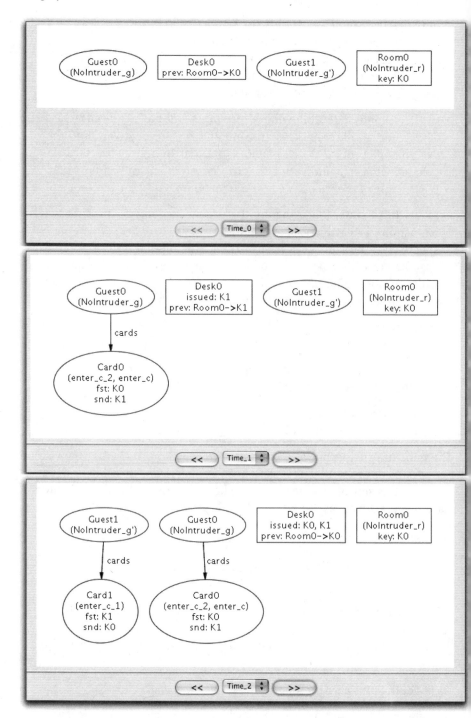

FIG. E.3 Counterexample to assertion of fig. E.2. Each panel corresponds to a state; execution beings in the top left, and continues from the bottom of the left-hand to the top of the right-hand page.

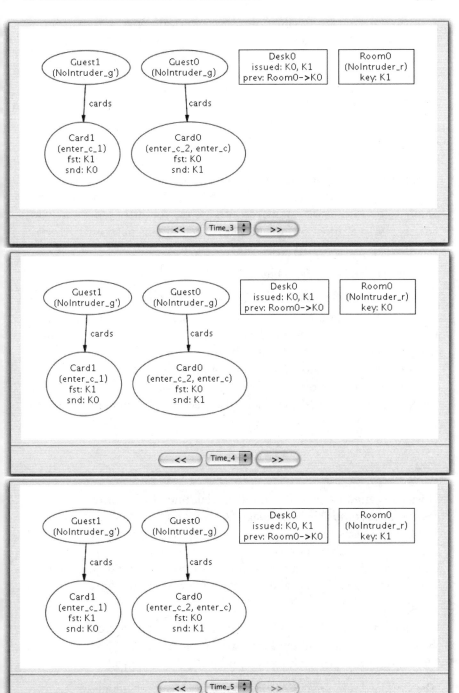

perform the 3 entries in violation of the assertion. We can fix this problem by only allowing guests to check in if they have returned cards they used previously. This can be modeled by changing one line of the *checkin* operation from

cards.t′ = cards.t + g -> c

to

cards.t′ = cards.t ++ g -> c

where the override operator now causes the guest's set of cards to be replaced, rather than augmented, by the new one. Now no counterexample is found, and we can increase the scope yet further for more confidence. With at most 6 cards and keys, 12 time instants, and 3 guests and rooms

check NoIntruder **for** 6 **but** 12 Time, 3 Guest, 3 Room

the space is exhausted in just under a minute. Of course, we have not *proved* the assertion to hold, and it is possible (though unlikely) that there is a counterexample in a larger scope. In a critical setting, it might make sense to attempt to prove the assertion at this point. Theorem provers can be applied to all of the approaches discussed here, even though our focus is on more lightweight tools. B and Z in particular are supported by readily available proof tools that are tailored to their particular forms.

E.2 B

B was designed by Jean-Raymond Abrial, one of the earliest contributors to Z. It comprises a language (AMN) and a method for obtaining implementations from abstract models by stepwise refinement. Starting with a very abstract machine, details are added one layer at a time, until a machine is obtained that can be translated directly into code. If each refinement step is valid, the resulting code is guaranteed to meet the top-level specification.

B is aimed primarily at the development of critical systems, and has been applied on a number of industrial projects. Its best known application to date was in a braking system for the Paris Metro.

The standard reference is Abrial's book [1]. More introductory texts are available [61, 76, 46], as well as a collection of case studies [62].

E.2.1 Modeling Notions of B

B's specification language, *Abstract Machine Notation* (AMN), reveals its focus in its name: a system is viewed (as in VDM and Z) as a state machine with operations over a global state. A model consists of a series of set declarations (akin to Alloy's signatures or Z's given sets); declarations of state components (called "variables"); an invariant on the state; an initialization condition; and a collection of operations.

State components are structured with sets and relations, as in Z; unlike in Alloy, higher-order structures are permitted. AMN does not separate type constraints from other, more expressive, invariants, so type checking has a heuristic flavor.

As in VDM, the precondition of an operation is explicit. In contrast to all the other approaches, the postcondition is not given as a logical formula, but as a collection of *substitutions*. A substitution is like an assignment statement, and can change the entire value of a state variable or update the value of a relation at a particular point. To partially constrain a state variable, one can assign to it an arbitrary value drawn from a set characterized by a formula.

The rationale for this style of specification is that it makes theorem proving easier: in manipulating operations syntactically, the postcondition can be treated literally as a substitution. The more operational style is also more familiar to programmers, and it makes more explicit the presence of non-determinism. Being programmatic in style, it is also more readily converted into an imperative program. The drawback is less flexibility in comparison to the other languages, and less support for incrementality: you have to give a substitution for every state variable (where, in Alloy for example, you can simulate an operation when constraints have been written for only some of the state components).

E.2.2 Sample Model in B

A version of the hotel locking model in B is shown in 3 figures: the top-level abstract machine in fig. E.4, and a refinement in figs. E.5 and E.6.

The abstract model (fig. E.4) has only a single state component—the room occupancy roster—which is updated by the *Checkin* operation, and guards the *Enter* operation. The special symbol +-> indicates a partial function; B and Z use a collection of special arrows in place of the multiplicity markings of Alloy and OCL.

```
1   MACHINE hotel1

2   SETS
3       GUEST = {g1,g2} ;
4       ROOM = {r1,r2}

5   VARIABLES  alloc

6   INVARIANT
7       alloc : ROOM +-> GUEST

8   INITIALISATION  alloc := {}

9   OPERATIONS

10  CheckIn(g,r) =
11      PRE
12          g:GUEST  &  r:ROOM
13      THEN
14          SELECT
15              r /: dom(alloc)
16          THEN
17              alloc(r) := g
18          END
19      END ;

20  Enter(g,r) =
21      PRE g:GUEST & r:ROOM THEN
22          SELECT
23              r |->g : alloc
24          THEN
25              skip
26          END
27      END ;
```

FIG. E.4 B model: most abstract machine.

B makes a distinction between the precondition of an operation and its
guard. When invoked in a state in which the guard is false, an operation
blocks; in contrast, an operation should never be invoked unless the
precondition holds (and if invoked, any outcome may result). For the
Enter operation, for example, the precondition says that the arguments
should be a guest and a room; the guard says that the operation cannot
proceed unless the guest is in the occupancy roster for that room.

The basic sets are given particular values in this specification to set bounds for analysis with the ProB tool. This is just like an Alloy scope specification, but is set globally rather than on a command-by-command basis.

The refined model in figs. E.5 and E.6 has exactly the same structure. The claim that this model, *hotel2*, refines the more abstract one, *hotel1*, is an assertion to be checked by a tool.

In this model, the state is more complex, since it includes the mechanism with cards and locks. The state is described as a collection of sets and relations, as in Alloy, OCL and Z. The expression *POW(e)* denotes the powerset of *e*—the set of sets of elements drawn from *e*—and the colon in each declaration denotes set membership. A declaration such as

key: POW(KEY)

is thus equivalent to the Alloy declaration

key: **set** KEY

even the right-hand expression is higher-order in B but not in Alloy. The arrow symbols >-> and -> denote injective and total functions respectively. The constraint of line 13 says that the first and second keys of a given card must be distinct. Including this as an invariant means that the operations are expected to preserve it. Although semantically this invariant is treated no differently from the declarations of *ckey1* and *ckey2* that precede it, type checking distinguishes them, and will fail if their order is reversed, with the invariant placed before the declarations.

Declaring *ckey1* and *ckey2* as state variables means that an operation can be defined that changes the keys on a card. They might have been declared instead as constants (as in the Alloy, OCL, and VDM models), which would rule this out.

The initialization condition illustrates non-determinism. The *ANY* clause binds an arbitrary set of keys to *ks*, and an arbitrary function from rooms to keys to *f*; the arrow symbol in the declaration of this function makes it injective, ensuring that no key is assigned to more than one room. The body of the clause assigns the set of keys to *key*, and the function to *lock* and *prev*. Note how the assignment of the non-deterministically chosen *f* to these two variables has the same effect as the equality

Desk.prev.t = key.t

```
 1  REFINEMENT hotel2

 2  REFINES hotel1

 3  SETS
 4     KEY = {k1,k2,k3,k4} ;
 5     CARD = {c1,c2,c3}

 6  VARIABLES
 7     alloc, key, cArd, ckey1, ckey2, lock, prev, guest

 8  INVARIANT
 9     key : POW(KEY) &
10     cArd : POW(CARD) &
11     ckey1 : cArd >-> key &
12     ckey2 : cArd >-> key &
13     !c.(c: cArd => ckey1(c) /= ckey2(c)) &
14     guest : cArd -> GUEST &
15     lock : ROOM >-> key &
16     prev : ROOM >-> key

17  INITIALISATION
18     ANY ks, f  WHERE
19        ks : POW(KEY) &
20        f : ROOM >-> ks
21     THEN
22        key  := ks ||
23        lock := f ||
24        prev := f ||
25        cArd, ckey1, ckey2, guest, alloc := {}, {}, {}, {}, {}
26     END

27
```

FIG. E.5 B model: state and initialization for refined machine.

in the Alloy model, ensuring that the room-key record at the front desk matches the keys of the actual locks, whatever it may be.

In this refined model, the *Entry* operation is split in two: *Enter1* for the normal case, and *Enter2* for the case in which the lock is recoded. In the other approaches, this is expressed with disjunction; in B, a non-deterministic choice operator could be used to the same effect.

```
1   OPERATIONS

2   CheckIn(g,r) =
3     PRE g:GUEST & r:ROOM THEN
4       ANY c, k WHERE
5         r : ROOM & r /: dom(alloc) &
6         c : CARD & c /: cArd &
7         k : KEY & k /: key
8       THEN
9         ckey1(c) := prev(r)  ||
10        ckey2(c) := k  ||
11        guest(c) := g  ||
12        prev(r) := k  ||
13        key := key \/ {k} ||
14        cArd := cArd \/ {c}  ||
15        alloc(r) := g
16      END
17    END ;

18
19  Enter1(g,r) =
20    PRE g:GUEST & r:ROOM THEN
21      ANY c, k WHERE
22        c:CARD & k:KEY &
23        c |-> g : guest &
24        ckey1(c) = lock(r)
25      THEN
26        lock(r) := ckey2(c)
27      END
28    END ;

29
30  Enter2(g,r) =
31    PRE g:GUEST & r:ROOM THEN
32      ANY c, k WHERE
33        c:CARD & k:KEY &
34        c |-> g : guest &
35        ckey2(c) = lock(r)
36      THEN
37        skip
38      END
39    END ;
```

FIG. E.6 B model: operations for refined machine.

E.2.3 Tools for B

Two commercial tools are available for B: Atelier-B from Steria, and the B-Toolkit from B-Core. Both focus on theorem proving and code generation, but also provide an animator for lightweight analysis.

ProB [49] is a very different tool. It offers very similar functionality to the Alloy Analyzer; of all the tools associated with these alternative approaches, it is the only one that can generate counterexamples to assertions fully automatically. B does not have a facility for defining arbitrary assertions, so ProB focuses on checking the proof obligations that are generated by invariants and refinement claims. Refinement is checked over traces rather than inductively over operations, so the user need not find an inductive invariant. ProB can also check the refinement relationship between a B model and a more abstract description written in the CSP process algebra.

E.3 OCL

OCL, the Object Constraint Language, is the constraint language of UML. It was developed by Jos Warmer and Anneke Klepper, based on Steve Cook and John Daniels's Syntropy language [10] and on modeling work done at IBM. Their book [73] provides an accessible overview. As part of UML, the language is an Object Management Group standard; the most recent specification is available online [53].

The early design of OCL placed less emphasis on precise semantics than the other approaches. Many researchers, in particular those associated with the Precise UML Group, worked to produce a formal semantics for OCL, but since the language was already standardized, it was too late to eliminate its complexities. So although OCL was designed in the hope that it would be simpler than languages such as VDM and Z, it actually ended up more complicated.

Our discussion is based on a variant of OCL designed by Mark Richters and Martin Gogolla [59, 58]. It has a formal semantics; a type system that supports subtyping; and a powerful animator and testing tool called USE.

When OCL was brought into the UML standard, it was viewed as an annotation language for UML class diagrams, so it was not given its own textual notation for declarations. This means that an OCL model, according to the standard, would have to include a UML diagram for the declarations of classes and relations—an inconvenience, especially for small models. The USE variant of OCL includes a textual notation for declarations, and thus overcomes this problem.

E.3.1 Basic Notions of OCL

An OCL model consists of a description of a state space (given in terms of classes, attributes and associations), some invariants, and a collection of operations. As in VDM, operations separate pre- and postconditions, and include invariants implicitly. In addition, however, OCL allows arbitrary predicates to be packaged, and in this respect, it has more in common with Alloy; the idiom used in the Alloy model, with explicit time instants, for example, can be cast fairly easily into OCL.

Like Alloy, OCL models the state with a collection of sets and relations. Surprisingly, however, a something-to-many relation, mapping an atom to more than one atom, is treated semantically not as a flat relation but rather as a function to sets, resulting in a model whose style is more reminiscent of VDM than of Alloy or Z. This gives a strong directionality to the relations of OCL; they cannot be traversed backwards. An association is thus accessed not as a single relation, but as a pair of relations derived from it called *roles*, one for navigation in each direction.

The multiplicity of a role is part of its type. Navigation is function application, and results in a set or scalar depending on the multiplicity (in contrast to Alloy, in which navigation is relational image, and always yields a set). The advantage of this is that the type checker can detect errors in which a navigation assumes a role to have a multiplicity incompatible with its declaration. The disadvantages are that multiplicities behave differently from explicit constraints that say the same thing; changing a role's multiplicities alters its type, and may require compensating changes where it is used; and conversions are needed between sets and scalars.

OCL has no transitive closure operator. To allow a multi-step navigation through a relation, therefore, it allows predicates and functions to be defined recursively. This brings useful expressiveness, but it has a downside: predicates no longer have a simple logical interpretation, but require a least fixpoint semantics. As a result, an OCL tool can't use a constraint solver in the style of the Alloy Analyzer or ProB, since it will generate spurious cases corresponding to non-minimal solutions.

In two respects, OCL is very different from the other approaches. First, its syntax stacks variable bindings in the style of Smalltalk, and treats the first argument of operators as privileged. Appropriately, it has a notion of *context* within which references to an archetypal member of a class are implicit. Second, like an object-oriented programming language, OCL distinguishes a class from the set of objects associated with it. This makes reflection possible, which is useful for metamodeling, but it also complicates the language.

The underlying datatypes of OCL are defined in library modules, which play a similar role in OCL to the mathematical toolkit in Z. In contrast, the basic types are built into the language in Alloy, B and VDM. This decision has some subtle implications for the type system. For example, unlike Alloy's type checker, a type checker for OCL cannot exploit the meaning of the set and relational operators, but must rely on their declared type alone.

An expression's value must belong to one of the library types. Since relations are not included, this means that, in contrast to the other languages, an expression cannot denote a relation. This does not reduce the expressiveness of the language, since arbitrary quantifications are allowed, but it does make some constraints more verbose.

E.3.2 Sample Model in OCL

An OCL version of the hotel locking model is shown in figs. E.7 and E.8.

The first figure, E.7, shows the declarations of classes and associations. The class *Desk* is included to provide a context for the state component representing the set of issued keys. As in the Alloy model, there is only one instance of *Desk*; this constraint is recorded as the invariant *oneDesk*. Note the use of the expression *Desk.allInstances*, meaning the set of instances of the class *Desk*; it would be illegal to write

```
Desk->size=1
```

instead because *Desk* denotes a class and not a set.

An association is a relation, and it may have any arity, as indicated by the number of roles: *fst* and *snd* have two roles and are binary, for example, whereas *prev* is ternary. This model follows the convention that a role of an association *a* that maps to instances of class *c* is named *c4a*.

For a binary association, the two roles are just binary relations that are transposes of one another. For a ternary relation, however, a role denotes a pair of binary relations, one for each possible source of a navigation (there being two other classes involved); and, in general, for an association with *k* roles, each role denotes *k*-1 distinct binary relations, with the appropriate relation selected according to the context.

Given a desk *d*, for example, the expression *d.key4prev* denotes the set of keys held at desk *d* as previous keys of some room; likewise *d.room4prev* denote the sets of rooms that have previous keys associated with them at desk *d*.

Roles give only a simplified view of higher-arity relations, which is not fully expressive. If there were more than one desk, one could not write an expression like Alloy's *d.prev[r]* for the previous key of room *r* at desk *d*. Fortunately, there is only a single desk, so the problem does not arise. When a truly higher-arity relation is needed in OCL, a different approach must be used, in which the relation is represented explicitly as a set of tuples. Richters explains this in section 4.9.2 of his thesis [58].

The second figure, E.8, shows the declaration of the class *Room*, and the definitions of the operations for checking in and entering a room. The operations are declared within the context of the *Room* class; this gives each an implicit argument that can be referred to by the keyword *self*, and which, unlike Alloy's *this*, can be omitted. The expression

    self.key4prev

on line 5, for example, denoting the previous key associated with the room in context, could be written instead as just *key4prev*—a shorthand not available in Alloy, since it would denote the relation as a whole.

Each operation has preconditions and postconditions that can be broken into separate, named clauses to allow a tool to give feedback about which clause is violated when checking a test case against the model. In a postcondition, roles and attributes that refer to values in the prestate are marked with the suffix *@pre*. The constraint

    g.card4cards = g.card4cards@**pre**->including(c) **and**

for example, says that the set of cards associated with the guest *g* in the poststate is the set in the prestate with the card *c* added.

The constraint

    self.key4prev=Set{c.key4snd}

on line 20 in the postcondition of *checkin* says that, in the poststate, the previous key is recorded to be the second key of the card. The *Set* key-

1 **model** hotel

2 **class** Key **end**
3 **class** Card **end**
4 **class** Guest **end**

5 **class** Desk **end**
6 **constraints**
7 **context** Desk **inv** oneDesk: Desk.**allInstances**->size=1

8 **association** fst **between**
9   Card [*] **role** card4fst
10   Key [1] **role** key4fst
11 **end**

12 **association** snd **between**
13   Card [*] **role** card4snd
14   Key [1] **role** key4snd
15 **end**

16 **association** key **between**
17   Room [*] **role** room4key
18   Key [1] **role** key4key
19 **end**

20 **association** prev **between**
21   Desk [*] **role** desk4prev
22   Room [*] **role** room4prev
23   Key [0..1] **role** key4prev
24 **end**

25 **association** issued **between**
26   Desk [*] **role** desk4issued
27   Key [*] **role** key4issued
28 **end**

29 **association** cards **between**
30   Guest [*] **role** guest4cards
31   Card [*] **role** card4cards
32 **end**

FIG. E.7 OCL model: state declaration.

```
1   class Room
2   operations

3     init()
4     post prev_eq_key:
5         self.key4prev = Set{self.key4key}
6     post issued_eq_room_key:
7         Desk.allInstances.key4issued = Room.allInstances.key4key
8     post no_cards:
9         Card.allInstances.guest4cards->isEmpty

10    checkin(g:Guest)
11    pre key_exists:
12        Key.allInstances->exists(k| Desk.allInstances.key4issued->excludes(k))
13    post fst_snd_ok_cards_issued_prev_updated:
14        Card.allInstances->exists(c|
15            self.key4prev->includes(c.key4fst) and
16            Desk.allInstances.key4issued->excludes(c.key4snd) and
17            g.card4cards = g.card4cards@pre->including(c) and
18            Desk.allInstances->forAll(d|
19                d.key4issued = d.key4issued@pre->including(c.key4snd)) and
20            self.key4prev = Set{c.key4snd})
21    post key_unchanged:
22        self.key4key@pre = self.key4key

23    enter(g:Guest)
24    pre key_matches:
25        g.card4cards->exists(c|
26            let k = key4key in c.key4snd = k or c.key4fst = k
27    post key_updated:
28        g.card4cards->exists(c|
29            let k = key4key in
30                (c.key4snd = k and self.key4key = self.key4key@pre) or
31                (c.key4fst = k and self.key4key = c.key4snd))
32    post issued_unchanged:
33        Desk.allInstances->forAll(d|d.key4issued@pre = d.key4issued)
34    post prev_unchanged:
35        Room.allInstances->forAll(r|
36            self.desk4prev@pre = self.desk4prev
37            and self.key4prev@pre = self.key4prev)
38    post cards_unchanged:
39        Card.allInstances->forAll(c|c.guest4cards@pre = c.guest4cards)

40  end
```

FIG. E.8 OCL model: operations.

word lifts the element *c.key4snd* to a set. You might think it's not necessary here, since the roles *key4prev* and *key4snd* have multiplicities of *[0..1]* and *[1]* respectively, which are type compatible. For a ternary relation, however, the multiplicity of a role *r* does not indicate the size of the set that *x.r* might represent. Rather, it indicates how many instances of that type are associated with a *combination* of instances of the other types. In this case, if there were multiple desks, *self.key4prev* might contain more than one key, despite the multiplicity, so any value equated to it must be a set and not a scalar.

E.3.3 Tools for OCL

Many tools are available for OCL. Some, such as Octopus (from Klasse Objecten, the company founded by Anneke Kleppe), are standalone tools; others are components in larger tools for model-driven development, such as the OCL component of Borland's Together Designer. Typical features are syntax and type checking, interpretation of OCL constraints over test cases, and generation of code in Java, SQL, etc, from OCL expressions.

Fewer tools support design-time analysis. The most powerful in this class seems to be the USE tool from the University of Bremen [71]. It offers an environment in which a modeler can construct test cases and evaluate OCL expressions and constraints over them. Recently, a facility for enumerating snapshots with user-provided generators has been added [18], which allows an exhaustive search over a finite space of cases in the style of Alloy. Its user interface integrates OCL with the graphical object model of UML, supporting visual editing of declarations and diagrammatic display of snapshots and executions.

With the USE tool, Martin Gogolla was able to simulate scenarios and uncover flaws, including the initialization error in the first variant of the Alloy model.

E.4   VDM

VDM stands for the "Vienna Development Method," so called because it grew out of work at IBM's Vienna Laboratory on programming language definition in the 1970's. The method, developed by Cliff Jones and Dines Bjørner, comprises a specification language and an approach to refining specifications into code. Many of the basic principles and ideas of logic-based specification first appeared in VDM.

Nowadays, the term "VDM" usually refers to the language, for which the classic reference is Jones's book [41]. The latest version of the language, VDM-SL (the VDM Specification Language), was standardized by ISO in the 1990's [47]; it has two syntaxes, one ASCII-based (used by most VDM tools), and one using special mathematical symbols.

VDM has been used in a variety of industrial settings; recent applications have included the development of electronic trading systems, secure smart cards and the Dutch flower auction system.

Two recent books explain the process of modeling in VDM; the first [16] uses the standardized language, VDM-SL, and the second [17] uses VDM++, an extension that includes object-oriented features and concurrency. Both books include case studies, and stress the use of light-weight tool technology for aiding dialog between engineers and domain experts. A paper by Jones discusses the rationale behind the design of VDM [42].

E.4.1 Basic Notions of VDM

A VDM specification describes a state machine comprising a set of states and a collection of operations. The states are given by a top-level declaration and auxiliary declarations to introduce any composite types that it uses. Each declaration can be accompanied by an invariant.

Operations have separate pre- and postconditions. Each operation must be *implementable*, meaning that the postcondition admits at least one poststate for each prestate satisfying the precondition. If an operation is written in an *explicit* style (that is, with a postcondition consisting of assignments to poststate components), it will be implementable by construction. The invariants, as in Alloy, OCL and Z, are implicitly included in the pre- and postconditions. Explicit operations must be preserve invariants.

The pre- and postcondition of one operation can be used in another by *operation quotation*, which treats the operation much like a pair of Alloy predicates. *Validation conjectures* play the role of Alloy's assertions, and are formulated in a tool-specific language extension, rather than in the VDM language itself.

In contrast to Alloy, B, OCL and Z (and in common with languages aimed more at describing code interfaces, such as JML [48] and the Larch interface languages [23]), VDM has *frame conditions* indicating which state variables may be read or written by an operation. A frame condition can make an operation much more succinct (since there is no need to mention components that don't change), and may make it easier to read at a glance. The downside is that frame conditions assume a more restrictive form of specification than languages such as Alloy and Z permit; you can't, for example, add redundant components to the state that are defined in terms of other components without changing all the operations.

E.4.2 Sample Model in VDM

A VDM version of the hotel locking model is shown in two parts: the type declarations in fig. E.9, and the operations in fig. E.10.

The type declarations begin with the declaration of *Key*, *Room* and *Guest* as "token" types, meaning that they denote sets of uninterpreted atoms. In contrast, *Card* and *Desk* are declared as record types. The special type *Hotel* corresponding to the global state is also a record type. Each type may be followed by an invariant; that of *Desk* (line 11), for example, says that the set of rooms that have a previous key associated with them is a subset of the set of rooms for which keys have been issued.

Alloy, in contrast, has no composite types (except for relations). The use of record types has benefits and drawbacks. The primary benefit is that a constructor can be used to create a fresh value (as in line 8), where Alloy requires a set comprehension or existential quantifier (as in line 2 of fig. E.2). The drawbacks are extra notation (note VDM's dot in *c.fst* but the brackets in *locks(r)*) and the problems they create for analysis.

Records can often be represented with signatures in Alloy, but the lack of constructors lies at the heart of the unbounded universals problem described in section 5.3. A record has no identity distinct from its value, so the VDM model does not distinguish two cards held by different guests that happen to have the same keys.

The more general, higher-order nature of VDM can be seen in the state invariant on line 16. The formula

dunion {{c.fst, c.snd} | c **in set dunion rng** h.guests}
subset h.desk.issued

says that the first and second keys on cards held by guests must be recorded as issued at the desk. Because the expression *h.guests* is a function from guests to sets of cards, its range, *rng h.guests*, is a set of sets, which must be flattened by taking a distributed union before determining whether card *c* belongs. In Alloy, sets of sets are not expressible, and this constraint would be written instead as

all t: Time | Guest.cards.t.(fst + snd) **in** Desk.issued.t

The time variable t plays the role of the state variable h in the VDM specification. Its placement is an artifact of the idiom chosen, and it would precede rather than follow the field names if the state were modeled as a signature instead, as in the memory or media asset examples of chapter 6.

An operation has a listing of arguments and their types, frame conditions, a precondition and a postcondition. Note how frame conditions shorten their associated postcondition; in *Enter*, for example, because only the *locks* components is writeable, there is no need for equalities on the other components, as in lines 17 and 18 of the Alloy model of fig. E.2.

The explicit precondition makes it easier to see when an operation applies, but it can make the operation more verbose: note how the precondition of *Enter* (line 17) is repeated in the postcondition, since the existential quantifier cannot span both.

VDM's pre- and postconditions are just logical formulas, like the body of an Alloy predicate. Unlike Alloy, and like the other approaches (although to a lesser extent Z), VDM assumes a particular state machine idiom, and provides special syntax to support it. The *state* declaration, unlike the other type declarations, defines a mutable structure, whose components have separate values in the pre- and poststate of an operation. The values of a component c in the pre- and poststates are referred to as $c\sim$ and c respectively. The special symbol & separates a quantifier's binding from its body.

This is convenient but less flexible than Alloy's approach. All mutations are confined to the top-level components of the state; you could not, for example, make cards mutable in order to model modifications to existing cards by hackers (as you could in Alloy by adding a time column to the relations of *Card*). VDM++, however, allows all structures to be mutable.

VDM distinguishes sets from relations. So where Alloy would use the single operator + for all unions, VDM uses *union* on sets and *munion* on maps. Being higher-order, it requires set former brackets to distinguish maps from tuples and sets from their elements. The initialization condition on line 21, for example, equates the range of the mapping from guests to sets of cards to {{}}—the set containing just the empty set—and writing {} here instead would mean something different. Simi-

```
 1  types
 2     Key = token;
 3     Room = token;
 4     Guest = token;

 5     Card ::
 6        fst : Key
 7        snd : Key;
 8     Desk ::
 9        issued : set of Key
10        prev : map Room to Key
11     inv d == rng d.prev subset d.issued;

12     state Hotel of
13        desk : Desk
14        locks : map Room to Key
15        guests : map Guest to set of Card
16     inv h ==
17        dom h.desk.prev subset dom h.locks and
18        dunion {{c.fst, c.snd} | c in set dunion rng h.guests}
19           subset h.desk.issued
20     init h == h.desk.issued = rng h.locks and
21        h.desk.prev = h.locks and rng h.guests = {{}}
22  end
```

FIG. E.9 VDM model: type declarations.

larly, the expressions used to extend the maps *guests* and *locks* require set brackets for one (as in *{r |-> new_k}*) but not the other (*{g |-> {new_c}}*).

To apply an animator (such as that of the VDMTools) to an operation, it must be written in an explicit form. An example, for the *Checkin* operation, is shown in fig. E.11. The existential quantifier has been replaced by a *let* statement; the constraints of the postcondition have been replaced by assignments; and the frame condition is no longer necessary. This notation is very similar to B.

```
1    operations
2       CheckIn(g:Guest,r:Room)
3          ext wr desk : Desk
4             wr guests : map Guest to set of Card
5          pre r in set dom desk.prev
6          post exists new_k:Key &
7             new_k not in set desk~.issued and
8             let new_c = mk_Card(desk~.prev(r),new_k) in
9                desk.issued = desk~.issued union {new_k} and
10               desk.prev = desk~.prev ++ {r |-> new_k} and
11               if g in set dom guests
12                  then guests = guests~ ++ {g |-> guests~(g) union {new_c}}
13                  else guests = guests~ munion {g |-> {new_c}};

14      Enter(r:Room,g:Guest)
15         ext wr locks : map Room to Key
16            rd guests : map Guest to set of Card
17         pre r in set dom locks and g in set dom guests and
18            exists c in set guests(g) & c.fst = locks(r) or c.snd = locks(r)
19         post exists c in set guests(g) &
20            c.fst = locks(r) and locks = locks~ ++ {r |-> c.snd} or
21            c.snd = locks(r) and locks = locks~;
```

FIG. E.10 VDM model: operations.

```
1       CheckInExpl: Guest * Room ==> ()
2       CheckInExpl(g,r) ==
3          let new_k:Key be st new_k not in set desk.issued in
4          let new_c = mk_Card(desk.prev(r),new_k) in (
5             desk.issued := desk.issued union {new_k};
6             desk.prev := desk.prev ++ {r |-> new_k};
7             guests := if g in set dom guests
8                then guests ++ {g |-> guests(g) union {new_c}}
9                else guests munion {g |-> {new_c}}
10            )
11         pre r in set dom desk.prev;
```

FIG. E.11 VDM model: operations.

E.4.3 Tools for VDM

Under the guidance of Peter Gorm Larsen, IFAD—a Danish company that offered VDM consulting in the 1990's—developed VDMTools, a toolkit for both VDM-SL and VDM^{++}. It included a type checker and theorem prover, and, for an executable subset of VDM, a facility for simulating and testing specifications, and a code generator. The toolkit is now owned by CSK Corporation of Japan. New tool support for VDM^{++} is being developed under the *Overture* open source initiative.

E.5   Z

Z was developed at Oxford University in the 1980's. It has been very influential in education and research, and has been applied successfully on several large projects, notably by Oxford University and IBM on the CICS system, in a series of projects by Praxis Critical Systems, and to the security verification of the Mondex electronic purse developed by NatWest Bank (the first ever product certified to ITSEC Level 6) [69, 68]. Z's clean and simple semantic foundation was an inspiration for the design of Alloy.

Although the language has been standardized by ISO [30], the version described in Mike Spivey's book [65] continues to be the most popular. Many books have been written about Z, including textbooks [40, 56, 74, 75], case study collections [26], and a guide to style [3].

E.5.1 Basic Notions of Z

Z, like Alloy, is at heart just a logic, augmented with some syntactic constructs to make it easy to describe software abstractions. In Alloy, these constructs are the signature, for packaging declarations, and facts/predicates/functions for packaging constraints. In Z, the same construct—the *schema* is used both to package declarations and constraints. The language of schemas, called the *schema calculus*, is rich enough to support a wide variety of idioms.

In practice, though, a particular idiom—called variously the "Oxford style," the "IBM style," and the "established strategy" [3]—has been adopted in almost all Z specifications since the earliest days. A collection of syntactic conventions have grown around it, and have become a de facto part of the language itself. The operator for combining operations by sequential composition, for example, assumes the use of this idiom; without it, the operator will not have the expected meaning.

Z, unlike B, does not have a built-in notion of refinement, and indeed many Z users view it as a system modeling language, and have no intent to prove conformance of their code to the model. There is, however, a well-established theory of refinement for Z, and the language is well-suited to developments by stepwise refinement. Woodcock's book [74] is an accessible introduction to this approach.

The sample model shown here is the first, most abstract, model in a development by refinement. Like the abstract B model of fig. E.4, it determines entry to the room by examining the room roster; in a subsequent refinement (not shown here), entry is determined by keys and locks alone. The abstract Z model does not, however, omit mention of keys and locks entirely: the recoding key on the card is selected on entry (rather than when checking in). The refinement will move this non-deterministic choice backwards in time to the checkin, with the same justification used for the example of section 6.4.6.

A Z specification is built as a series of schema declarations. A declaration has two parts: a series of variable declarations, and a predicate constraining them. When a reference is made to a previously declared scheme, both its variable declarations and predicate are incorporated implicitly. A schema representing state typically builds on previous state schemas by adding new components and constraining the state further with additional invariants. A schema representing an operation may incorporate state schemas for the pre- and poststates, or it may extend a previous operation schema, adding constraints to make its behaviour more specific.

Because incorporating a schema brings the variables it declares into scope, there is often no explicit declaration for a variable that appears in a schema's predicate. As a result, Z specifications can be very succinct—sometimes mysteriously so. Exactly the same power, with the same potential for succinctness and obscurity, is found in the inheritance mechanisms of object-oriented programming languages, and in Alloy's signature extension mechanism (which was, incidentally, designed explicitly to support schema-style structuring).

In the Oxford style, state invariants are declared with the state declarations and are thus incorporated implicitly into operations, as in VDM, and in marked contrast to B, where invariants must be shown to be preserved by operations. Preconditions of operations are not separated from postconditions. It is regarded as good style for the precondition to appear explicitly in the operation schema, but it is not necessary. In place of the implementability check of VDM, a Z specifier *derives* a precondition from an operation schema and compares it to the one expected.

Sets and relations are the predominant datatypes in Z. In this respect, Z is similar to B—which is not surprising, since B's inventor, Jean-Raymond Abrial, was one of the early developers of Z (and had worked before that on database semantics). For both Z and B, sets are seen as fundamental and relations as derived; Z is so named because of its roots in ZF (Zermelo-Fraenkel) set theory. Alloy is also based on sets and relations, but its logic is more influenced by the relational formalisms of Tarski's calculus [70] and Codd's relational database model [9], with sets regarded as a special case of relations.

Like VDM, however, Z does include record types. The same schema construct that is used syntactically for grouping declarations together can be used semantically to declare a 'schema type', whose values are bindings of values to field names. Schema types are more powerful than Alloy's signatures, because they provide constructors. Unlike signatures, however, schemas have no subtyping. One schema can be defined as an extension of another schema, but the types of the two schemas are unrelated. For example, if you declared a schema for a file system object, and extended it into two other schemas corresponding to files and folders, you would not be able to insert an instance of the file or folder schema into a set or relation declared over file system objects.

Z has a distinctive appearance, with boxes drawn around schemas, and its own collection of mathematical symbols. Here we use the "horizontal form," which, although less elegant, can be produced without special layout tools.

E.5.2 Sample Model in Z

A Z specification of the hotel locking problem is shown in figs. E.12, E.13 and E.14.

The first figure (E.12) shows the declaration of the state and initialization. Guests, keys and rooms are declared as *given sets*: uninterpreted sets of atoms that become the basis for type checking. A global variable *initkeys* is declared that represents the function associating room locks with the initial values of their keys. A *Msg* datatype is declared to represent the possible outcomes of operations.

Hotel is our first schema declaration. It introduces 3 variables that will represent the state components of the system: *firsttime*, a set of rooms; *key*, a function from rooms to keys (representing the keys held in their

[Guest, Key, Room]

initkeys: Room ⤔ Key;

Msg ::= okay
　| room_already_allocated
　| guest_already_registered
　| room_not_allocated
　| wrong_guest
　| key_not_fresh

Hotel ≜ [
　firsttime: ℙ Room
　key: Room ⤔ Key
　guest: Room ⤀ Guest
　]

InitHotel ≜ [
　Hotel′
　|
　firsttime′ = ∅
　key′ = initkeys
　guest′ = ∅
　]

FIG. E.12 State and initialization in Z.

locks in a particular state); and *guest*, a function from rooms to guests (representing the occupancy roster). The kind of arrow indicates the multiplicities: that *key* is a partial injection, and *guest* is a partial function.

This model, because it is the first in a development by refinement, will describe exactly when an entry should be permitted, and when a lock should be rekeyed; a later refinement would describe the mechanism by which entry is determined by checking keys. This explains the *firsttime* component, which did not appear in the Alloy model, but is used to mark the set of rooms which, when subsequently entered, should have their locks recoded (since a new guest will be entering for the first time).

```
1   Checkin0 ≙ [
2       Δ Hotel
3       g?: Guest
4       r?: Room
5       |
6       r? ∉ dom guest
7       g? ∉ ran guest
8       firsttime' = firsttime ∪ {r?}
9       key' = key
10      guest' = guest ∪ {r? ↦ g?}
11     ]

12  EnterFst ≙ [
13      Δ Hotel
14      g?: Guest
15      r?: Room
16      k?: Key
17      |
18      r? ∈ firsttime
19      r? ∈ dom guest
20      guest r? = g?
21      k? ∉ ran key
22      firsttime' = firsttime \ {r?}
23      key' = key ⊕ {r? ↦ k?}
24      guest' = guest
25     ]

26  EnterSnd ≙ [
27      Ξ Hotel
28      g?: Guest
29      r?: Room
30      |
31      r? ∈ dom guest
32      guest r? = g?
33      r? ∉ firsttime
34     ]
```

FIG. E.13 Checkin and Enter operations in Z.

InitHotel, the second schema, describes the initialization. Unlike *Hotel* which included only variable declarations, this schema has both declarations and a predicate. The declarations are those of *Hotel*, imported by mentioning the schema's name. Notice the prime mark appended to the name. This is called *decoration*; its effect is to include not exactly the declarations of *Hotel*, but versions in which each variable is likewise primed. These primed variables are used in Z to refer to the values of state components after execution of an operation (in this case, the initialization).

A schema predicate is just a constraint, formed by conjoining the constraints on each line. Each line's constraint is a simple mathematical formula, with the equals sign denoting equality (and not assignment). So there is no semantic significance to the ordering of the terms in these equations, and we could reverse each equation without changing its meaning. This specification has been written, however, in a form that suggests how it might be executed, with the primed variables on the left. This allows it to be animated using a tool such as Jaza. The same rationale explains why the initialization equates *keys'* to the previously declared function *initkeys*, just as the corresponding component was initialized in the B model (on line 23 of fig. E.5). A more traditional Z style would simply not mention *keys'*, leaving its value unconstrained.

The second figure (E.13) shows the checkin and entry operations for normal cases; the exceptional cases are described in separate operations in the next figure. There are three schemas corresponding to checking in, and two forms of entry—one which recodes the lock, and one which does not.

The first two, *Checkin0* and *EnterFst*, mention Δ *Hotel* in their declarations. This is a schema, defined implicitly by convention, that includes *Hotel* and *Hotel'*, thus introducing standard and primed versions of each state variable, to represent the state components before and after execution. The third schema, *EnterSnd*, mentions Ξ *Hotel*. This refers to a similar schema, also including *Hotel* and *Hotel'*, but additionally a constraint equating each state variable to its primed version. Its use, therefore, indicates an operation that has no effect on the state.

Each operation also declares some variables decorated with question marks. By convention, these represent input arguments; semantically, they are no different from the variables representing the state components. When an operation schema is used elsewhere, these arguments are bound by a syntactic substitution that replaces every occurrence of an argument variable in the schema with a variable name from the new context. In comparison to the explicit parameterization of Alloy, this can be a bit awkward: an expression cannot be substituted for a variable, so if no variable already exists for the actual argument, it must be de-

Success ≜ [m!: Msg | m! = okay]

EnterRoomNotAllocated ≜ [
    Ξ Hotel
    r?: Room
    m!: Msg
    |
    r? ∉ **dom** guest
    m! = room_not_allocated
    ]

EnterWrongGuest ≜ [
    Ξ Hotel
    g?: Guest
    r?: Room
    m!: Msg
    |
    r? ∈ **dom** guest
    guest r? ≠ g?
    m! = wrong_guest
    ]

Enter ≜ EnterFst ∧ Success ∨ EnterSnd ∧ Success ∨
    EnterRoomNotAllocated ∨ EnterWrongGuest

FIG. E.14 Variant operations in Z.

clared with an existential quantifier. On the other hand, when the actual and formal arguments have the same name, no substitution is necessary and the resulting text is uncluttered by argument lists.

Z does not distinguish pre- and postconditions syntactically, and there is no need to make preconditions explicit at all. It is regarded as good style to list preconditions in full, however, above the constraints of the postcondition. The precondition of *Checkin0*, for example, is that *r?* is not in the domain of *guest*, and *g?* is not in its range—that is, the room requested is not already occupied, and the guest is not already assigned to another room. This stylistic guideline is not generally checkable by simple syntactic means, since the explicit precondition might admit states for which the postcondition cannot be satisfied, so that the actual precondition is stronger. A theorem asserting that the operation has the expected precondition can be formulated. For *Checkin0*, this theorem is:

Theorem preCheckin0
∀ Hotel; g?: Guest; r?: Room |
    r? ∉ **dom** guest ∧ g? ∉ **ran** guest • **pre** Checkin0

This kind of theorem is not expressible in Alloy, as explained in section 5.3. Unintentional overconstraint is mitigated instead by simulating the operation.

The operation predicates are unsurprising. *Checkin0*, for example, adds to the *guest* relation a mapping from *r?* to *g?*; *EnterFst* recodes the lock by overriding the *key* relation with a mapping from *r?* to the new key *k?*. Note that, as in Alloy and OCL, a state variable that is unmentioned is unconstrained, so if a component is unchanged, an explicit equality is needed (as in line 24).

The third figure, E.14, shows how the behavior of these operations is augmented to cover exceptional cases. The schema *Success* simply introduces an output argument *m!* and equates it to the message *okay*. The next two schemas specify the conditions under which an entry should be regarded as impermissible, because the room has not been allocated to a guest at all, or because the guest attempting entry is not the legitimate occupant. These conditions are expressed as preconditions, and are accompanied by postconditions that constrain the value of the message accordingly.

Finally, a schema is declared that brings the different cases together: *Enter* is an operation that describes all the scenarios of attempted entry to a room. Note its assembly using just disjunction and conjunction. This simplicity is a consequence of operations being no more than logical formulas. Alloy took this idea from Z, and thus supports the same kind of structuring.

E.5.3 Tools for Z

Most tool support for Z has focused on theorem proving. The most widely used proof tools are ProofPower (from Lemma 1 Ltd), and Z/Eves, a front-end to the Eves theorem prover (from ORA Canada). The sample model was analyzed with Z/Eves. The tool can calculate preconditions and perform "domain checks" (which ensure that partial functions are never applied outside their domains), as well as performing general theorem proving. Although many steps in a proof are executed automatically, complex theorems tend to require guidance from an experienced user.

A number of animators have been built for Z. The sample model was tested using Jaza [72], an animator developed by Mark Utting at the University of Waikato. Jaza can execute operations written in an explicit style, and can do a certain amount of constraint solving over small domains. The entire sample model above can be handled in Jaza. We noted how the initialization, for example, assigns the global function *initkeys* to *keys'* rather than leaving it unconstrained; this allows the initialization to be executed given a value of *initkeys* by the user. Like the USE tool and the animator of the VDMTools, Jaza can evaluate expressions, check given states against invariants and transitions against operations, and can simulate an execution trace with the user selecting operations and providing input arguments.

References

[1]   Jean-Raymond Abrial. *The B-Book: Assigning Programs to Meanings.*
      Cambridge, UK, Cambridge University Press, 1996.

[2]   Sten Agerhold and Peter Gorm Larsen. The IFAD VDM tools: Light-
      weight formal methods. In Dieter Hutter, Werner Stephan, Paolo Tra-
      verso, Markus Ullmann (eds.), *Applied Formal Methods—FM-Trends 98,
      International Workshop on Current Trends in Applied Formal Methods,*
      Boppard, Germany, October 1998. Lecture Notes in Computer Science,
      Vol. 1641, Berlin, Springer-Verlag, 1999, pp. 326–329.

[3]   Rosalind Barden, Susan Stepney and David Cooper. *Z in Practice.* Engle-
      wood Cliffs, New Jersey, Prentice-Hall, 1995.

[4]   Kent Beck. *Extreme Programming Explained.* Boston, Addison Wesley,
      1999.

[5]   Armin Biere, Alessandro Cimatti, Edmund M. Clarke, and Yunshan Zhu.
      Symbolic model checking without BDDs. In Rance Cleaveland (ed.),
      Tools and Algorithms for Construction and Analysis of Systems, Neth-
      erlands, March 1999. Lecture Notes in Computer Science, Vol. 1579,
      Berlin, Springer-Verlag, 1999, pp. 193–207.

[6]   Egon Börger, Erich Grädel and Yuri Gurevich. *The Classical Decision
      Problem.* Berlin, Springer-Verlag, 1997.

[7]   Alex Borgida, John Mylopoulos, and Raymond Reiter. On the frame
      problem in procedure specifications. *IEEE Transactions on Software
      Engineering,* 21(10):785–798, 1995.

[8]   E.J.H. Chang and R. Roberts. An improved algorithm for decentralized
      extrema-finding in circular configurations of processes. *Communica-
      tions of the ACM,* 22(5):281–283, 1979.

[9]   E. F. Codd. A relational model of data for large shared data banks. *Com-
      munications of the ACM,* 13(6):377-387, 1970.

[10] Steve Cook and John Daniels. *Designing Object Systems: Object-Ori-
      ented Modelling with Syntropy.* Englewood Cliffs, New Jersey, Prentice-
      Hall, 1994.

[11] Craig A. Damon, Daniel Jackson and Somesh Jha. Checking relational
      specifications with binary decision diagrams. In *Proceedings of 4th
      ACM SIGSOFT Conference on Foundations of Software Engineering,* San
      Francisco, CA, October 1996, pp. 70–80.

[12]   Edsger W. Dijkstra. Where is Russell's paradox?, EWD-923A, May 1985.
       Available at *http://www.cs.utexas.edu/users/EWD*.

[13]   Edsger W. Dijkstra. On the Reliability of Mechanisms. In *Notes on
       Structured Programming*, EWD249, Second Edition, April 1970. Avail-
       able at *http://www.cs.utexas.edu/users/EWD*.

[14]   Jonathan Edwards, Daniel Jackson, and Emina Torlak. A type system for
       object models. In *Proceedings of ACM SIGSOFT Conference on Founda-
       tions of Software Engineering*, Newport Beach, CA, November 2004.

[15]   Michael Ernst, Todd Millstein, and Daniel Weld. Automatic SAT-com-
       pilation of planning problems. In *Proceedings of the Fifteenth Interna-
       tional Joint Conference on Artificial Intelligence*, Nagoya, 1997. Morgan
       Kaufmann Publishers, 1997.

[16]   John Fitzgerald and Peter Gorm Larsen. *Modelling Systems: Practical
       Tools and Techniques for Software Development*. Cambridge, UK, Cam-
       bridge University Press, 1998.

[17]   John Fitzgerald, Peter Gorm Larsen, Paul Mukherjee, Nico Plat, and
       Marcel Verhoef. *Validated Designs for Object-Oriented Systems*. Berlin,
       Springer-Verlag, 2005.

[18]   Martin Gogolla, Jörn Bohling, and Mark Richters. Validation of UML
       and OCL models by automatic snapshot generation. In Grady Booch,
       Perdita Stevens, and Jonathan Whittle (eds.), *Proceedings of Sixth Inter-
       national Conference on the Unified Modeling Language*, San Francisco,
       2003. Lecture Notes in Computer Science, Vol. 2863, Berlin, Springer-
       Verlag, 2003, pp. 265–279.

[19]   Eugene Goldberg and Yakov Novikov. BerkMin: a Fast and Robust SAT-
       Solver. In *Proceedings of the Conference on Design, Automation and Test
       in Europe*, Paris, 2002. Washington, DC, IEEE Computer Society, pp.
       142–149.

[20]   Erich Grädel. Decidable fragments of first-order and fixed-point logic:
       from prefix-vocabulary classes to guarded logics. In *Proceedings of
       Kalmär Workshop on Logic and Computer Science*, Szeged, 2003. Avail-
       able at *http://www-mgi.informatik.rwth-aachen.de/Publications/pub/
       graedel/Gr-kalmar03.ps*.

[21]   John Guttag and James J. Horning. Formal specification as a design tool.
       In *Proceedings of the Seventh ACM SIGPLAN-SIGACT Symposium on
       Principles of Programming*, Las Vegas, 1980, pp. 251–261.

[22]   John V. Guttag and James J. Horning. Preliminary report on the Larch
       Shared Language. Technical Report MIT/LCS/TR-307, MIT Laboratory
       for Computer Science, Cambridge, MA, 1983.

[23] John V. Guttag and James J. Horning. *Introduction to LCL: A Larch/C interface language*. Research Report 74, Digital Equipment Corporation Systems Research Center, Palo Alto, CA, July 1991. Available at: *http://gatekeeper.research.compaq.com/pub/DEC/SRC/research-reports/abstracts/src-rr-074.html*.

[24] Paul R. Halmos. *Problems for Mathematicians, Young and Old*. Mathematical Association of America, 1991.

[25] David Harel. *Algorithmics: The Spirit of Computing*. Reading, MA, Addison-Wesley. 1st ed., 1987; 2nd ed., 1992; 3rd ed. (with Yishai Feldman), 2004.

[26] Ian Hayes, editor. *Specification Case Studies*. London, Prentice Hall International (UK), 1987.

[27] Eric C.R. Hehner. Bunch theory: a simple set theory for computer science. *Information Processing Letters*, 12(1):26–30, 1981.

[28] C.A.R. Hoare. Proof of correctness of data representations. *Acta Informatica*. 1:271–281, 1972.

[29] C.A.R. Hoare. The emperor's old clothes. *Communications of the ACM*, 24(2):75–83, 1981.

[30] *Information technology – Z formal specification notation – Syntax, type system and semantics*. International Standard ISO/IEC 13568, July 2002.

[31] Daniel Jackson. Boolean compilation of relational specifications. Technical Report MIT-LCS-TR-735, MIT Laboratory for Computer Science, Cambridge, MA, December 1997.

[32] Daniel Jackson. An intermediate design language and its analysis. In *Proceedings of ACM SIGSOFT Conference on Foundations of Software Engineering*, Lake Buena Vista, FL, November 1998, pp. 121–130.

[33] Daniel Jackson. Alloy: a lightweight object modelling notation. *ACM Transactions on Software Engineering and Methodology*, 11(2):256–290, 2002.

[34] Daniel Jackson, Craig A. Damon, and Somesh Jha. Faster checking of software specifications. In *Proceedings of ACM Conference on Principles of Programming Languages*, St. Petersburg Beach, FL, January 1996, pp. 79–90.

[35] Daniel Jackson and Craig A. Damon. Elements of style: analyzing a software design feature with a counterexample detector. *IEEE Transactions on Software Engineering*, 22(7):484–495, 1996.

[36] Daniel Jackson, Somesh Jha, and Craig A. Damon. Isomorph-free model enumeration: a new method for checking relational specifications. *ACM*

Transactions on Programming Languages and Systems. 20(2):302–343, 1998.

[37] Daniel Jackson and Jeannette Wing. Lightweight formal methods. In Hossein Saiedian (ed.), Roundtable contribution to: An invitation to formal methods, *IEEE Computer,* 29(4):16–30, 1996.

[38] Michael Jackson. *Software Requirements and Specifications: A Lexicon of Software Practice, Principles and Prejudices.* Boston, Addison Wesley, 1995.

[39] Michael Jackson. *Problem Frames: Analyzing and Structuring Software Development Problems.* Boston, Addison Wesley Professional, 2000.

[40] Jonathan Jacky. *The Way of Z: Practical Programming with Formal Methods.* Cambridge, UK, Cambridge University Press, 1996.

[41] Cliff Jones. *Systematic Software Development Using VDM,* 2nd ed., Englewood Cliffs, New Jersey, Prentice-Hall, 1990.

[42] Cliff B. Jones. Scientific decisions which characterize VDM. In *Proceedings of the 1999 World Congress on Formal Methods in the Development of Computing Systems,* Toulouse, France, September 1999. Jeannette Wing, Jim Woodock, and Jim Davies (eds.), Lecture Notes in Computer Science, Vol. 1708, Berlin, Springer-Verlag, 1999, pp. 28–47.

[43] Henry Kautz and Bart Selman. Planning as satisfiability. In *Proceedings of the Tenth European Conference on Artificial Intelligence,* Vienna, 1992. John Wiley & Sons, 1992, pp. 359–363.

[44] Viktor Kuncak and Daniel Jackson. Relational analysis of algebraic datatypes. In *Proceedings of Foundations of Software Engineering,* Lisbon, September 2005.

[45] Viktor Kuncak and Martin Rinard. Decision procedures for set-valued fields. In *Proceedings of First International Workshop on Abstract Interpretation of Object-Oriented Languages,* Paris, 2005.

[46] Kevin Lano and Howard Haughton. *Specification in B: An Introduction using the B Toolkit.* London, Imperial College Press, 1996.

[47] P.G. Larsen, B.S. Hansen, H. Brunn, N. Plat, H. Toetenel, D. J. Andrews, J. Dawes, G. Parkin et al. *Information technology – Programming languages, their environments and system software interfaces – Vienna Development Method – Specification Language – Part 1: Base language.* International Standard ISO/IEC 13817-1, December 1996.

[48] Gary T. Leavens, Albert L. Baker and Clyde Ruby. JML: a notation for detailed design. In Haim Kilov, Bernhard Rumpe, and Ian Simmonds (eds.), *Behavioral Specifications of Businesses and Systems,* Chapter 12, pp. 175–188, Amsterdam, Kluwer, 1999.

[49] Michael Leuschel and Michael Butler. ProB: a model checker for B. In *Proceedings of International Symposium of Formal Methods Europe*, Pisa, 2003. Lecture Notes in Computer Science, Vol. 2805, Berlin, Springer-Verlag, 2003, pp. 855–874.

[50] Zohar Manna and Amir Pnueli. *The Temporal Logic of Reactive and Concurrent Systems: Specification*. Berlin, Springer-Verlag, 1992.

[51] John McCarthy. Situations, actions, and causal laws. Technical Report, Stanford University, Stanford, CA, 1963. Reprinted in Marvin Minsky (ed.), *Semantic Information Processing*, Cambridge, MA, MIT Press, 1968.

[52] Stanley Milgram. The small world problem. *Psychology Today*, 2:60-67, 1967.

[53] Object Management Group. *UML 2.0 OCL Specification*. OMG Final Adopted Specification, ptc/03-10-14. October 2003. Available at *http:// www.omg.org/docs/ptc/03-10-14.pdf*.

[54] Carroll Morgan. Telephone network. In [26], pp. 73–87.

[55] M.W. Moskewicz, C.F. Madigan, Y. Zhao, L. Zhang, and S. Salik. 2001. Chaff: engineering an efficient SAT solver. In *Proceedings of the 38th Conference on Design Automation*, Las Vegas, June 2001. New York, ACM Press, pp. 530–535.

[56] Ben Potter, David Till and Jane Sinclair. *An Introduction to Formal Specification and Z*. 2nd ed. Upper Saddle River, NJ, Prentice Hall PTR, 1996.

[57] Raymond Reiter. The frame problem in the situation calculus: a simple solution (sometimes) and a completeness result for goal regression. In V. Lifschitz, (ed.), *Artificial Intelligence and the Mathematical Theory of Computation: Papers in Honor of John McCarthy*, San Diego, Academic Press, 1991, pp. 359–380.

[58] Mark Richters. *A Precise Approach to Validating UML Models and OCL Constraints*. PhD thesis, Universitaet Bremen. Berlin, Logos Verlag, BISS Monographs, No. 14, 2002.

[59] Mark Richters and Martin Gogolla. On formalizing the UML object constraint language OCL. In *Proceedings of 17th International Conference on Conceptual Modeling*, Singapore, 1998. Tok Wang Ling, Sudha Ram, and Mong Li Lee (eds.), Lecture Notes in Computer Science, Vol. 1507, Berlin, Springer-Verlag, 1998, pp. 449–464.

[60] Mark Richters and Martin Gogolla. Validating UML models and OCL constraints. In *Proceedings of Third International Conference on the Unified Modeling Language: Advancing the Standard*, York, UK, Oc-

tober 2000. Andy Evans, Stuart Kent, and Bran Selic (eds.), Lecture Notes in Computer Science, Vol. 1939, Berlin, Springer-Verlag, 2000, pp. 265–277.

[61] Steve Schneider. *The B-Method: An Introduction*. Cornerstones of Computing Series, Hampshire, UK, Palgrave, 2001.

[62] Emil Sekerinski and Kaisa Sere, eds. *Program Development by Refinement : Case Studies Using the B Method*. Formal Approaches to Computing and Information Technology Series, Berlin, Springer-Verlag, 1999.

[63] Ilya Shlyakhter. Generating effective symmetry-breaking predicates for search problems. In *Proceedings of LICS 2001 Workshop on Theory and Applications of Satisfiability Testing*, June 2001, Boston, MA. Henry Kautz and Bart Selman (eds.), Electronic Notes in Discrete Mathematics, Vol. 9, 2001.

[64] Ilya Shlyakhter. Declarative symbolic pure-logic model checking. PhD Thesis, Department of Electrical Engineering and Computer Science, Massachusetts Institute of Technology, Cambridge, MA. February 2005.

[65] J. Michael Spivey. *The Z Notation: A Reference Manual*, 2nd ed. Upper Saddle River, NJ, Prentice Hall, 1992.

[66] G. Stalmarck and M. Saflund. Modeling and verifying systems and software in propositional logic. In *Proceedings of International Conference on Safety of Computer Control Systems*. Oxford, Pergamon Press, 1990, pp. 31–36.

[67] P. R. Stephan, R. K. Brayton, and A. L. Sangiovanni-Vincentelli. Combinational test generation using satisfiability. Technical Report M92/112, Departement of Electrical Engineering and Computer Science, University of California at Berkeley, Berkeley, CA, October 1992.

[68] Susan Stepney, David Cooper and Jim Woodcock. More powerful Z data refinement: pushing the state of the art in industrial refinement. In *Proceedings of Z User Meeting*, Berlin, Germany, 1998. Jonathan P. Bowen, Andreas Fett, and Michael G. Hinchey (eds): *ZUM '98: The Z Formal Specification Notation*, Lecture Notes in Computer Science, Vol. 1493, Berlin, Springer-Verlag, 1998, pp. 284–307.

[69] Susan Stepney, David Cooper, and Jim Woodcock. An electronic purse: specification, refinement, and proof. Technical Monograph PRG-126, Oxford University Computing Laboratory, Oxford, July 2000.

[70] Alfred Tarski and Steven Givant. A formalization of set theory without variables. *American Mathematical Society Colloquium Publications*, Vol. 41, 1987.

[71] USE: A UML-based specification environment. University of Bremen, Germany. Available at *http://www.db.informatik.uni-bremen.de/projects/USE/*.

[72] Mark Utting. *The Jaza Animator*. University of Waikato, New Zealand. Available at: *http://www.cs.waikato.ac.nz/~marku/jaza*.

[73] Jos Warmer and Anneke Kleppe. *The Object Constraint Language: Getting Your Models Ready for MDA*. Boston, Addison-Wesley, 2003.

[74] Jim Woodcock and Jim Davies. *Using Z: Specification, Refinement, and Proof*. Upper Saddle River, NJ, Prentice Hall, 1996.

[75] John Wordsworth. *Software Development With Z: A Practical Approach to Formal Methods in Software Engineering*. Boston, Addison-Wesley, 1992.

[76] John Wordsworth. *Software Engineering With B*. Boston, Addison Wesley Longman, 1996.

Index

Symbols

! (not) 69, 284, 286
\# (cardinality) 80, 282
&& (and) 69, 286
& (intersection) 52, 279
* (reflexive transitive closure) 65, 279
+ (in signature declaration) 92
+ (integer plus) 80, 282
+ (union) 52, 279
++ (override) 67–68, 279
- (difference) 52, 279
- (integer minus) 80, 282
-> (product) 55, 279
. (join) 57, 279
< (less than) 80, 283
<=> (iff) 69, 286
= (equals) 52, 285
= (integer equals) 80, 283
=< (less than or equal to) 80, 283
=> (implies) 69, 286
> (greater than) 80, 283
>= (greater than or equal to) 80, 283
@ (suppress expansion) 119, 269, 278
[] (join) 61, 279
^ (transitive closure) 63–65, 279
|| (or) 69, 286
~ (transpose) 62, 279

A

Abrial, Jean-Raymond 306, 326
Abstraction function 220
Abstractions
    not well expressed in code 2
    why key to software design xiv, 1

abstract keyword 84, 91, 93, 102, 254, 268
Abstract signature 91, 93, 102, 268, 276
Acyclicity
    constraint 35, 115, 130
    exercise 234
Address book
    informal description 5
Algebraic property 15, 208, 214
Alias
    for module 131
    in address book 5
all keyword 70, 254, 285, 286
Alloy Analyzer 4, 150–152
Alloy grammar 255
AMN (Abstract Machine Notation) 307
Analysis
    cf. manual review xiii, 30
    mechanism 150–152
    vs. theorem proving 15
Analysis constraint 144
Analysis variable 144
and keyword 69, 254, 286
Arithmetic 134
Arity
    defined 36
    error 110, 261
    highest used in practice 43
Arrow product
    defined 55, 280
    universal relation 51
as keyword 131, 254, 266
Assertion
    anonymous 126

P

Q

R